Running a Bed & Breakfast For Dummies®

Cheat Sheet

W9-BRM-579

Readying Your Guest Rooms

Use this checklist to make sure your guest rooms make a good first impression.

- ✔ Clean guest bedroom (dust; vacuum; change sheets; make bed; empty trash cans; check under beds, in drawers, and behind curtains for anything left by previous guests; note anything broken; reset thermostat).
- ✔ Check guest bedroom amenities (fresh glassware and beverage coasters, TV and DVD remotes on night stand, guest welcome letter, and so on).
- ✔ Stock guest bedroom closet (fresh robes hanging and arranged properly with belts tied, luggage rack open, wooden hangers — ten men's/ten women's, and extra pillows and blankets).
- ✔ Add the finishing guest bedroom touches (check clock radio to be sure the time is set correctly and the alarm is turned off, adjust all blinds to the same level, display current magazines, add fresh candy to a dish, stage guest book with pen, and so on).
- ✔ Clean guest bathroom (dust; vacuum; mop; clean shower, toilet, mirrors, and vanity; empty trash cans).
- ✔ Check guest bathroom amenities (replace bath, hand, and face towels; replace bathmat; stock basics such as soap, shampoo, conditioner, lotion, toilet paper, tissue, and fresh glassware).
- ✔ Add the finishing guest bathroom touches (add bath gel, mouthwash, makeup remover pads, hair dryer, deodorizer, and so on).

Taking Complete Reservations

You need to gather essential information when taking guest reservations by phone, and you'd be surprised how easy it is to forget the basics. To cover all the bases, begin by taking down the following information:

- ✔ Date reservation taken and who took the reservation
- ✔ Guest name(s), address, telephone (day, evening, cell), and e-mail
- ✔ Arrival and departure dates (confirm number of nights)
- ✔ Room selected and special add-ons
- ✔ Reason for visiting the area and whether this is a special occasion
- ✔ Referral source (how they originally found you)
- ✔ Credit card number, expiration, 3 digits on back (4 digits on front of AMEX)

Wrap things up by

- ✔ Confirming the rate plus tax and any additional charges
- ✔ Reviewing policies (especially deposit and cancellation policies) and check-in time (ask for approximate arrival time)
- ✔ Noting any dietary restrictions or allergies
- ✔ Offering to make reservations for dining, events, tours, and so on
- ✔ Telling guest the next step such as a follow-up confirmation by e-mail

Copyright © 2009 Wiley Publishing, Inc. All rights reserved. Item 2682-1.

For more information about Wiley Publishing, call 1-800-762-2974.

For Dummies: Bestselling Book Series for Beginners

Running a Bed & Breakfast For Dummies®

Cheat Sheet

Keeping Important Phone Numbers Handy

The time to search for a drain-cleaning service is not when you have guests waiting for breakfast. Keep this list on hand for quick fixes to ensure your guests' comfort, enjoyment, and safety.

Plumbing and drain-cleaning service _____

Heat/AC equipment person _____

Electrician _____

Carpenter/Contractor _____

Roofer _____

Septic tank info _____

Propane gas supplier _____

Cable _____

Internet provider _____

Power company _____

Phone service provider _____

Hot-tub repair _____

Appliance repair _____

Snow-removal service _____

Landscaper/tree-removal service _____

(Other)_____ _____

Prepping for Breakfast Before Bed

Mornings are a scramble, and not just of eggs; so use this checklist to have breakfast practically ready before you go to bed. See Chapter 11 for essential breakfast supplies to have on hand.

- Review menu choices.
- Check guest register for dietary restrictions and guest allergies.
- Check for all ingredients; decide on quick substitutions if necessary.
- Set out all cooking utensils by recipe.
- Set out serving dishes and utensils.
- Measure all dry and nonperishable ingredients.
- Take frozen items out of the freezer to defrost.
- Set breakfast table(s).
- Set up early departure "to go" bags.
- Set up early-morning coffee and tea service.

Taking Care of Business

Use this list (and the help of your accountant, lawyer, consultant, and/or broker) to ensure you have the accounts and paperwork you need before opening day (then mark renewal dates on your calendar). These include your

- Conditional use and sign permits (if required)
- Business license
- Business name and/or DBA registration
- Certificate of occupancy
- Account for transient/lodging taxes
- Sales tax account (seller's permit)
- Federal and State Tax ID
- Business checking credit accounts
- Merchant account (to process credit cards)
- ServSafe food certification (if required)
- Health Department inspection
- Fire Department inspection
- Liquor license, if applicable
- Insurance (business, liability, property, and liquor liability if applicable)
- Property management/reservation and accounting software

For Dummies: Bestselling Book Series for Beginners

Running a Bed & Breakfast

FOR DUMMIES®

by Mary White

WILEY

Wiley Publishing, Inc.

Running a Bed & Breakfast For Dummies®

Published by
Wiley Publishing, Inc.
111 River St.
Hoboken, NJ 07030-5774

www.wiley.com

Copyright © 2009 by Wiley Publishing, Inc., Indianapolis, Indiana

Published by Wiley Publishing, Inc., Indianapolis, Indiana

Published simultaneously in Canada

For general information on our other products and services, please contact our Customer Care Department within the U.S. at 877-762-2974, outside the U.S. at 317-572-3993, or fax 317-572-4002.

For technical support, please visit www.wiley.com/techsupport.

Wiley also publishes its books in a variety of electronic formats. Some content that appears in print may not be available in electronic books.

Library of Congress Control Number: 2009923066

ISBN: 978-0-470-42682-1

Manufactured in the United States of America

10 9 8 7 6 5 4 3 2 1

WILEY

About the Author

Mary White is the President and Founder of www.BnBFinder.com, a leading bed & breakfast directory.

In 1998, after many years as a securities broker, Mary decided to embark on a new venture — Internet publishing. With a Bachelor of Arts and a Master of Business Administration, she developed a simple business model: offering consumers exciting, innovative ways to access practical information in easy-to-use formats. She decided to test this concept in a field she believed in, the bed & breakfast industry. Mary's mission was to provide an easy-to-use Web site that could effectively put B&Bs and inns on a level playing field with larger hotels and resorts, convey the uniqueness and special features of B&Bs, and provide consumers with the information they need in order to choose a B&B. Today her site, www.BnBFinder.com, consistently earns the industry's highest ratings by providing interesting content and comprehensive search features while incorporating the latest technology for both the novice and experienced Web user.

Mary enjoys every aspect of working with new and seasoned innkeepers and has helped thousands of innkeepers to market their inns. She does numerous radio and podcast interviews each year, is a frequent contributor to major newspapers and magazines, and has presented workshops at several Professional Association of Innkeepers International conferences.

Mary lives in New York City with her husband, Greg, and is the proud mother of two exceptional teenagers.

For more information on B&Bs, feel free to contact Mary at www.BnBFinder.com, (888) 547-8226, or mary@BnBFinder.com.

Dedication

This book is dedicated to the thousands of wonderful innkeepers I've worked with over the years who have created places where guests can wake up someplace special. It's a privilege and true pleasure to work with you and to promote your inns on `BnBFinder.com`.

And, of course, to my wonderful family and special friends who have helped and supported me without hesitation. To Greg, Steven, and Kristin, you guys are the best part of my life; to Joe, who helped me to create `BnBFinder.com` and who is always there when I need him; to Loretta, Patti, Steve, Ed, Daria, Gabe, Erika, Jane, and Lorraine; and because I am so blessed, there are too many others of you to name individually. You know who you are and how much I love and appreciate you, especially my parents who taught me that a mom can work hard, run her own business, and be a good mom.

Author's Acknowledgments

I, and everyone who reads this book, owe a huge debt of gratitude to five very special and dedicated innkeepers and inn consultants who generously shared their time, experience, and expertise to guide me in assembling the valuable resource that I know this book will be for aspiring innkeepers. Thank you Diane and Michele DiNapoli, Innkeepers at Journey Inn (`www.journey inn.com`) in Hyde Park, New York; Dottie Musser, Innkeeper at Bradford Place Inn and Gardens (`www.bradfordplaceinn.com`) in Sonora, California; Linda Hayes, Innkeeper at Inn at Riverbend (`www.innatriverbend.com`) in Pearisburg, Virginia; Hilary Jones, Innkeeper at Admiral Peary House (`www.admiralpearyhouse.com`) in Fryeburg, Maine, and professional inn consultant (`www.inngenium.com`) specializing in strategic and business planning for the small lodging industry; and Hugh Daniels, professional inn consultant (`www.askhugh.com`) and a retired 22-year innkeeper with an MBA and a head for numbers. When you assemble a good team, great things happen; each of you — and your sometimes diverse views — made this a fabulous team that I can't thank you enough for being a part of.

Thank you also to those of you who have shared with me the vision of `BnBFinder.com` and devoted your efforts to making it a great resource for innkeepers and travelers.

Finally, thank you to my technical editor, Diane Callahan, and to Mike Lewis, Alissa Schwipps, Christy Pingleton, Elizabeth Rea, and everyone else in the Wiley organization who knew and appreciated the need for a comprehensive resource such as this book for aspiring innkeepers.

Publisher's Acknowledgments

We're proud of this book; please send us your comments through our Dummies online registration form located at `http://dummies.custhelp.com`. For other comments, please contact our Customer Care Department within the U.S. at 877-762-2974, outside the U.S. at 317-572-3993, or fax 317-572-4002.

Some of the people who helped bring this book to market include the following:

Acquisitions, Editorial, and Media Development

Senior Project Editor: Alissa Schwipps

Acquisitions Editor: Michael Lewis

Copy Editor: Christy Pingleton

Assistant Editor: Erin Calligan Mooney

Editorial Program Coordinator: Joe Niesen

Technical Editor: Diane Callahan

Senior Editorial Manager: Jennifer Ehrlich

Editorial Assistants: Jennette ElNaggar, David Lutton

Cover Photo: © Botanica

Cartoons: Rich Tennant (`www.the5thwave.com`)

Composition Services

Project Coordinator: Katherine Key

Layout and Graphics: Samantha K. Allen, Reuben W. Davis, Christine Williams

Proofreaders: Laura Albert, Joni Heredia

Indexer: Potomac Indexing, LLC

Special Help: Elizabeth Rea

Publishing and Editorial for Consumer Dummies

    Diane Graves Steele, Vice President and Publisher, Consumer Dummies

    Kristin Ferguson-Wagstaffe, Product Development Director, Consumer Dummies

    Ensley Eikenburg, Associate Publisher, Travel

    Kelly Regan, Editorial Director, Travel

Publishing for Technology Dummies

    Andy Cummings, Vice President and Publisher, Dummies Technology/General User

Composition Services

    Gerry Fahey, Vice President of Production Services

    Debbie Stailey, Director of Composition Services

Contents at a Glance

Table of Contents

Part IV: Up and Running: Day-to-Day Operations 217

Chapter 11: Communicating with Potential Guests and Taking Reservations 219

Chapter 12: Taking Care of Guests 235

Introduction

Running a bed & breakfast is a dream that many inn guests take away from their B&B getaways, and I'm thrilled that you're exploring this vision. If you're like many, you've been thinking about it for years, you've been cutting out recipes, and you can envision your ideal inn with you as the innkeeper. Some of your friends think you're crazy and others think you'll be a natural. This book is your guide to getting started, being prepared, and running a successful bed & breakfast.

To be an innkeeper and run a profitable bed & breakfast, you need to see past the idyllic notions of innkeeping and be ready for the tough choices and sacrifices that you'll make as an innkeeper; and this book addresses them directly. I help you take off your rose-colored glasses, sit down, and examine your motivations; make a plan for your business; set up everything from your records to your rooms; and give you inside tips on what to expect and how to handle a variety of situations that you'll encounter as an innkeeper. With this information you'll figure out things ahead of time, get answers to the most frequently asked questions, and enter the world of innkeeping with enthusiasm and confidence. *Running a Bed & Breakfast For Dummies* helps you realize your dream of owning and operating a successful bed & breakfast.

About This Book

No book can tell you exactly how to run a bed & breakfast because no two bed & breakfasts are alike. Every area has different restrictions, requirements, and appeal, and innkeepers add their own personalities to their inns. What this book does is tell you what you *need* to know, what you should consider, and where to turn for answers to any questions that are unique to your situation.

Each chapter is divided into sections, and each section contains information to help you run a successful bed & breakfast, including:

- How to get started, what to look for in a location, and how to make an offer to purchase your inn
- The biggest problems new bed & breakfasts encounter and how to avoid them
- What you need to know about taking reservations and using property management software

✔ How to market your bed & breakfast, including creating a Web site, getting your inn listed on the search engines, and navigating the confusing advertising choices that you'll be confronted with so you know what works and how to spend your advertising dollars wisely

✔ How to get extra help when you need it

✔ The best ways to furnish your inn

✔ Ways to save time cleaning and preparing breakfast

The best part about this book is that *you* decide where to start and what to read. It's a reference, so if you forget something or want to review it again, you can easily refer back to that section. Let the table of contents and the index be your guides.

Conventions Used in This Book

The following conventions are used throughout the text to make things consistent and easy to understand:

✔ All Web addresses appear in `monofont`.

✔ New terms appear in *italic* and are closely followed by easy-to-understand definitions.

✔ **Bold** is used to highlight the action parts of numbered steps and keywords in bulleted lists.

In the bed & breakfast industry, the terms bed & breakfast, bed & breakfast inn, B&B, and inn are used interchangeably. Throughout this book I have incorporated this same terminology.

What You're Not to Read

I've written this book so that you can find the most important information quickly and easily and also skip over some of the finer details. While I'd love for you to read every word, I've set some text off from the main information, text you can live without if you're just after the reference material. Don't get me wrong — this stuff is interesting material, and I think you may find it helpful. But if you're just after the nuts and bolts, you can come back to the text in sidebars later. Sidebars are shaded boxes that usually give detailed examples or flesh out historical perspectives on the topic at hand.

Foolish Assumptions

As an innkeeper you're going to have to make some assumptions about your guests, and in writing this book I've made some assumptions about you and why you're reading this book:

✔ You love staying at bed & breakfasts and you've dreamed for a long time about owning your own inn.

✔ You're an excellent host or hostess looking for a new career, and friends have told you that you should open a bed & breakfast.

✔ You've found a beautiful old home and you're trying to figure out how you can afford it so you're exploring the possibility of turning it into a bed & breakfast.

✔ You want to get away from the corporate world, be your own boss, and unleash your creativity.

✔ You're already an innkeeper and you're looking for tips and advice to make your business more profitable and successful.

How This Book Is Organized

This book is organized into six parts, each an ingredient in the recipe for running a successful bed & breakfast inn.

Part 1: Inn the Beginning

In this part, I get you ready to enter the bed & breakfast industry. I outline the basics for you so you have an overview of what a bed & breakfast is and what some of your marketing obstacles may be. I also give you the information to analyze the social skills and the commitment necessary to be a successful innkeeper, and help you to pick a location and size for your B&B.

Part 11: Transitioning from Inn Goer to Inn Owner

In this part, I help you get started by giving you ideas to create a plan for your business. I suggest important steps you can take on your own and when you should engage outside professionals. This section also covers the important information you need to know when you're buying an existing bed & breakfast — from making an offer to closing the sale — as well as information you need if you're building a new inn from the ground up or converting an existing property or your home into a B&B.

Part III: Getting Ready for Guests

In this part, I get you ready to greet guests. First I help you to get organized by setting up your records. This section gives you the information you need to set up your books as well as choose a property management system, set your rates, and establish your policies. Then I help you get a basic marketing plan in place so that guests will find you, and I include important information that you must know when designing or updating your Web site. I won't have you ready to welcome guests until I help you furnish your inn and create a plan for your all-important breakfasts, so I also share some of my favorite tried-and-tested sample menus and recipes.

Part IV: Up and Running: Day-to-Day Operations

In this part, I guide you through taking reservations. This may be when guests get their first impression of your inn, so you want to do it right. I help you take care of guests, including checking them in and getting them settled, and, for those rare occasions when you have problem guests, I give you some suggestions on how to handle them. We all know cleaning isn't fun, but keeping a clean inn is an important part of your business, so I share some tips and tricks to help you get this job done as quickly and efficiently as possible. You're taking on a big job as an innkeeper, so I give you advice on how to get extra help when you need it — including how to take a vacation.

Part V: Taking It beyond Breakfast and the Basics

In this part, I make sure you don't feel left on your own just because you've made it to the point of opening and running a bed & breakfast. I help you analyze your results and make future projections. For those of you whose goal is to build your business further, I provide concrete marketing advice tailored specially to the bed & breakfast industry. I encourage you to recognize how important it is to take care of yourself on both the personal and professional levels, and give you ideas and suggestions for doing so. And finally, I help you consider your future plans and give you ideas on how to implement them, including selling your B&B and moving on when the time comes.

Part VI: The Part of Tens

In this standard *For Dummies* section, I give you tips and tricks that save you time and money when cleaning the inn. I also provide concrete ideas and examples for making every guest a return guest.

Icons Used in This Book

To make this book easier to read and simpler to use, I include some icons that can help you find and fathom key ideas and information.

This icon appears whenever an idea or item can save you time, money, or stress.

Any time you see this icon, you know the information that follows is so important that it's worth reading more than once.

This icon flags information that highlights dangers that are easily overlooked and that you want to avoid.

Where to Go from Here

This book is organized so that you can go wherever you want and find complete information or just an overview of a topic. Want to know the biggest roadblock new innkeepers encounter? Head to Chapter 5 for important information on zoning and permits. Looking for some tested innkeeper recipes and tips to make breakfast prep simpler? Jump to Chapter 10 for sample menus and recipes. Want tips on getting your inn listed on the Internet? You'll find this information in Chapters 8 and 15.

If you're not sure where you want to start, begin with Part I. It gives you all the basic info you need to understand what it takes to be a successful innkeeper. It also points to places where you can find more detailed information in this book and in the B&B industry, including the support of other innkeepers.

Part I
Inn the Beginning

The 5th Wave — By Rich Tennant

"After 30 years on the police force, Beth and I decided to open this B&B. You want to keep your hands where I can see them and empty your pockets?"

In this part . . .

You take a look at what a B&B really is and get an overview of the bed & breakfast industry to help you to decide if running a place of your own is right for you. I help you determine if you have what it takes to be a successful innkeeper. I also break down the process of picking the right location, which is a key factor in the success of your business, and help you figure out what size and what type of bed & breakfast to open.

Chapter 1

So You Want to Open a B&B

In This Chapter

▶ Understanding what a bed & breakfast is and isn't

▶ Surveying the skills and personality traits being an innkeeper requires

▶ Looking at the pros and cons of being an innkeeper

▶ Filling in the gaps: Ways to find out more of what you want to know

You've been cutting out recipes for years, everyone tells you you're the perfect host or hostess, and you've stayed at more B&Bs than you can count — but will you be a good innkeeper? Maybe. The fact that you can cook doesn't mean you have the persistence and stamina to run an inn, nor does being handy at restoring an old building mean you have the leadership skills it takes to run a business.

Some equate the job of an innkeeper to that of an actor or actress in that you must be "on" whenever you're working. The differences are that you can't be acting, and the show never ends. When you're an innkeeper, it's show time 24 hours a day.

In this chapter, I give you a clear vision of what a B&B is (and isn't) and what being an innkeeper entails — without rose-colored glasses. Parts of this chapter may sound discouraging, but they're not meant to dishearten you. Rather, the intention is to make sure you enter the world of innkeeping with your eyes wide open, the skills you need to succeed, and the support you need to thrive. I want you to be sure that you have what it takes not only to run a successful inn but also to be happy in your new profession.

Defining B&B: It's Not Just a Bed and a Breakfast

A bed & breakfast is more than the simple combination of a bed and a breakfast. It's a business and a unique lodging experience for your guests. You can be the best host or hostess in the world, but if you don't run your B&B

as a business, you run the risk of not being able to pay your bills. Equally as important, you must see your customers as guests. If you run a rigid business without providing warmth and hospitality, you miss out on the joys and satisfaction of innkeeping, and your guests leave your inn deprived of the special B&B lodging experience.

The next sections clarify exactly what constitutes a B&B, and point out some fallacies you may encounter among those who are less enlightened.

Clearing up confusion: What a B&B is

You may be a bit confused by various impressions that you've had over the years about the term B&B, so before taking the leap into innkeeping you want to know: *What exactly is a bed & breakfast?* You can't run something if you don't have a clear picture of what it is in your mind.

Comparing a B&B to a country inn and home-stay

Because the word inn is used interchangeably when referring to bed & breakfasts and country inns, and because home-stays rent rooms and provide breakfast, there can be confusion in the distinctions between B&Bs, country inns, and home-stays.

✔ **Country inn:** This kind of lodging property has many of the characteristics of a B&B, but serves an evening meal in addition to breakfast. Some country inns serve dinner to overnight guests only, and the cost of dinner and breakfast is generally included in the room rate (called the *Modified American Plan*). A country inn with a *full-service restaurant* serves meals to the general public. Generally the owner or owners are actively involved in the daily operations of the inn, and often live on site. To be a country inn, a property does not have to be located in a rural area, although historically restaurants were added so that travelers in remote locations could enjoy a good evening meal.

✔ **Home-stay:** This is an owner-occupied private home that rents rooms to earn additional income while the owners continue their present employment or retirement. Although breakfast may be included in the room rate, in general, home-stays lack the emphasis on unique accommodations and personal service typical of a B&B stay.

If you provide a high level of service with a personal touch, offer generous hospitality and good value with unique ambiance and surroundings in individually decorated rooms that are clean and comfortable, then you are providing your guests with a fabulous lodging experience — no matter what you call it!

According to the Professional Association of Innkeepers International (PAII), a bed & breakfast is a lodging establishment where the owner/host typically lives on the premises. Breakfast is served to overnight guests and may be quite lavish. A professional B&B meets all the appropriate zoning, safety, health, and legal requirements of the state and local government. The owner or owners provide a high degree of personal service to guests. Many B&Bs have been inspected by state associations or inspection rating services such as AAA, Mobil guides, or Canada Select. Small B&Bs usually provide a part-time or seasonal occupation for the owners, who do most of the work, often with some help for housekeeping and other chores. Larger B&Bs provide the primary financial support for the owner(s) and generally require their full-time, active involvement in the daily operations with the help of employees.

From there, the choice is yours. You can open a bed & breakfast in the city or in the country, in a quaint Victorian mansion or in a conventional home (see Chapter 2 for more about your options). I've even heard of B&Bs on boats, in treehouses, and in old jails!

Dispelling myths: What a B&B is not

As an innkeeper, you need to know and confront head-on some of the misconceptions and general perceptions that the traveling public and the media may have about bed & breakfasts. Some of these are based on out-dated notions, and others have evolved as a result of confusion with home-stays. Tackling these mistaken beliefs and knowing what information you need to provide, especially for first-time B&B goers, is helpful in your marketing efforts (see Chapters 8 and 15). Some mistaken notions and their clarifications are:

- **B&Bs are cheap and second-rate.** While the values offered by bed & breakfasts can make them an economical alternative to other accommodations, B&B guests generally find upscale amenities, such as luxury linens, fresh flowers, fine china, gourmet breakfasts, and special touches not found even at higher-priced hotels.

- **Breakfast is family-style with other guests.** This is true at many inns, and part of the appeal of a B&B is the camaraderie. However, many B&Bs offer individual tables or even breakfast delivered to the guest's room. Knowing who your guest is allows you to offer a breakfast setting conducive to your target guest (see Chapter 10 for information on breakfast settings).

- **Bathrooms are shared.** According to PAII, nearly 95 percent of inns include private baths, and many now offer private in-room Jacuzzis for two.

- ✔ **Privacy is limited.** Actually, professional innkeepers use their people skills and know when to engage guests in conversation and when to give them privacy (see Chapter 12 for more on honing your communication skills). They also take into account thin walls and squeaky staircases by soundproofing when possible.

- ✔ **The breakfasts are fattening and unhealthy.** Most innkeepers offer a variety of food choices at breakfast, and many ask about dietary restrictions when taking guests' reservations. (See Chapter 10 for information about dietary requests that you will encounter.)

- ✔ **Running a bed & breakfast is a hobby.** By reading this book and following the advice it contains, you know this notion is far from true; however, don't be surprised by how often guests will ask *"So, what do you really do?"*

- ✔ **B&Bs are just a room, and they're boring.** On the contrary, many bed & breakfast inns provide activities for their guests free of charge or have deals with local vendors to offer guests discounted rates. Embrace this aspect of a B&B stay and offer activities and services appropriate for your guests.

- ✔ **B&Bs have too many rules.** While it is true that a few innkeepers take creating policies to such an extreme that guests can't relax and enjoy their getaway, the majority of innkeepers focus their concern on the safety, comfort, and enjoyment of their guests. (Chapter 7 focuses on establishing your policies.) Not furnishing your inn with irreplaceable, valuable personal property and priceless family heirlooms will help you to relax, welcome, and enjoy your guests.

Finding Out What It Takes to Be an Innkeeper

You must have multiple skills, personality traits, and personal characteristics to be a successful innkeeper. The following sections describe these qualities in greater depth and comprise a job description of sorts for aspiring innkeepers.

Communicating effectively

Before taking the plunge into innkeeping, you need to take an inventory of your own people skills, past the point of being a friendly person. To be a successful innkeeper, you must like people, be willing to interact with them on many levels, and possess some innate higher-level communication skills, such as:

- ✔ **You should have the ability to break down communication barriers gently and graciously by taking cues from your guests.** This means being able to figure out what the guests' needs are and what, if possible, can be done to make your guests comfortable. It also means knowing when guests want to be engaged in conversation and when they'd rather be left alone. Some people are naturally better than others at reading situations, but luckily, making guests comfortable is a skill that you can continue to perfect with each guest interaction.

- ✔ **You need to be a skillful leader, which means being competently in charge.** Guests sense incompetence, so you always want to appear confident and in control. If you're not in charge, guests will immediately try and take advantage of you. From your first contact with each guest, be it by e-mail, by phone, or in person, always remain in charge by creating policies and an environment that you're comfortable offering to guests; then stick within the boundaries that you create for this environment. Guests will try and dictate everything from your reservation policies to room assignments and menu choices, but you must remain in control.

- ✔ **You need to be skillful at communicating nonverbally.** Studies have shown that only 7 percent of what we "hear" from in-person communication is actual words. The remaining 93 percent of the message we receive comes not from the literal words spoken, but rather from the following:

  - The tone and pitch of a voice

  - The speed at which words are delivered

  - Facial expressions, including mouth, chin, eye and eyebrow movements, and the position of the head as well as hand and body gestures and eye contact

  - Emotional responses such as sighing, laughing, snickering, and crying

  - Physiological responses such as rapid breathing, eyes filling with tears, choking on words, and so forth

These signals make nonverbal communication a very powerful way of "hearing" guests and communicating with them. Listening to guests' nonverbal communication and being in command of your own nonverbal correspondences is an art and a skill that savvy innkeepers employ and perfect over time.

Examining other necessary traits

Don't underestimate the value of your strong passion to become an inn-keeper. Not only is it an important factor in determining your success, it's also what carries you through the roughest and most exhausting times. But passion and determination alone aren't enough to make your bed & breakfast successful. In addition to the high-level communication skills I discuss in the preceding section, here are some other key traits you must possess:

- **Endurance and stamina.** This is a biggie and a lot tougher than it sounds. Even when you're tired or don't feel well, beds have to be made, breakfast must be prepared, toilets must be cleaned, and everything must be done in a cheerful manner. At 10 p.m., you may find yourself still manning the fort because guests you're expecting haven't called to let you know they're running late or, worse, not coming at all. And so you wait, knowing all the while that you need to be up at 6 a.m. to start breakfast.

- **A willingness to see damages as a part of doing business.** Even when you take precautions to protect your inn, some damages are bound to occur. Guests spill things, drop things, break things, wet the bed, and more, so you should never put anything in your rooms or common areas that you can't bear to part with.

- **Tolerance to entertain a variety of people — even those you don't like.** You know who I mean, those who insist on talking politics from their point of view as if it were the only point of view, discuss their medical conditions with a level of detail that is not only inappropriate but annoying, share their religious views with complete disregard for anyone else's beliefs, or monopolize the conversation and talk only about themselves. Add to this the fact that many of these people are always complaining about something. Not only do you need to entertain these people, but you also need to skillfully manage the situation to minimize their interference with your other guests' enjoyment.

- **An affinity for multitasking.** You need to be adept at working in a fast-paced environment with frequent interruptions. This could mean anything from taking a reservation while cleaning a bathroom to telling guests about area activities while buying tomatoes.

- **Organizational skills.** You need to be organized in order to keep a housekeeping schedule, plan and prepare meals, shop for the inn, manage your advertising, take care of bookkeeping and banking, handle repairs, meet required reporting deadlines, take care of current and future guests, and more.

- **Willingness to learn from your experiences.** Successful innkeepers con-stantly find more efficient ways to use their time, from streamlining meal preparation to making their housekeeping routine more productive. They discover new bookkeeping functions and marketing techniques. Having an open and flexible mind makes the job easier over time.

✔ **Patience.** An innkeeper's days are filled with answering the same questions over and over, even after the requested information has been provided. Say you show a couple at check-in how to use the remote for the TV and point out the card in the room that provides complete instructions on operating the TV. You go to their room later and patiently help them with it again, only to get another call from them that night asking you to show them how to use the remote. Each time, you respond with patience and a smile, even though you can't help thinking to yourself, *Why don't they get it?* or *How many more times will I have to show them?* At first, you're happy to help your guests, but fast-forward to the 100th and then the 1,000th time you've answered the same question: Can you still do it with the same patience and smile?

✔ **Willingness to make personal sacrifices.** Being an innkeeper invariably means missing some family and personal functions. When this happens, you must be able to hide your feelings of disappointment for your guests' sake.

In addition to all of this, you must find time to take care of yourself. An innkeeper's job is never done. Even on days when there are no guests at your inn, you should expect to be preparing for them by working on your marketing plan, baking ahead, cleaning, and performing maintenance and upkeep. When guests are staying at the inn, you may be hoping for a little quiet time alone in the afternoon, only to find that your guests prefer to hang around and visit. None of these dynamics are bad; they're simply a reality of innkeeping and the lifestyle you sign on to when you decide to run a bed & breakfast. But remember, your job description doesn't come with personal leave, vacation time, or days off, so you have to carve out this time for yourself (Chapter 16 shows you how). Be wise, and build it into your business plan.

Being a Jack or Jill of all trades

If I were to write a job description for the position of innkeeper it would probably read something like this: *Knowing how to do everything and being ready to do it at any time.* Innkeepers wear many hats and walk in many shoes, from cook to cleaner and from greeter to gardener. I can't think of any other profession that combines the knowledge from as many different disciplines as innkeeping does.

Many new innkeepers make the mistake of downplaying the need for experience, or at least a little knowledge, and overestimating their abilities in the many areas that affect the success of a bed & breakfast. While many jobs can be outsourced, knowledge in some areas is indispensable. For example, you may outsource your accounting and tax preparation to a CPA or accountant, but knowing how to generate and read a profit and loss statement (also called an income statement) from your bookkeeping software is essential for gauging the health of your business and comparing its success from year to year (see Chapter 15 for details on assessing your success).

Making personal sacrifices

Many stories come to mind of professional innkeepers who understand that it's show time 24/7/365. One in particular is of innkeepers who were welcoming their guests when one of the innkeepers excused himself to take a phone call. It was on this call that he found out that his father had passed away. His partner continued checking in the current guests and the next group of guests. By the time yet another group of guests arrived, he was back helping to check them in. The guests never knew what the innkeeper was going through personally and enjoyed their stays immensely. It's this type of personal sacrifice that many innkeepers make. Situations like these are also why it's important to have an interim innkeeper or competent staff on hand should you need to be away from the inn suddenly. (See Chapter 14 for information on finding an interim innkeeper.)

While the following list by no means includes every role an innkeeper may be called upon to play, it gives you an idea of those areas in which a degree of proficiency is necessary. How do you measure up? You should be prepared to be a

- ✔ Bookkeeper
- ✔ Chef/short order cook
- ✔ Concierge
- ✔ Gardener
- ✔ Handyman/woman
- ✔ Housekeeper
- ✔ Interior decorator
- ✔ Safety coordinator
- ✔ Negotiator/mediator
- ✔ Marketer
- ✔ Personnel Director
- ✔ Webmaster

Lucky for you, this book helps you brush up on these skills and more. Turn to Chapter 6 for information on record-keeping, Chapter 10 for food preparation and recipe suggestions, Chapter 14 for help with hiring help, and Chapter 9 for decorating tips. Chapter 13 gives you the lowdown on inn maintenance. Chapters 11 and 12 cover communication and guest relations, while Chapter 8 provides an overview of marketing, including capitalizing on the possibilities offered by the World Wide Web.

Making your job look easy (and other secret skills)

The best innkeepers have a secret: They make everything look easy. Because successful innkeepers are so good at this, new innkeepers often underestimate the variety of skills required to be a successful innkeeper, the energy necessary to be on duty 24/7/365, and the stamina to bring it all together.

Guests can't enjoy themselves if they feel they are an imposition, so innkeepers go out of their way to hide the fact that, sometimes, they are.

In addition to making your job look easier than it is, to be a successful innkeeper you need to have the following "secret" skills, which aren't always revealed to your guests:

- ✔ **A competitive streak:** Even though you may be on friendly terms and generally work cooperatively with other innkeepers in your area, innkeepers are competitive. You want your inn to be the best at meeting your guests' needs and expectations.

- ✔ **A talent for managing time wisely:** Out of sheer necessity, you must call upon your creative flair to practice good time management. You need to quickly decide which items or tasks are time wasters and must be eliminated, which tasks need to be minimized, and which need to stay in place and be streamlined so that more time is carved out for running the B&B and taking care of yourself.

- ✔ **A well-calculated focus:** Innkeepers are akin to magicians in a lot of ways — their focus, preparation, and practice make everything fall into place and seem so easy! With a lot of hard work and a little bit of magic, your guests can enjoy the fabulous mouth-watering breakfast you prepare, your immaculately clean inn, and your beautifully manicured lawn without ever knowing how many hours go into the details to make all of this possible during their brief visits.

Knowing What You Want from Your B&B

If you have the personality traits and skills described in the previous sections of this chapter, you have most of what it takes to be a successful innkeeper. But while having these skills and traits may enable you to go through the motions of being an innkeeper, to be a really great innkeeper you need to have a clear understanding of what you expect to get out of your B&B.

In much of the rest of this book, the focus is on what you will provide to your guests, but this section is about what's in it for *you*. Will you be happy? You probably won't be a good innkeeper if you're not. Will your bed & breakfast and the love and sweat that you put into it provide you with a good return? This doesn't have to be defined only in terms of monetary success. Your success is also defined by the achievement of the goals that you set for yourself — your reasons for running a bed & breakfast. Figuring out how you define your own success and happiness can help you decide whether running a bed & breakfast is the right choice for you.

Looking at your motivation: The pros and cons of innkeeping

The most common reason to start a new business is to make money. While innkeepers do want to run a profitable bed & breakfast, this is often not the only reason — and many times not the first reason — they give for getting into the industry. Although this doesn't mean you won't make money, the point is to understand fully what you plan to invest in the business in terms of money, time, energy, and commitment, and then decide whether you have realistic expectations of what you intend to get out of it.

If you decide to forgo taking a salary in the beginning, be sure to get financial advice. Although you'll be working, you won't be contributing to social security, which could adversely affect your benefits later in life.

Ask ten innkeepers why they decided to become innkeepers and you'll probably get ten different answers. Popular reasons include, but are not limited to,

- ✔ To be my own boss
- ✔ To live in a nicer home than I could afford otherwise
- ✔ To work from home so I can be around my family and my children
- ✔ To work with my spouse or chosen partner
- ✔ To meet new and interesting people and/or relieve loneliness
- ✔ To take advantage of my love to cook, entertain, and be creative
- ✔ To be able to restore an old property

Your list may look completely different than the list above, or it may be a combination of some of the above reasons and some of your own. The most important thing is to have a firm list of your goals and a clear understanding of your motivation and expectations before you start out.

You can't look only at the bright side. Before making the decision to become an innkeeper, you need to weigh the disadvantages of innkeeping as well, some of which include:

- ✔ Long hours
- ✔ Limited income
- ✔ Heavy startup costs
- ✔ Lack of privacy for you and your family
- ✔ Reduced family time
- ✔ Hard manual labor
- ✔ Menial and repetitive tasks that are performed over and over

Pulling all the pieces together

Being an innkeeper can be exciting. However, just because it seems like a good idea, it may or may not enable you to meet your personal and financial goals. Without setting these goals, you can't judge your success. Start by making a clear list of what you want to achieve personally, then figure out exactly what type of commitment you're willing to make to get there. With all this in mind, use your business plan to determine how closely you will come to meeting your financial goals. (See Chapter 3 for help in creating a business plan and using it as a road map for your business's growth.) By looking at the combination of your business plan and your personal and financial goals, you'll be able to clearly define what success means to you and whether innkeeping is the best means to achieve it.

Juggling the Lifestyle of Innkeeping

Adapting to the innkeeping lifestyle is tough for new innkeepers. Figuring out how to juggle the reality of the demands that this lifestyle brings is no easy task.

Balancing your business and personal lives

When you live where you work and work where you live, separating your business life from your personal life can be a challenge, but it's a necessity. Even if you're among the nearly 15 percent of innkeepers who live off property, you still have a lot invested in your bed & breakfast and a vested interest in making sure it maintains your personal touch. Either way, you're going to find yourself juggling business decisions and personal obligations.

Running a bed & breakfast involves a huge time commitment. If your family will live at the inn, they should be involved in your decision to open a bed & breakfast because entertaining guests in your home will affect them. If you expect them to work in the business, you need an even greater commitment from them, and they should be part of establishing the division of labor.

See Chapter 3 for help allocating the responsibilities of various tasks, and check out Chapter 14 for details on getting extra help when you need it.

Family and friends may not share your devotion to your new profession. Some may think you've gone overboard, and many may not understand the tremendous commitment you are undertaking. When possible, educate them and enlist their support.

Life happens, and you need to have a plan for how you intend to handle personal invitations and commitments that come up, such as attending a family wedding or scheduling required medical treatment for yourself. If you're running the bed & breakfast with a partner, discuss ahead of time how you'll handle various job duties and situations. If you're a solo innkeeper, spend some time planning how you'll make time for yourself and handle emergencies.

Budget time for yourself, whether it's to take a walk in the park or to take a vacation. Personal time has a different meaning for everyone. Know what you need for yourself and carve out time for it in advance. (See Chapter 16 to find out how.) Otherwise, you're unlikely to find the time you need, a situation that can lead to bitterness and, ultimately, poor guest services.

Understanding uncertainty

Getting used to uncertainty is part of settling in as an innkeeper. The best way to handle uncertainty is with flexibility. Being flexible means creating a plan for your business and understanding that your projections are only an educated guess. It also means knowing that your plans for each day are always tentative. You may begin your day with a list of chores and baking that you plan to do and end up spending the entire day rebuilding your kitchen drain after the waste disposal fails in the middle of breakfast.

Check references for repairmen and have their emergency numbers on hand ahead of time — preferably programmed into speed dial. You never know when you'll need them. Don't forget numbers for services such as pest control and tree removal.

As an innkeeper, you need to be flexible and ready for the unexpected not only in your activities, but in cash flow as well. This might sound scary — and it is. However, those who don't overextend themselves — in either time or financial resources — can usually weather any storm.

One way to be prepared for uncertainty is for you, your partner, or a family member to keep an outside job. This may be beneficial for a variety of reasons, two of which include:

✔ **Extra income:** Having an outside income may provide the necessary cash flow to support your lifestyle and bed & breakfast until the inn begins to turn a profit. Even after your inn is profitable, you may continue to work outside the inn to provide additional income or to enable you to hire staff. Having an outside source of income also helps to insulate you from the effects of uncertain economic and environmental factors that may affect your revenues. If you're counting on an outside income to support your bed & breakfast, be sure you're prepared for the possibility of losing your job.

> ✓ **Benefits:** Providing your own health and retirement benefits is expensive, and many innkeepers keep their day jobs in order to keep their benefits.
>
> If you have benefits for yourself through your inn, you may be required to provide the same level of benefits to all employees. Check with your attorney to find out what's required.

Your business plan (see Chapter 3 to devise one) can help you determine the projected amount of time you'll need to spend working a job outside of the inn. Innkeepers juggle the running of their inns with their day jobs in a variety of ways, including:

✓ Hiring an assistant innkeeper either full- or part-time

✓ Catering only to weekend guests

✓ Running the inn on a part-time or seasonal basis

✓ Working just part-time outside the inn

Before You Take the Plunge: Finding Out All You Can about the B&B Biz

Fortunately, a plethora of resources is available to show you what it's like to be an innkeeper before you invest a substantial amount of time or money. Use this book as your guide, and read and re-read every chapter to ensure you absorb all the valuable information. Then seek out and talk to other innkeepers by looking for one or more innkeeper networks, which offer a wealth of information and support. Too often, innkeepers fail or burn out because they haven't done their research or feel alone in the major endeavor of running a bed & breakfast. With so many good resources available, there's no reason for this to happen to you!

Talking to other successful innkeepers

No matter what stage of innkeeping you're in, you're not alone and never need to feel that you are. Savvy innkeepers take part in industry associations and forums to get support from others and answers to their questions. New innkeepers benefit from the wisdom of experienced innkeepers, and seasoned innkeepers benefit from the energy and enthusiasm of new innkeepers. Innkeeper groups come in all shapes and sizes. I encourage you to get in touch with several. Here is some help in finding them:

✔ **Innkeeper recommendations:** Ask local innkeepers what associations and forums they find helpful. In addition to organized associations, many innkeepers have informal gatherings amongst themselves and you may be invited to participate.

✔ **Local and regional associations:** You can find these associations by doing a Google search. Enter your city or region and then the keyword phrase "bed breakfast association," for example, *Mystic CT bed breakfast association.*

✔ **State associations:** Innkeepers in many states have joined together to form state associations. To see whether such an association exists in your state, perform a Google search by entering your state followed by the keyword search phrase "bed breakfast association," for example, *West Virginia bed breakfast association.*

Many state B&B associations have kits, research, and courses specifically for aspiring innkeepers who are thinking of opening a bed & breakfast in their state.

✔ **The Professional Association of Innkeepers International:** Known as PAII (pronounced "pie"), you can look them up at www.paii.org. This worldwide organization provides education, information, networking, advocacy, business opportunities, online forums, and industry research for all aspects of the bed & breakfast industry. Each year the association hosts an industry conference and trade show that offer a wealth of educational seminars, panels, demonstrations, and opportunities and bring aspiring and seasoned innkeepers together with industry vendors and suppliers.

The PAII annual conference and trade show and many state bed & breakfast associations offer seminars just for aspiring innkeepers.

✔ **Innkeeper forums:** A forum is an online discussion group. It can be private or public, and may or may not be monitored by a forum leader or group. Many forums are open to all innkeepers — all you have to do is register or join a particular association. Private forums are by invitation only. These forums aren't trying to be exclusive; rather, they're formed by innkeepers who want to converse freely amongst themselves without moderation or vendor involvement. Here are two of the most popular forums:

  • **The PAII Forum (www.paii.org):** Participation in this active forum requires membership in the PAII. Innkeepers, aspiring innkeepers, and vendors interact, seeking and giving advice and referrals.

  • **Innspiring Forum (www.innspiring.com):** This active forum is comprised of a group of innkeepers and a few vendors who daily share stories, ask each other questions, and discuss topics of interest to the group, such as vendor recommendations, occupancy rates, handling specific guest situations, and so on.

Finding a class for aspiring innkeepers

Many classes and workshops are devoted to training aspiring innkeepers. The format and schedule of these classes differ, so take some time to find a class that you feel is best geared toward your needs. Classes are offered across the country and at a variety of times during the year, so with a little research, you should be able to find a convenient class near you. For help in finding classes for aspiring innkeepers, check these resources:

- **PAII.** Go to www.paii.org and click on Resources, Vendor Marketplace, Education & Events, and Workshops, respectively.

- **State, local or regional B&B associations.**

- **Industry consultants.** (See Chapter 3 to find a consultant.)

- **Online B&B directories.** (See Chapter 8 for information on how to find an online B&B directory.)

Taking a test drive

If you're ready to roll up your sleeves and give innkeeping a test drive, you may want to consider taking a hands-on course offered at an individual inn or volunteering as an innkeeper.

- **Hands-on training at an individual inn:** Inns across the country offer these classes, usually on an individual basis. You should expect the class to be about a week in length with an organized course outline. At the beginning of the week, you typically learn through observation, and by the end of the week, most classes have you taking care of guests with the help of an experienced innkeeper in the background. The best way to find a hands-on training class is through bed & breakfast associations, by asking for a referral in an innkeeper forum, or by checking the new innkeeper resources section in many online directories.

- **Volunteering as an innkeeper:** You may consider contacting some inns in the area where you live to see whether any B&B owners would be interested in having you as a volunteer innkeeper. This arrangement could be for a few hours each day or for a few days at a time. While you aren't paid, the experience you receive is invaluable, and you have a B&B owner or manager to ask questions about the business. If you volunteer, remember that your primary focus is to be dedicated to keeping their inn running — not to constantly be asking questions.

Chapter 2

Deciding on the Location and Style of Your B&B

. . . .

In This Chapter

▶ Finding a location you'll be happy and successful in

▶ Figuring out the personality and style of your B&B

▶ Deciding how big your bed & breakfast should be

. . . .

Choosing the location and style of your bed & breakfast are important decisions in the formation of your business. By making these choices, you're choosing your work environment, the location of the inn, and the type of guests you'll attract.

In this chapter I help you balance the pros and cons of bed & breakfast locations and styles to meet your goals, whether you're searching for a new location or trying to decide whether your existing residence would be a good spot for a B&B. This is your business and you're the boss, so I help you use that power to find a location and style for your business that make sense not only financially, but emotionally as well.

Choosing a Location for Your B&B

Location, location, location is a phrase that should ring in your mind as you search for the perfect spot for your bed & breakfast. The location you choose for your B&B will have a huge impact on your happiness, your inn's success, and your ability to meet your goals, but you can't find a good location until you know what you're looking for. As you search for the perfect location, look for a venue that can fulfill both your business and personal goals.

When analyzing locations, the four most important questions to ask are:

- ✔ Will you be happy in the area?
- ✔ Will guests come?
- ✔ Will zoning be an issue?
- ✔ What do current area innkeepers have to say?

Whatever your reasons for opening a bed & breakfast, your location needs to be a balance between your personal preferences and business reality. In this section, you evaluate what you want in an area, look at whether the location can draw enough guests to keep you in business, make sure zoning laws fit your plans, and get some feedback from local innkeepers.

Identifying what you want in an area

When you choose the location for your inn, you make two decisions in one — where you will live and where you will work — and you need to be happy on both counts. The best way to prevent burnout is to love where you are and what you're doing, so finding a location that you like is an important step in ensuring a great and long-lasting innkeeping career.

If you don't choose your location carefully, you may find yourself loving your business but being unhappy in your location or loving your business and your location but not being as successful as you want to be. When you're an innkeeper, changing your work environment — the location of your inn — isn't as feasible as it is with most jobs, so choosing a comfortable environment at the outset is important.

You can open a bed & breakfast practically anywhere, so pick an area that makes sense to you. There are many questions you need to ask yourself and some self-analysis you need to perform in choosing your location. Even if the location is your current residence, you must conduct all the same evaluations that you would for any other property. Some things to consider are

- ✔ **Local activities and attractions that interest you:** Basing your initial property search on your hobbies and interests increases the likelihood of your happiness, which in turn can lead to greater business satisfaction and help you to avoid burnout. Do you want an area that offers skiing? Historical significance? The ocean?

- ✔ **Climate:** Conduct your search in an area where you find the climate agreeable. If, for example, you like cold weather, opening a B&B on a ski slope in Vermont may be a good match for you.

✔ **Downtime and seasonal closures:** How much to do you want to work? Do you want to work 7 days a week, 365 days a year, or do you only want to work on the weekends? Do you want to be able to take several months off to travel on your own?

If you'd like to take winters off, for example, you might want to start your search in an area like central Maine, where few guests visit during the winter. Because winter is the slow season there, you wouldn't be giving up a great deal of income by being closed then. On the other hand, if you want a full-time inn, you'd be better off in a location where it makes more sense from a financial point of view to be open year-round.

✔ **Outside employment opportunities:** If you or your partner intend to work outside of the inn, are there sufficient job opportunities in the area?

After you narrow down your choices to an area that seems right for you, you need to determine whether it makes business sense, that is, whether guests will come.

If you build it, will they come? Gauging an area's drawing power

While it's important to be happy in the area where you live, the only way to run a successful bed & breakfast is to be located in an area that guests will visit. The bed & breakfast inn experience is unique, but it's rarely a destination in and of itself, so you need to look for area events, attractions, activities, and businesses that can bring guests to your inn.

To determine an area's potential as a location for your bed & breakfast, you need to conduct a *market analysis.* This is the process of taking a close look at your area to understand who the potential guests are; what the competition is like; when guests are most likely to visit; and what activities, attractions, and events bring them to the area. In this section, I discuss what draws guests to a region, what may keep them away, and how to analyze whether an area can likely support your inn.

Knowing what brings guests to an area

Guests need a reason to visit your area and things to do while they're there before they're likely to stay with you. Knowing the types of activities, attractions, events, and businesses that bring guests to a given area helps you determine how good that potential location would be. Use Table 2-1 as a starting point to check off what brings guests to the area you're considering and what they do once they get there.

Look beyond peak weekends and special events, when you should expect to be full. Analyze what brings guests to the area mid-week and during slower seasons.

Table 2-1	Analyzing What Brings Guests to an Area			
Points of Interest	**Natural Attractions**	**Activities**	**Events**	**Businesses**
Amusement parks	Beaches	Antiquing and shopping	Art fairs	Colleges & universities
Archaeological sites	Cave systems	Biking	Concerts	Corporations
Casinos	Fall foliage	Boating and fishing	Conventions	Fine dining
Churches	Hot springs	Golfing	Cultural and regional fairs	Funeral homes
Covered bridges	Lakes	Hiking	Dance performances	Government agencies
Gardens	Mountains	Horseback riding	Film festivals	Hospices
Historic sites	National parks	Hot air ballooning	Flea markets	Hospitals
Mansions	State parks	Hunting	Plays and musicals	Retirement homes
Monuments	Wetlands	Swimming	Races	Spas
Museums	Wildlife reserves	Water sports	Spectator sports	
Wineries		Winter sports		

Red flags: Recognizing what keeps guests away

Buying or starting up a bed & breakfast is a big investment. Picking the wrong location could mean losing your life's savings and your home, so knowing what to avoid is just as important as knowing what to look for in a location. Think twice before ignoring any of the following red flags:

- ✔ **An overabundance of lodging choices with low occupancy:** If a number of B&Bs and hotels are already struggling to survive in an area, your inn is unlikely to be able to attract guests that they couldn't.

- ✔ **A location that's not a destination and on the way to nowhere:** You'll have a tough time filling your rooms in a location that doesn't draw guests through attractions and isn't a convenient stopover point on a popularly traveled route.

- **A place that's hard to get to:** Your inn needs to be accessible. Say you fall in love with a beautiful seaside cottage that you think would make the perfect B&B, but the roads to get to the town it's located in are nearly nonexistent. Although the privacy such a location offers is appealing, your target market would be very limited and you'd have to spend a lot of effort and money advertising to fill your rooms.

- **An area that's economically depressed:** Not only are economically depressed areas usually not tourist attractions, but you also need to consider whether you or your partner would be able to find desirable jobs outside of the inn if your business plan requires a second income to sustain the inn.

Checking the numbers: Analyzing an area's potential market

A variety of resources can help you conduct a market analysis to weigh the pros and cons of your potential location. They can assist you in determining whether an area you're considering has the potential to attract guests and sustain your bed & breakfast. Here are some good places to start:

- **SCORE:** SCORE (www.score.org) is a nonprofit association and a resource partner of the U.S. Small Business Administration (SBA). SCORE counselors are usually retired business owners, executives, and corporate leaders who are experienced in analyzing business situations. They volunteer their time to help new small business owners, like you, get started. Contact SCORE to see whether your local chapter has anyone who can help you perform your market analysis.

- **Inn consultants:** Inn consultants are professionals who can help you objectively evaluate an area and its viability as the location for your bed & breakfast. (See Chapter 3 for help in finding an inn consultant.)

- **State and local tourism boards:** Contact by phone or, if possible, visit your state tourism board and introduce yourself as a prospective innkeeper. Ask for a list of lodging establishments and tourist attractions in the area you're considering for your bed & breakfast. Develop a rapport, and ask about high and low seasons and the main reasons guests visit the area. You should be able to get a wealth of information on lodging statistics, occupancy rates, and area attractions. Use Table 2-1 to keep track of the unique characteristics of each area you're interested in.

- **Chamber of commerce or visitors bureau:** As with the state tourism board, introduce yourself as a prospective innkeeper. This visit should always be in person. Let them know how excited you are about the possibility of opening a B&B in their area. Solicit their advice and engage their help by asking them for detailed information about what brings guests to the area and what the high and low seasons are for tourism. Continue to add to Table 2-1 with any additional information that they provide. Ask them about the occupancy of other lodging establishments in the area.

If you find yourself evaluating extremely positive reports on how popular the area is, remember that the chamber's purpose is to serve as a cheerleader for the area, so the advice you receive may not be completely objective.

Watching out for unfriendly zoning laws

Without proper zoning, you won't be able to operate your business. Many bed & breakfasts have failed because of unfriendly zoning restrictions. Check local zoning laws and restrictions before falling in love with a location or property, and you'll save yourself a lot of grief, wasted time, and aggravation.

Among other restrictions, states and local areas may

- Prohibit bed & breakfasts entirely
- Limit the number of rooms and overnight guests you can have
- Dictate the type of kitchen you must install (commercial kitchens are very expensive)
- Regulate what you can serve for breakfast
- Prohibit you from having a sign outside your inn

Going into an area thinking you can get a conditional use permit is risky and rarely pays off. Make sure you can live with all applicable zoning laws and that the restrictions they pose fit into your business plan. (See Chapters 4 and 5 for more info on zoning considerations.)

Asking other innkeepers about the area

When you're seriously considering an area because you want to find a property for your bed & breakfast there or because you've found a property that you're seriously thinking about making an offer on, staying at other local lodging accommodations, as a paying guest, is recommended. (Before doing so, be sure to read the section "Getting ideas by staying at other B&Bs" later in this chapter for some important warnings and considerations.) When you take these scout-it-out trips, try to find out the following:

- Are there area associations that the innkeeper belongs to or recommends?
- How long has the innkeeper been in the area?
- What does the innkeeper like and dislike about innkeeping in the area?

Envisioning Your B&B Style

After you've narrowed down some possible locations, the next step is to determine the type of B&B you'd like to own. The best way to think about this is to consider what you'd be comfortable selling. Your bed & breakfast is a business, and you are selling the experience of staying at your inn. Bed & breakfast shapes, sizes, and personalities are as unique as those of their innkeepers. Your goal is to find a balance between the style of B&B that you want to own, who you want your potential guests to be, and the personal and financial goals you have for your business.

Finding a style that best reflects you

Basing your inn's focus on your likes and hobbies — such as restoring old homes, gardening, wine, motorcycles, skiing, hunting, antiquing, and so on — helps everything else fall into place. Oftentimes the personality of a property is defined by the type of property that it is, be it a farm, a historic property, an elegant Victorian, and so on. You want to be sure that your personality and the inn's personality are in synch.

For instance, consider Pleasant Bay Bed & Breakfast & Llama Keep, which has been serving guests for nearly 20 years. More than 50 percent of their business comes from repeat guests and referrals. When looking for their location, the couple who own the inn knew that he had always wanted to be a farmer and she loved llamas from her days in the Peace Corps. When they found a large piece of property on the coast of Maine, they knew they had found a comfortable place where they could welcome guests, he could live his dream of farming, and she could have her llamas. Today the bed & breakfast is run on a 110-acre working llama farm. This works for them because the location they chose and the property's personality support the lifestyle they were seeking.

In contrast, the owners of Blair Hill Inn in central Maine had traveled for their corporate careers and wanted to get away from hotels. They knew they liked skiing, cooking, entertaining, keeping grounds, historic properties, and renovating. They wanted to be busy most of the year, but also wanted a B&B that would allow them some time for themselves. With these aspects in mind, they looked for a location that had natural seasonal closures and times when few guests visited (they usually close in April and November, accordingly). They found an historic inn in need of renovation, and have turned it into a successful bed & breakfast business.

Innkeeping is a full-time job, so just because you love to ski and find the perfect location for your inn in a ski area, don't be surprised if you don't have as much time — or any time in the start-up years — as you'd like to devote to skiing.

Matching your B&B style to the guests you want to attract

Part of an innkeeper's job is to make innkeeping look easy. Hosting and serving people is easier when you know what they want and can relate to their needs. For example, it would be easy for you to host business travelers if you'd just left the corporate world, because you'd understand the needs and demands of business travelers. However, it would be difficult for you to host guests who came to visit your area's many wineries if you didn't know anything about wine.

The style of your inn and the service you offer should support the guests you're trying to attract. Characterizing those guests can help define the style of your bed & breakfast. Here's how to create a style targeted to your guests:

1. **Start by identifying who your guests will be.**

   Ask yourself what type of people will be staying at your inn. For example, will they be families on vacation, business travelers, or couples seeking a quick weekend getaway?

2. **Create a guest profile.**

   Think about the age, education, hobbies, interests, affiliations, preferences, and income level of the guests you hope to attract, as well as the geographic location you expect to draw them from.

3. **Identify the reasons for their travel.**

   Make a list of the reasons guests will be visiting your area. For example, will they be sightseeing, visiting wineries, or passing through on their way to another destination?

4. **Decide how your inn will accommodate your target guests.**

   Make sure your inn will offer what the market wants. For example, if you want to cater to business travelers, your guest rooms don't need to be drenched with antiques, but they need to be large enough to provide comfortable work areas. Guests on romantic getaways, on the other hand, may care less about early breakfast times and more about whirlpools and fireplaces.

5. **Define what makes your B&B distinctive and unique.**

   Because guests have many lodging choices, it's your job to define what makes your inn unique and why guests should choose your inn over another B&B or hotel in the area. Perhaps you'll offer flexible breakfast times to business travelers or breakfast in bed for those on a romantic getaway. Or maybe you'll serve as an expert concierge who's able to handle special requests or suggest the best places to visit.

Getting ideas by staying at other B&Bs

Because good innkeepers make the job of innkeeping look easy, merely staying at other B&Bs is not a good indication of what the lifestyle of innkeeping is like or what the job of an innkeeper entails. (See Chapter 1 for information on what it's like to be an innkeeper.)

Staying at other B&Bs is a good way, however, to get an idea of what you like and don't like as a guest. It's a great way to figure out what you want to offer your own guests and how you may or may not want to do things at your own bed & breakfast. You can and should sleep around. When you do, be on the lookout for

- ✓ Amenities you like
- ✓ Policies you like and don't like
- ✓ Room furnishings you like
- ✓ Breakfast ideas and settings

You may want to explain the vision of your B&B to the innkeeper and ask for his opinion. This is a touchy exercise, but one I recommend. Use your people skills to determine how comfortable the innkeeper is talking with you. The level of support you're likely to receive differs by areas. Some areas are very competitive and others are very collaborative; you should quickly assess this and tailor your questions accordingly.

It's important to remember that no matter how much help an innkeeper wants to offer you, he's running a business. To get the most out of the encounter and be considerate of the innkeeper's time, keep your questions brief and targeted. He has other guests to serve, bathrooms to clean, and errands to run. Here are two important "don'ts":

- ✓ Don't monopolize innkeepers' time, thus keeping them from their other guests or duties.
- ✓ Don't expect them to provide you with training. You are only paying to be a guest, not to take a workshop. (See Chapter 1 for advice and training resources.)

Deciding How Big Your B&B Should Be

Ask ten people how big your bed & breakfast should be, and you'll probably get ten different answers. The size of your B&B is ultimately determined by local zoning laws, your personal and financial resources, your objectives, and careful planning and projections. Here are some things to consider when trying to decide how big your bed & breakfast should be:

✔ **What you can afford:** How much you can afford is directly related to how much money you can put down and what you'll have in reserve. At a minimum, you need money for a down payment. While not easy to secure, this amount can range from as little as 10 percent down with an SBA 7A loan program to 25 percent down for a commercial loan through a bank. (See Chapters 4 and 5 for information on financing.)

You may need money for closing costs, renovations, or improvements, and, often, to bring a property up to code. You also need funds for marketing and furnishing the inn. All of these calculations should be worked out by creating a business plan to determine what you can realistically afford. (See Chapter 3 for help in creating a business plan.)

✔ **How many rooms you need to be profitable:** I often hear that you need at least 5 to 10 rooms to be profitable. While this is not an unrealistic number, many things contribute to the calculation of profitability, including the cost of your debt service and your occupancy rate.

For example, in 2007 InnMatchmakers, specialty inn brokers in Colorado, helped a young couple purchase a small, non-operating, historic B&B in the Colorado mountains for $350,000. With only three guest rooms, the couple worked hard to market the property. They expanded by adding a fourth guest room, and at the end of their first year in business, had booked nearly $90,000 in gross revenues. Sometimes, size isn't all that matters!

✔ **How much staff you plan to hire:** The bigger the inn, the more likely you'll need to hire staff to assist you.

✔ **How much you want to work:** The bigger the inn, the bigger the mortgage and the more nights you'll need to fill your rooms.

✔ **Local and state zoning and licensing laws:** Zoning and licensing laws often restrict such things as the number of rooms you may have at your inn, the maximum length of guest stays, breakfast regulations, and how big each room must be. (See Chapters 4 and 5 for more information on zoning.)

Ensuring room to grow

Entering innkeeping with the vision of success means considering how you will grow your business not only at the outset but also well into the future. At some point, you may decide to grow your business through expansion, so it's a good idea to allow for that possibility from the get-go. Factors that may affect your ability to expand in the future include

✔ Whether local and state zoning laws allow expansion

✔ Whether the building lends itself to additions

✔ Whether there's enough physical property to support expansion, including room for additional parking

Consider these issues before investing time and money in either buying an existing inn or in finding a suitable location to build your bed & breakfast business.

Part II
Transitioning from Inn Goer to Inn Owner

The 5th Wave   By Rich Tennant

"We can get this B&B back up and running. It just needs some fresh flowers and some potpourri simmering on the stove. Oh, and let's get rid of those alligator motels."

In this part . . .

Turn your dream into a reality by putting your vision on paper and developing a road map for your success. I show you how to create a business plan and go about getting advice from experts in the field. I also help you weigh the decision of purchasing an existing inn or building one from scratch. If you decide that buying an existing inn is the way to go, you come to understand the process from offer to close, what to be careful of, and how to transition the inn from the previous innkeeper's turf to something you can call your own. If your plan is to build an inn or convert an existing property, I give you an overview of this process and warn you about the most common pitfalls other innkeepers have encountered.

Chapter 3

Creating the Plan for Your Business

In This Chapter

▶ Getting expert advice from CPAs or accountants, lawyers, and consultants

▶ Creating a road map for your business with a business plan

▶ Creating financial forecasts

C reating a plan for your business is as important as creating a plan for any major event in your life. Created correctly, your business plan will give you clear direction through the start-up phase of your business. In the process, you'll be assembling the information you need to create a loan package to secure financing. After your new business is up and running, your plan will keep you focused and on track as your business grows and matures.

In this chapter, I help you find the resources and experts who can help you answer the tough questions it takes to decide whether the lifestyle of innkeeping can meet your financial goals. I help you create a plan for your business that can be used to get financing, and then I help you plan for the future prosperity of your bed & breakfast.

Getting Expert Advice

If you're like most innkeepers, you're investing your life's savings into your home and business together. Knowing how to separate your business and personal space from a legal and financial point of view has some unique twists and requires advice from experts.

Bringing an accountant and lawyer on-board

Two of the most important experts you need to hire at the onset are an accountant and a lawyer. They can assist you in making crucial organizational decisions, and make sure you've covered all the bases.

Hiring an accountant

Finding an accountant or certified public accountant (CPA) who is familiar with the lodging industry — and bed & breakfasts in particular — helps to ensure that you set up your books to record your business and personal expenses correctly from the start. Asking other innkeepers or innkeeper consultants for recommendations is the best way to find a CPA or accountant who understands the nuances of bed & breakfast accounting procedures. (See Chapter 1 for help in finding innkeeper resources.) If you can't find someone with first-hand knowledge of the industry, make sure the person you select is used to accommodating the individual needs of small businesses.

Have your CPA or accountant help you customize your accounts to meet your business's needs. (Table 6-1 in Chapter 6 shows a sample chart of accounts for a bed & breakfast.) At the end of the year, ask her to prepare the journal entries for more complicated items, such as depreciation.

Seeking advice from a lawyer

Finding a lawyer with a good corporate, business, and contract law background who understands the needs of a small business will help you get the best answers to your legal questions. You want a lawyer who can help you determine the best organization for your business. During the course of operating your bed & breakfast, you'll probably also want legal advice on such matters as the wording of your policies (to be sure they're clear but not discriminatory) and the handling of gift certificates, as well as the review of contracts and other documents that affect the business.

Many innkeepers have difficulty finding lawyers who have experience in the bed & breakfast industry. Remember that your lawyer (and CPA or accountant for that matter) doesn't necessarily need to live close to you. Of course, she must know federal tax laws, and if she doesn't live within your state or jurisdiction, be certain she has an extensive working knowledge of the tax laws in your state or jurisdiction. You can contact B&B organizations such as the Professional Association of Innkeepers International (PAII; www.paii.org) or your local B&B association for lawyer recommendations (see Chapter 1 for help in finding innkeeper resources).

Asking key questions of your lawyer and accountant

Just like every other small business owner, you'll have specific questions about running your business that should be reviewed by a lawyer, CPA, or accountant. In the bed & breakfast industry, the answers are very seldom simple or mutually exclusive. For example, living in the same building and space that houses your business creates issues about how much space is used for personal purposes and, therefore, what percentage of your expenses qualifies as a business deduction. This, and many other questions unique to your B&B, cannot be covered in a book like this, but the next sections help you put together a list of questions to get the ball rolling.

Structuring your business

Your business is a legal entity, and you need to decide what legal form the business should take. The most common choices are sole proprietorships, general partnerships, limited partnerships, C corporations, S corporations, and limited liability companies (LLCs). Each has advantages and disadvantages. Some forms are more restrictive than others, and, depending on your personal situation, some may have greater tax benefits. Hugh Daniels, a long-time innkeeper and industry consultant (www.askhugh.com), advises his clients against sole proprietorships; although they are easy to set up, the liability and tax issues can be huge. Consult both your CPA or accountant and your lawyer to determine the legal structure that's best for your business.

Making smart legal and tax moves

Decisions that you make as you're setting up your business affect how your business is taxed while you own it and when you sell it. Seeking both legal and tax advice early in the process is important because your lawyer and accountant will help you address questions that you may not think to ask, such as:

- Should you separate the real estate from the business and have each owned by a different entity? If so, which entity should own the real estate portion of the business?
  - Are there tax considerations if there are two forms of ownership, whereby one entity owns the real estate and rents it to the other entity, which owns and operates the business?
  - What effect does this arrangement have on either entity's legal exposure?
- Are there benefits of putting the real-estate portion of the business into a trust?
- If the business name is jointly owned, should the business be in both parties' names?

Consulting an inn consultant

You may decide to seek the advice of professionals to help you determine whether your plan is realistic and then help you put it in writing. (Even if you write your plan yourself, you may want to engage a consultant to help you review it.) Inn consultants can help in this respect; in fact, many of them have walked in your shoes as innkeepers themselves.

In addition to helping you put together your business plan, inn consultants can recommend accountants and lawyers or coach you on how to pick professionals familiar with the issues that you'll face as a B&B owner.

Table 3-1 lists the key industry consultants who can help you create a strong, clear plan for your business.

Table 3-1	Professional Inn Consultants
Company	*Web Site*
Ask Hugh Consulting	www.askhugh.com
Bushnell & Bushnell	www.bushnellandbushnell.com
Hiler Hospitality	www.hilerhospitality.com
Inngenium LLC	www.inngenium.com
Innseminars	www.innseminars.com
Inn Consulting Partners	www.innpartners.com
Lodging Resources	www.lodgingresources.com
The B&B Team	www.bbteam.com

Brushing Up on Business Plan Basics

Creating a business plan is a step many small business owners, especially busy innkeepers, are tempted to skip over. Most business plans are created in order to secure financing, so while it's not as much fun as picking out amenities and planning menus, creating your plan is probably the most important thing you can do to ensure your B&B's success. Without a good plan, you end up with chaos, and no business can succeed for long without clear direction. Your business will have a greater chance of success if you go through the exercise of setting your goals and analyzing your projections, your break-even point, and your best- and worst-case scenarios.

If you decide to create your business plan on your own, there are many templates that you can use. The Small Business Administration (SBA) offers a wealth of information on its Web site (www.sba.gov). Also check out *Business Plans Kit For Dummies,* 2nd Edition, by Steven D. Peterson, PhD, Peter E. Jaret, and Barbara Findlay Schenck (also published by Wiley). But remember that your business plan should be unique to your B&B. So if you use a template, make sure that the person reading your plan can't tell. By simply filling in the blanks, you're unlikely to be able to adequately convey your passion and vision for your business and the research that should go into your plan.

Although it's important to create a business plan that presents an organized look and feel and makes a good first impression, your focus should be on the planning process rather than the actual document itself. When you present your plan, by all means, ensure that it is well laid out and professionally proofed. However, don't spend valuable time on colors, graphs, and diagrams that could be better spent refining your data and assumptions.

Why you need a business plan

The main reasons to create a business plan are

- ✔ **To create a road map for your business:** Your business plan should chart the course and direction you think your business will take by clearly defining your business structure, goals, and projections.

- ✔ **To secure financing:** Done correctly, you can create a plan that will convince a bank to loan you money.

- ✔ **To evaluate your performance against your projections:** Once you're in business, your business plan serves as a tool to help you analyze whether you're meeting, exceeding, or falling below your expectations.

The process of creating your business plan is an exercise that forces you to anticipate what may happen and set your goals and strategies accordingly. When you write down your goals and refer to them often, you're more assured of achieving them.

Your business plan is not just your proposal and request for financing; it's also a commitment that you're making to yourself, your family, any investors, and your business. Because all important commitments require time to consider, writing a business plan requires a significant allocation of your time. Whether you seek outside advice from consultants or decide to create the plan yourself, you need to schedule time to do the proper research, gather documentation, and perform the analysis necessary to write a sound plan. Don't underestimate this time commitment — keeping on track and meeting the deadlines that define your B&B purchase or startup is your responsibility.

And while you should be passionate about your business, don't miss the opportunity to see flaws in your plan. If, during your research, you find that achieving the occupancy rate necessary to meet your goals is going to be difficult, stop and take a good, hard look at your motivation and the realistic prospects for your bed & breakfast. Think of the money, time, and aggravation you'll save by using the planning process to discover major obstacles to the success of your business.

Looking at the parts of your plan

To give you an idea of the scope of a well-written business plan, the main sections should include

- ✔ **A cover page** that serves as an introduction to the plan and includes your contact information.

- ✔ **A table of contents** so those reading your plan can quickly find the specific information that's of interest to them. Your table of contents says a lot about your plan — the more organized it appears, the better the first impression it makes on the reader. A comprehensive plan contains 20 or more pages, so organization is key.

- ✔ **An executive summary** that serves as an introduction to your bed & breakfast. This should be a comprehensive description of your business, including your vision and goals for your B&B as well as the services that you plan to offer. In defining the vision for your B&B, include the major features of your inn and how you intend to operate it. Also identify in detail what makes your bed & breakfast special and unique, and why someone would choose your inn over the competition.

- ✔ **A company description** outlining your corporate form and any partners involved in the business.

- ✔ **A market analysis** that outlines the strengths and weaknesses of any competitors in the area, who you expect your guests to be, the benefits of your location, and the niche your bed & breakfast will fill.

- ✔ **A product and services analysis** describing the types of accommodations and services your bed & breakfast will provide.

✔ **A marketing plan** that includes one of the following:

  • **For an existing inn:** How you plan to fill your rooms and grow your business beyond the current level of occupancy.

  • **For a new inn:** How you plan to bring guests to the inn.

✔ **A funding request** that outlines the financing you're applying for if you're using the plan as a loan request document.

✔ **Financial statements** that include such reports as budgeted income and cash flow statements, a break-even analysis, and one-, two- and three-year forecasts of each report. This section should include supporting documents to back up your figures and forecasts. Use the example in Figure 3-1 for help in understanding how to forecast the figures you need to create these reports. Figure 3-2 shows you an example of how these figures are used to compile a budgeted income statement. When the plan is presented to a potential lender, you'll also need to include personal tax returns and credit history information.

✔ **Appendixes** that can include more information about your background and your qualifications to run a successful B&B, as well as information about your lawyer, CPA or accountant, consultant, bank, and so forth.

For many years, lenders made loans based on projections of future cash flows. Today, however, they want hard facts and solid numbers before granting loans. Additionally, in the past, many bed & breakfasts were financed with residential loans, whereas most new bed & breakfast loans must now go through the rigorous application process for a commercial loan. Thus, a good, solid business plan, backed up by historical performance numbers, is a necessity. (See Chapters 4 and 5 for more information on financing.)

A five-step plan for writing a business plan

Hilary Jones of Inngenium (www.inngenium.com), who has written hundreds of business plans for bed & breakfasts, outlines five steps that can guide you toward the proper preparation crucial to your success as an innkeeper:

1. Start early.

2. Get organized.

3. Dig deep with your research.

4. Consider adversity.

5. Back up all assumptions with credible sources.

Figure 3-1: The types of numbers you need to prepare a budgeted income and cash flow statement with room revenue forecasting.

	January	February	March	April	May	June	July	August	September	October	November	December	TOTAL
REVENUES													
Room rental *	$ 5,813	$ 5,250	$ 6,975	$ 6,750	$ 8,138	$ 13,500	$ 13,950	$ 13,950	$ 7,875	$ 6,975	$ 5,625	$ 5,813	$ 100,614
Gift shop sales	50	50	50	50	75	150	150	150	150	50	50	50	1,175
Other income	10	10	10	10	10	10	10	10	10	10	10	10	120
Total Revenues	5,873	5,310	7,035	6,810	8,223	13,660	14,160	14,210	8,035	7,035	5,685	5,873	101,909
EXPENSES													
Cost of goods sold -- gift shop	17	17	17	17	26	51	68	85	51	17	17	17	400
Professional fees	–	–	100	250	–	–	250	–	–	–	–	200	800
Utilities	180	150	180	200	200	170	205	300	350	180	150	200	2,465
Repairs/Maintenance	200	200	200	200	200	200	200	200	200	200	200	200	2,400
Insurance	175	175	175	175	175	175	175	175	175	175	175	175	2,100
Office supplies/Postage	80	80	80	80	80	80	80	80	80	80	80	80	960
Food expense	400	400	400	500	500	600	650	700	600	500	400	400	6,050
Room/Building supplies	150	150	150	200	275	300	350	400	350	200	150	150	2,825
Garden	50	50	100	100	150	200	200	200	125	100	50	50	1,375
Hot tub	25	25	25	25	25	25	25	25	25	25	25	25	300
Linens	104	94	125	121	146	242	250	250	141	125	101	104	1,803
Training/Seminars	–	–	400	–	–	–	–	–	–	–	–	–	400
Travel	–	–	375	375	–	–	–	–	–	–	–	–	750
Advertising/Printing	200	200	500	500	500	250	250	200	200	200	200	200	3,400
Dues/Subscriptions	150	20	20	20	20	200	20	20	20	20	20	20	550
Taxes/Licenses	200	200	200	200	200	200	200	200	200	250	250	250	2,550
Interest expense (mortgage)	2,000	2,000	2,000	2,000	2,000	2,000	2,000	2,000	2,000	2,000	2,000	2,000	24,000
Bank charges	25	25	25	25	25	25	25	25	25	25	25	25	300
Travel agent commission	25	25	30	50	50	100	100	100	50	25	25	25	605
Credit card fees	200	200	200	250	300	400	500	600	500	250	200	200	3,800
Amortization of organizational costs	167	167	167	167	167	167	167	167	167	167	167	167	2,004
Depreciation	833	833	833	833	833	833	833	833	833	833	833	833	9,996
Miscellaneous	10	10	10	10	10	10	10	10	10	10	10	10	120
Total Expenses	5,191	5,021	6,312	6,298	5,882	6,228	6,558	6,570	6,102	5,382	5,078	5,331	69,953
Net Income	$ 682	$ 289	$ 723	$ 512	$ 2,341	$ 7,432	$ 7,602	$ 7,640	$ 1,933	$ 1,653	$ 607	$ 542	$ 31,956

Budgeted Cash Flow Statement

	January	February	March	April	May	June	July	August	September	October	November	December	TOTAL
Net income	$ 682	$ 289	$ 723	$ 512	$ 2,341	$ 7,432	$ 7,602	$ 7,640	$ 1,933	$ 1,653	$ 607	$ 542	$ 31,956
Add: Non-cash expenses													
Amortization of organizational costs	167	167	167	167	167	167	167	167	167	167	167	167	2,004
Depreciation	833	833	833	833	833	833	833	833	833	833	833	833	9,996
Less: Other cash expenditures													
Capital expenditures	(400)	(400)	(400)	(400)	(400)	(400)	(400)	(400)	(400)	(400)	(400)	(400)	(4,800)
Mortgage principal payments	(833)	(833)	(833)	(833)	(833)	(833)	(833)	(833)	(833)	(833)	(833)	(833)	(9,996)
Cash inflow (Outflow)**	$ 449	$ 56	$ 490	$ 279	$ 2,108	$ 7,199	$ 7,369	$ 7,407	$ 1,700	$ 1,420	$ 374	$ 309	$ 29,160
** before any income taxes													
* Room Rental Revenue													
Occupancy rate [A]	25%	25%	30%	30%	35%	45%	45%	45%	35%	30%	25%	25%	25%
# of rooms [B]	5	5	5	5	5	5	5	5	5	5	5	5	5
# of nights available [C]	31	28	31	30	31	30	31	31	30	31	30	31	31
Actual room rate [D]	150	150	150	150	150	150	150	150	150	150	150	150	150
Room Rental Revenue [A x B x C x D]	$ 5,813	$ 5,250	$ 6,975	$ 6,750	$ 8,138	$ 13,500	$ 13,950	$ 13,950	$ 7,875	$ 6,975	$ 5,625	$ 5,813	$ 5,813

REVENUES

Room rental	$100,614
Gift shop sales	1,175
Other income	120
Total Revenues	101,909

EXPENSES

Cost of goods sold -- gift shop	400
Professional fees	800
Utilities	2,465
Repairs/Maintenance	2,400
Insurance	2,100
Office supplies/Postage	960
Food expense	6,050
Room/Building supplies	2,825
Garden	1,375
Hot tub	300
Linens	1,803
Training/Seminars	400
Travel	750
Advertising/Printing	3,400
Dues/Subscriptions	550
Taxes/Licenses	2,550
Interest expense (mortgage)	24,000
Bank charges	300
Travel agent commission	605
Credit card fees	3,800
Amortization of organizational costs	2,004
Depreciation	9,996
Miscellaneous	120
Total Expenses	69,953

Net Income* $31,956

*before debt principal payments and any income taxes

Figure 3-2:
An example
budget
income
statement.

Creating Your Financial Forecasts

All of your well-thought-out planning comes down to the numbers. The numbers you use in your forecasts are only as good as the research that goes into getting them. Without good, honest, up-to-date research, your forecasts and budget will be unrealistic.

Your finances are one of the primary areas that your banker looks at when determining your loan value, so they should be a major factor in all your decisions concerning your B&B. Spend time to get numbers you can trust for revenues, wages, operating expenses, marketing, renovations, insurance and licenses, start-up costs, legal and accounting expenses, and so forth.

If you don't have a background in finance or accounting, it's a good idea to prepare your forecasts with professional assistance.

Forecasting your revenue

Revenue is the money that you take in from all aspects of your business. Revenue is primarily generated by guests paying to stay in your rooms, but it can also come from selling items in a gift shop, hosting special events, and the like. The more room nights your inn is booked the higher your revenue will be, so the price of your rooms and how many nights they are occupied are used to calculate your revenue.

Estimating occupancy

According to the 2007-2008 PAII Industry Study of Operations and Finance, the average annual occupancy rate of participating inns was 43 percent. Your occupancy rate may vary significantly from this depending on many factors, such as location, amount of time in business, and whether the B&B has been marketed effectively in the past.

If you're taking over an existing inn, in your first year of operation, you should forecast your occupancy rate monthly by looking back at the numbers from previous years and deciding what, if anything, you want to change to bring more guests to your business. Making projections on a monthly basis helps you to factor in the high- and low-season variables, as well as account for any local events and activities. Add up the monthly occupancy rates for the year, and then divide by 12 to estimate your first year's average occupancy rate. If you're starting your B&B from scratch, most experts advise taking no more than 50 percent of the average occupancy rate of similar, established properties in the area as a first-year estimate of occupancy.

Others suggest estimating 10 to 15 percent as your total-year figure. Because there is no right answer and your situation and location are unique, do as much research as possible to get the most realistic evaluation. Here are some sources of data as well as trends and events to consider when creating your occupancy estimate:

- ✔ **Historical occupancy,** if you're taking over an existing inn.

- ✔ **Occupancy of other properties.** Yours will be less if you're a start-up business.

- ✔ **Festivals and events that bring guests to the area.** Look at your target market and determine dates that are important to those guests. For example, if you're in or near a college town, check the dates that parents and students will be touring prospective colleges, settling new students in, and visiting for special events and graduations.

- ✔ **Occupancy predictions** from the chamber of commerce and/or the convention and visitors bureau.

  Be careful about using published occupancy figures from these sources as your estimate if your location includes a number of large or chain hotels and motels. Occupancy rates of large lodging properties are commonly up to two times those of a small B&B in the same area. These figures can therefore skew your projections and give you an overly optimistic view.

- ✔ **Seasonal patterns.** Determine the time of year guests are most likely to visit (high season) and when it's most likely to be quiet (low season) and estimate your occupancy accordingly.

- ✔ **Economic predictions.** You can't ignore what's going on around you. If the economy is heading into a downturn, expect occupancy rates to decline from the same period last year. If the economy is on an upturn, you should be more optimistic, but realistic, in your occupancy estimates.

Calculating your revenue

To be successful, you'll need a steady stream of revenue and guests flowing through your inn, and the two are directly related to each other. In order to estimate your revenue, you need

- ✔ Your estimated occupancy rate (calculated above)

- ✔ The number of rooms you have available for rent

- ✔ The number of days you're open each month

- ✔ Your room rates (see Chapter 7 for help in calculating your room rates)

Your estimated revenue is the product of these four figures. For example, the inn in Figure 3-1 estimated their revenue in January as follows:

Estimated occupancy rate	25%
Number of rooms available	5
Number of days in January	31
Actual room rate	$150

$.25 \times 5 \times 31 \times 150$ = January revenue of $5,812.50 (rounded up to $5,813.00)

Including other revenue

In the beginning, it's best to focus on your core business — filling your guest rooms. You may, however, be purchasing an existing inn that hosts bridal showers, corporate events, or weddings, and/or has a gift shop. In this case, add the expected revenue from each income producer to your total revenue calculations. (Once your business is established, see Chapter 17 for information on increasing revenue by adding services and a gift shop.)

Projecting costs and expenses

When projecting your costs and expenses, you'll break them down into three categories: organizational costs (sometimes called start-up costs), capital expenditures, and operating expenses:

✓ **Organizational costs** are those expenses that you incur while getting ready to open your doors for business. These expenditures are accounted for on your balance sheet and are amortized over at least five years. They include

- Legal fees in setting up your business

- Registration/filing fees

- Accounting fees to set up your accounting system

- Expenses in investigating the industry and business, such as conventions and training

- Consultant expenses prior to opening

- Most expenses incurred prior to opening that are not capital or operating expenses

✓ **Capital expenditures** are those items that generally have a life of greater than one year and a value of over $1,000, though the definition can be adjusted depending on your circumstances. These also are accounted for on your balance sheet and are depreciated over the life of the asset. These items may include your building, furniture, towels and linens, appliances, renovations, fixtures, and equipment.

✓ **Operating expenses** are the ongoing expenses that include everything you use to produce income, such as food, supplies, wages, utilities, insurance, advertising, memberships, and so forth.

Because it's assumed you'll have greater expenses in your first year due to the costs of getting your bed & breakfast off the ground, your financial plan should contain projections for at least three years.

It generally takes about three years to get enough historical information to be able to accurately forecast expenses and revenues.

This area can be confusing and technical, which is exactly why you need a competent CPA or accountant and/or consultant.

It takes money to make money, and there is no way to avoid the operating (ongoing) expenses necessary to run your B&B. In order to predict when your business will reach the break-even point and then be profitable, you must estimate all your expenses and then subtract them from the revenue that you expect your business to generate (which you forecasted earlier in this chapter). The next sections help you to create forecasts for the biggest and most common operating expenses associated with running a bed & breakfast.

Creating a schedule of payments

Your business will have expected and unexpected expenses. Creating a spreadsheet of known, recurring expenses will help you estimate your financial obligations on a monthly basis.

There are three types of expenses: fixed, variable, and discretionary. Sometimes an expense is a little of two, sometimes it falls into all three. Some payments, such as your mortgage and taxes, don't change during your busy season, whereas others, like your utility payments, probably do. For example, the more guests you entertain at your inn, the higher your utility bill is likely to be. In this case, you can expect the higher revenue coming in (as a result of greater occupancy) to cover the added expense. However, your mortgage and taxes must be paid even during the off-season or when your inn is closed. (Mortgages that have seasonal payments are the exception, and some states treat tax payments similarly.) Having a schedule from which you budget expenses helps your business run smoothly during all seasons.

Create a list of your expected expenses and estimated payments, broken down by month, such as those shown earlier in Figure 3-1. If you're using accounting software, which I highly recommend, you can set up your budget figures for the year and the software will then calculate the monthly estimates automatically. When you're finally up and running, the software will also do actual versus budget comparisons for you.

Forecasting food and amenities expenses

Creating a luxurious guest experience is the goal of most innkeepers, but at what cost? Champagne and caviar are great only if your room rates support the cost of providing them and still allow you to be profitable. Figure out, then, what amenities you can offer within the price of your rooms.

Knowing what other B&Bs in the area offer from an amenity standpoint is a good place to start. Next, draw up a list of the amenities you plan to offer, including both food and non-food items, and then figure out what it will cost you to provide these amenities. (It's important to note that some people define amenities as disposables, such as shampoo, soap, and so on, while others define amenities as encompassing everything that they provide, including concierge services, breakfasts, flat panel TVs, jetted tubs, fire-places, and so forth. You may want to break down your expenses in terms of disposable items versus services, but to keep things simpler, I use the term to discuss both here). This part of the process requires planning, research, and some estimation on your part.

Calculating food costs begins by breaking down the cost of what you plan to serve on a per-person basis. As you get busier, this is an exercise you may not have time for and you may use your weekly grocery bill for budgeting, but in the beginning, it's a good exercise to get an idea of your true costs:

1. **Start by creating several typical sample breakfast menus.**

   List all ingredients required to prepare the meal.

2. **Calculate the cost of the ingredients to prepare each recipe.**

   For staples such as flour, sugar, salt, and so forth that you may have on hand, divide the price of the package size by the amount you use. For example, if you need 1 cup of flour to make a batch of muffins that serves 12, your calculations for the flour are

   $ price of 5-lb bag of flour ÷ 24 (5 pounds of flour = 24 cups)

3. **Add up the cost of the ingredients for each recipe, and divide it by the serving size.**

   You now have the approximate cost per serving for each item on your sample menu.

4. **Add up the cost per serving for each item on your sample menu.**

   This allows you to calculate the approximate cost per person for each sample menu.

   Each person won't necessarily eat one serving, a factor you need to take into consideration when calculating your menu costs. For buffet-style breakfasts, calculate the number of servings you anticipate each guest eating (more food is wasted with buffet breakfasts), and for plated breakfasts, don't forget to take into account that some guests may ask for seconds. Once you've adjusted the number of servings you need to accommodate these estimates, you can more accurately determine the anticipated cost per guest for each recipe.

5. **For other complimentary food services, such as welcome drinks, afternoon tea, cookies, snacks, and so on, you need to start with your best guess of what guests will consume.**

   Other innkeepers may be willing to share their experiences with you for budgeting purposes. As you begin welcoming guests, keep track of the complimentary food and beverages consumed and the number of guests served. These figures will help you calculate the average cost of complimentary items on a per-guest basis, allowing you to eliminate some of the guesswork in your second-year projections.

Your food expenses per guest will be less when you have a full house than when you have only a couple of guests. This is because serving a smaller number of people always generates more waste. With many recipes, you can reduce the number of servings by only so much: For example, you can't use half an egg. So if the smallest number of muffins you can make is 6 (using one egg) but only three muffins are consumed by guests, you have three that must be disposed of. Your cost per muffin, therefore, doubles in these instances, to account for the fact that three out of the six are wasted.

Creating menus with the same approximate total cost is helpful for budgeting and pricing your rooms. Knowing the approximate cost of a variety of your favorite recipes helps you mix and match items to create menus that you will be pleased and proud to serve.

To forecast your expenses for non-food amenities, start by making a list of the items that you plan to provide to each guest, such as shampoo, conditioner, soap, lotion, turn-down chocolates or mints, and flowers in the room.

If you plan to use an amenities dispenser, calculate the cost divided by the number of nights you think it will take guests to use up your supply. This is another calculation you'll be able to forecast better in your second year of operation, if you keep track of guests' actual use. For individual bottles of shampoo, lotion, and conditioner, and bars of soap, calculate how much each one costs. For purposes of initial forecasting, budget for one of each for each room per night. Although you'll find that, in practice, most two-night stays only require one bottle of each amenity, you may get guests who ask for more. If your inn will be attracting high-end guests, consider purchasing larger, 2-ounce bottles rather than standard 1- or 11/2-ounce bottles.

Adding advertising expenses

Your advertising costs will probably be highest in the first three years of your business because this is the average number of years it takes to achieve the same occupancy as your competition. Additionally, you need to budget for creating or updating your Web site. (See Chapter 8 for information on creating a Web site and utilizing various types of advertising.) How much you budget for advertising depends on a variety of factors. Costs are highest for those who are opening a new bed & breakfast, buying an existing B&B that doesn't have a strong Internet presence, or purchasing a distressed inn that needs lots of help. No matter what, it takes advertising to bring guests to your inn, so don't skimp on this expense.

Don't make the mistake of cutting back on your advertising after you're established because this can be disastrous. Also consider that the Web is ever-changing and that new technologies (such as Web 3.0) will show up eventually!

Budgeting for room & housekeeping supplies

Everything from cleaning supplies to toilet paper to light bulbs can land in this category. Bed & breakfasts are so diverse that this number may vary greatly. The PAII Industry Study of Operations and Finance suggests that, depending on the size and location of your inn, the cost of room and housekeeping supplies should run between $1^1/_2$ and $2^1/_2$ percent of your estimated revenues.

Anticipating staffing costs

If you have partners involved in the business, you need to divide up job responsibilities early in the planning process and then determine what you can and will outsource. Not only does this prevent misunderstandings, but it also helps you to analyze the talent already on your team. Having a real strength in one area doesn't make up for deficiencies in other areas. For example, having two partners with a strong background in marketing doesn't make up for the fact that no one on the team has any bookkeeping or accounting experience.

To determine partnership roles and how to divvy up the responsibilities, or to determine which tasks require outside help, begin by making a list of the areas that need to be covered at your inn. Then decide who should be responsible for each of them. If this is a family business, everyone involved needs to be consulted. Your list may look something like this:

- ✔ **Bookkeeping:** Banking, bill paying, payroll
- ✔ **Food Service:** Breakfast and menu preparation, shopping, baking
- ✔ **Marketing:** Managing advertising, creating brochures, handling Web site
- ✔ **Housekeeping:** Cleaning guest rooms, common areas, and bathrooms; trash removal; laundry; and so on

> ✔ **Gardening:** Maintaining yard and gardens
>
> ✔ **Guest Services:** Taking reservations, greeting guests, handling guest requests, answering the phone, returning phone calls and e-mails
>
> ✔ **Maintenance:** Basic upkeep, preventative maintenance, snow removal

You may find that some areas can be split up, with some tasks handled by someone at the inn while others are outsourced. For example, as the innkeeper, you could pay bills and do the banking, but payroll could be outsourced.

While innkeepers do the majority of the work at the inn themselves, hiring some form of outside help is an eventual reality for most (see Chapter 14 for information on getting extra help when you need it). Calculating staffing costs helps you to determine how much assistance you can afford.

First, make a list of jobs that you plan to outsource or hire additional help for. The larger your B&B, the more people you'll need to have on your team. Participants in the PAII Industry Study of Operations and Finance employed an average of 4.3 employees, including full-time, part-time, hourly, and salaried personnel. Larger inns and those with higher rates had more employees than average, while inns with one to four rooms typically had fewer than two employees. When assembling your team, decide whether you're going to hire an innkeeper, assistant innkeeper, cook, housekeeper, bookkeeper, gardener, maintenance person, and so on, and outline it in your plan. Note that despite the number of inns that do employ staff, 58 percent of innkeepers in the study also worked outside of the inn and relied on additional sources of income in addition to innkeeping.

Next, calculate and record the estimated wages for these employees, including any associated or required payroll costs, such as the employer's portion of FICA (Medicare and Social Security), unemployment, disability, workers compensation, and other taxes your state or city may require you to withhold. For help in calculating base wages, look at classified ads to see what similar jobs are paying (not just jobs at B&Bs, but in the lodging industry in general) or consult other innkeepers in local associations and on innkeeper forums (see Chapter 1 for info on benefitting from other innkeepers).

Workers compensation insurance is generally expensive. Whether or not you offer benefits to your employees, this is a requirement that you must budget for, even if you only employ one part-timer.

Making insurance part of your business plan

When you insure your bed & breakfast, you want to be certain that both your home and your business are covered in the event of loss, damage, or injury. For most, it's not a question of whether you'll need to file a claim, but when, so having good coverage from the start is essential to protect yourself, your investment, and your business. Note that a homeowners' policy doesn't cover your business, and a straight business policy doesn't cover you personally, so look for a specialized policy that covers both.

Your insurance policy will be broken into two main areas: property (the building and its contents) and causality (also known as liability). Because many different types of coverage are available, it's a good idea to find an insurance agent with experience in the lodging industry to help you determine what coverage you need. Once you have a good idea, shop for the most competitive price by comparing the features of several policies.

Asking other innkeepers is a good way to begin your search for an insurance carrier. (See Chapter 1 for help in finding innkeeper resources.) PAII also maintains a list of insurance carriers that serve the bed & breakfast industry. Go to www.paii.org, click on Resources, and then click on Vendor Marketplace. Use this list as a starting point for comparing recommended coverage and rates, and then check references with other innkeepers. You may be able to find a local carrier who can serve your needs, but remember that typical homeowners' insurance won't provide the protection you need.

Shop around. It isn't possible for one broker to obtain quotes from every company. Some companies only sell through their own agents. Some brokers have more clout with different insurance companies, so you could get two different quotes from the same company from two different brokers!

Request any clarifications you have about coverage in writing from the carrier, not the broker or agent.

Including other expenses

You'll have a variety of other expenses, both expected and unexpected. Review the expense section of your chart of accounts (Chapter 6 helps you set up your chart of accounts, and Table 6-1 shows a sample chart of accounts for a bed & breakfast) and budget for each line item.

Making the numbers work

If you've worked through this chapter, you've calculated, estimated, and researched the numbers. Don't cut corners. With the help of your accountant or inn consultant or on your own, create an estimated monthly forecast (refer to Figure 3-1) and use it to create a budgeted income statement (refer to Figure 3-2). Keep in mind that net income does not represent the cash flow generated by your inn. Your accountant or inn consultant can help you understand how this works, but you can estimate your cash flows by adjusting your net income for noncash expenses (like depreciation and amortization) and other cash expenditures (like capital expenditures and principal payments on your mortgage).

Now take time to review your business plan and — no matter how excited you are about your new business — ask yourself seriously: Do the numbers work? Do they make sense? Combine your conclusions with your personal goals, remembering to consider:

- ✔ How long do you estimate it will take for your business to break even? Can you live with this time frame?

- ✔ Will you need an outside income to make your business plan work? If so, have you considered what would happen if you lost this job or if this additional income was greatly reduced for some reason?

- ✔ How much do you have saved for the unexpected?

- ✔ How much of these savings are you willing to invest in the business?

If your break-even projected timeline isn't what you anticipated, it's better to know now in the planning stage, when you can make changes or even abandon your plans for this business. In any event, you should plan to put aside 6 to 12 months' worth of money to cover operating expenses and debt service for your first year. This is called *working capital* and if you're applying for a loan, the bank will want to see that you've accounted for it.

Chapter 4

Purchasing an Existing B&B

. . . .

In This Chapter

▶ Searching for your dream inn

▶ Crunching numbers: Making an offer and securing financing

▶ Managing the transition of inn ownership

. . . .

*F*inding and buying the right inn is the beginning of what will hopefully be an exciting journey for you as an innkeeper. As with most journeys in life, you'll encounter a few bumps along the way, so in this chapter I help you to prepare for them with information you need to move through the purchase process. At times, you may become frustrated in your search for the inn of your dreams — or simply one that you can afford. Or you may find the perfect inn and then discover that the costs of bringing it up to code or making major repairs mean you have to scratch it off your list. The good news is that this chapter prepares you for all possible scenarios by telling you what to look for when searching for the bed & breakfast that you'll ultimately pour your love, sweat, and tears into.

In this chapter, I help you to find your inn by showing you where to look. Then I take you through the process of making an offer, conducting your due diligence, and getting ready for opening day!

Weighing the Pros and Cons of Buying an Existing Inn

Buying and taking over an existing inn, building your own inn, or converting a property into a bed & breakfast each has a unique set of advantages, drawbacks, and challenges. Like many innkeepers, you may find that the advantages of buying an existing bed & breakfast far outweigh the disadvantages. Being informed and evaluating the tradeoffs will help you determine whether buying an existing inn is the right choice for you. Following are some pros and cons:

✔ **Existing business records to evaluate:** An existing inn that has been run professionally as a business should have financial records that will help you determine your future at that B&B. (For a brand new inn, you have to rely solely on your projections.) You shouldn't expect a seller to divulge all the records and financial information in the early stages of negotiations. Asking questions about occupancy rate, average daily rate, and the types of guests that the inn caters to will give you a preliminary idea about the business. When you get to the point where you're seen as a serious buyer, have qualified as such with the seller's broker (see more on this later in this chapter), and are proceeding with the purchase of the property, you'll have the benefit of seeing the actual numbers for the current revenue and expenses of the business.

Engaging an inn consultant or inn broker familiar with the bed & breakfast industry early in your search not only helps you to move the entire process along but also helps you get and interpret the information you need during the purchase process. (Chapter 3 tells you how to find an inn consultant, and Table 4-1 later in this chapter directs you in finding an inn broker.)

✔ **Having furnishings in place:** When you buy an existing bed & breakfast, you may be buying a *turnkey operation,* meaning the furnishings and equipment necessary to run the inn are already in place. Keep in mind, however, that an owner rarely leaves absolutely everything that you see when you walk in the door. What's turnkey to one seller may not be turnkey to another. During negotiations, ask for a list of items that will be removed from the inn (see information on inclusion and exclusion lists later in this chapter, in the "Outlining basic terms" section).

✔ **Living with someone else's decorating style:** You may find an existing B&B that makes sense from a business point of view and fits into your business plan, but you may not like how it's decorated or currently laid out. This isn't a serious issue if the drawbacks are cosmetic and you can live with them for a while, but you should factor the cost of redecorating and/or major renovations into your business plan.

If you really don't like the look and feel of the inn, even if it fits many of your other criteria such as location, price, current cash flow, and so on, stop and seriously consider looking for another property that you can be excited about. Remember, you have to live and work there, probably for several years or more!

✔ **Hosting guests immediately:** When you buy an existing inn, you don't have to wait for advertising to kick in for guests to find you. There even may be some future reservations already on the books, depending on how the business was run previously. As you move through the purchase process, you can evaluate the value of the established business based on the current revenue stream and expenses. The value to you of buying that business will vary depending on these numbers, as well as on whether the business is attracting the type of guests that you intend to cater to.

For example, if the inn specializes in romantic getaways and your plan is to target business travelers and host business meetings, you have to work harder than if the inn already caters to this type of guest. You need to create a timeline for the transition. As you gear up for new guests, you wind down and honor reservations from existing guests. You need to provide for both. Your breakfast hours may be longer because business travelers usually want early breakfast times, whereas those enjoying a getaway like to sleep in. Your rooms need to offer the amenities for both groups — the inn may already have hot tubs, but you may need to add desks and wireless Internet. You have to ramp up your advertising to target your new group of guests.

At the end of the day, you have a lot of room nights to fill and it may not be a good idea to make a complete change immediately. My advice: Don't try and fix what's not broken. Look at the value of the inn's existing business and see how you can enhance it, paying attention to who your weekend guests will be and who your mid-week guests will be.

✔ **Having zoning, licenses, and permits in place:** Generally speaking, when you purchase an existing bed & breakfast, most zoning, licenses, and permits are in place and the legal issues have been handled. (Check out the "Verifying zoning, permits, and codes" section later in this chapter for important considerations in this area.)

If permits and licenses are in a sole proprietor's name and not in the name of the business, you have to change them when you purchase the inn. This process may prove time-consuming and/or costly.

Finding Inns for Sale

The decisions that you make to find and buy a bed & breakfast to call both home and work are exciting, important, difficult, and confusing. If you've identified and done your research on the type of B&B you want to run and you've found a geographical location that makes sense (see Chapter 2 for help in these areas), the next step is to find the specific property that fits your business model.

Keep your business brain and your emotions separate. Yes, you need to find a location and a property that you're passionate about, but you also need to find a property that meets your business expectations and not be tempted to change those expectations and your business model to fit the property. If you do, you could end up living in a beautiful property only temporarily because you won't be able to support it if you don't have enough guests to fill your rooms.

Bed & breakfast buyers and sellers meet in a variety of places, from conferences to coffee shops to the Internet to the inns themselves. As an inn buyer, your concern is finding an inn that fits your business model and plan. Fortunately for you, there are many ways and places to find inns for sale.

Doing the legwork yourself

Many of the best inns sell without ever officially being for sale, according to Bill Oates of Inn Consulting Partners (www.innpartners.com). He advises clients to look at every inn (both those for sale and those not for sale) in a market-place that fits their business model and eliminate the ones that don't. Narrow the list down to six inns that fit your profile, and stay at each one as a guest.

While you're staying at an inn, discreetly let the current innkeepers know that you're an aspiring innkeeper and interested in owning an inn somewhat like theirs. This should be a friendly, informal conversation, but one that you've thought through ahead of time. Tread carefully: If the innkeepers aren't interested in selling, they may end up being your new neighbors (and competition!), so you don't want to establish a bad impression. Also, the innkeepers usually know which inns in the area or region are for sale and can help direct your search. If you find out that the innkeepers may be interested in selling, arrange to have a professional inn consultant perform an evalua-tion of the property and construct a financial packet. (See the next section for information on inn consultants.)

Even if you don't find your B&B through this research method, you haven't wasted time or money because you should stay in many of the inns in the area that you're considering for your bed & breakfast. This practice helps you get to know the area, find out what other inns are offering, and establish relationships with other innkeepers.

The Internet is an excellent place to find inns for sale; numerous Web sites are devoted to listing them. Here are some suggestions on where to turn online:

- ✔ **Internet search engine:** Perform an Internet search for "bed breakfast for sale [desired location]," filling in the state or region you've identified in your business model for the location of your inn. For example, "bed breakfast for sale California" produces a list of sites offering inns for sale in California.

- ✔ **Associations:** Check the Web sites of state and local bed & breakfast associations in your preferred area for listings of inns for sale. For an example, see the Indiana Bed & Breakfast Association Web site, (www.Indianabedandbreakfast.org), which has links to inns for sale at the top and bottom of the right side of their home page. The Professional Association of Innkeepers International (www.paii.org) is also a great association resource for listings.

- ✔ **Online directories:** Several leading online directories, such as www.bbonline.com and www.bnbfinder.com, devote sections of their Web sites to listings of inns for sale. (You can find a more complete list of popular directories in Chapter 8.)

Consulting an inn broker, inn consultant, or real estate agent

Wondering what the difference is between an inn broker, an inn consultant, and a real estate agent? *Inn brokers* and *inn consultants* have an in-depth understanding of the uniqueness of the bed & breakfast industry. Each can work to protect either the buyer or the seller and be the facilitator to ensure a good deal reaches successful completion.

Because so much specialized knowledge is necessary for the proper handling of the purchase or sale of a bed & breakfast, many inn brokers also offer inn consulting services. But not all inn consultants are brokers in that they're not licensed to sell real estate and therefore don't represent any inns for sale. However, consultants often specialize in other areas, such as business planning, and can be a good resource to help you plan for and find your inn, and advise you on decisions regarding a purchase, particularly if there's no inn broker in your area and if your accountant, lawyer, and real estate agent are unfamiliar with the bed & breakfast industry.

Real estate agents sell real estate. Some are knowledgeable about commercial transactions, and some aren't. Many innkeepers who are ready to sell their B&Bs list with local real estate agents who may not have handled the purchase or sale of a B&B. And that inexperience means that there are some serious downsides to using a real estate agent for a B&B sale or purchase. For example, a real estate agent who doesn't specialize in B&B transactions is unlikely to be able to review an inn's books, records, and income tax returns in order to put together an overview evaluation of the business for you. Here's another example: Residential real-estate agents may not have any experience selling turnkey operations and so may not know the importance of creating inclusion and exclusion lists early in the process. Also, residential real-estate agents often aren't familiar with commercial mortgages, which are the most common financing method behind the sale of a bed & breakfast. For these reasons I strongly encourage you to consult an industry professional during your search process. (Start with the inn consultants in Chapter 3 or the inn brokers in Table 4-1).

Table 4-1 presents some of the better-known companies offering listings of bed & breakfasts for sale; some of these companies also offer inn consulting services. An industry professional can guide you through the process and make up for a local agent's inexperience in inn sales. Chapter 3 helps you find an inn consultant. To find additional professionals with knowledge of inn sales, visit PAII's Vendor Marketplace at `www.paii.org`. Look under Resources, click on Vendor Marketplace, and then click on Appraisal/Valuation/Real Estate Agent or Accounting/Bookkeeping/Consulting/Legal.

Table 4-1	Specialists in Bed & Breakfast Sales	
Company	**Web Site**	**Listing Area**
The B&B and Country Inn Marketplace	www.innmarketing.com	Worldwide
The B&B Team	www.bbteam.com	Worldwide
Bed & Breakfast Inn Brokers	www.bbinnbrokers.com	California
BnB4Sale	www.BnB4Sale.com	Worldwide
Bushnell & Bushnell	www.bushnellandbushnell.com	United States
The Inn Broker	www.innbroker.com	Michigan
Inn Consulting Partners	www.innpartners.com	United States
InnMatchmakers	www.innmatchmakers.com	Colorado
Lodging Resources Partners	www.lodgingresources.com	United States
TMG Real Estate Consultants/Virginia Inn Brokers	www.virginiainnbroker.com	Virginia

Being seen as a serious buyer

Plenty of folks explore the dream of owning a bed & breakfast. Before sellers get their hopes up that you're their buyer, and before they share sensitive financial information with you, they want to know that you're a serious buyer. By reading this book, you're on your way to proving you're serious because you're taking the time to understand what it takes to run a bed & breakfast. However, some other signs are just as important when approaching a seller or broker. Consider the following recommendations:

✔ Have at least 20 percent in cash for a down payment, plus additional money for operating funds.

✔ Have a model for your business. (Review Chapter 3 for help in building the model for your business.)

✔ Assemble your team of inn broker, inn consultant, accountant, and lawyer. (See Chapter 3 for help in finding these experts and developing a business plan.)

✔ Join innkeeper associations and attend their aspiring innkeeper workshops and conferences. All associations welcome aspiring innkeepers and are anxious to help you. You will miss out on valuable resources by waiting to own an inn before joining B&B associations. (Chapter 16 has information on professional innkeepers' associations.)

✔ Take a class for aspiring innkeepers. (See Chapter 1 for help in finding innkeeper training.)

✔ Work or volunteer at a bed & breakfast to gain experience.

Deciding What to Offer

When you find inns that you're interested in, how do you figure out what the inn, its property, and its potential are worth? How much should you pay? Deciding the value of almost anything is a tough job, and as you've probably realized, given the uniqueness of the bed & breakfast industry and each B&B, figuring out what to offer for an existing inn can be even tougher. Naturally you have to keep in mind the asking price when making an offer, and then negotiations go back and forth because of the many complex considerations to be made, until hopefully you and the seller reach a compromise. Of course, you want to buy the inn at the lowest price possible, and the seller wants to receive the highest price possible. Here are some variables to help you formulate an offer that makes sense to you and satisfies everyone:

✔ **Cash flow:** With 20 percent down, does the anticipated cash flow, which is based on your projections by analyzing the inn's current cash flow and your realistic expectations of future cash flow, cover the *debt service* — your mortgage payment? Ideally, the property should generate a cash flow of about 120 percent of the debt service after covering all other expenses. So your net income before you've paid your mortgage needs to be at least 1.2 times the debt payments. For example, if your mortgage payments for the year total $50,000, you should expect the property to have a cash flow of at least $60,000, after operating expenses.

✔ **Down payment:** You shouldn't buy what you can't afford. When making offers, look for properties for which you can afford to put up a minimum of 20 percent as a down payment.

✔ **Other calculations, such as price per square foot, price per room, return on investment, capital rate, and gross rent multiplier:** These calculations are all useful tools but complicated to calculate and interpret and not infallible. A good inn consultant can help you with them.

Determining the value of the property

The value of the property is determined by the value of the real estate plus the value of furniture, fixtures, and equipment and/or by how the business itself is doing.

The same features that make the property appealing to you as a buyer also make it more valuable to you someday when you're the seller. Some of the characteristics that add value to a bed & breakfast property are

- Private baths
- Up-to-date zoning and permits
- Modern, heavy-duty appliances
- In-room fireplaces
- Whirlpool tubs
- Curb appeal (including landscaping and the building exterior)
- Location
- Large rooms
- Large, comfortable innkeeper's quarters
- Status as inspected and accepted by various accreditation organizations (Select Registry, AAA Diamond awards, Canada Select, and so on)
- Expansion capabilities (including available space and friendly zoning laws)

If the historical numbers (revenue and expenses) don't seem to justify the purchase price, you need to pull back and seriously consider whether opportunities exist to increase the numbers. If the answer's yes, are they realistic? Don't let your excitement for the property get in the way of a smart decision. Low numbers could be a loud and clear warning sign that running the property as a B&B is not a good investment and one that you should steer clear of. Conversely, low numbers could mean that something has occurred in the current operation of the inn that has kept the numbers low, giving you an opportunity for growth.

Here are some ways to evaluate the future potential of an inn:

- **Look at the competition.** Compare this inn to other similar inns in the area, and answer these questions:

    - **Are the rooms priced too high or too low in comparison?** Remember that when prices are set too high, guests may choose other properties. When they're set too low, not only is potential revenue lost, but also guests may think that the property is inferior and therefore choose other accommodations. Refer to Chapter 7 for information on setting prices.

- **Do other properties have similar occupancy rates?** Is it located in an area that guests visit, and does the area have activities to attract guests? Refer to Chapter 2 for help in determining whether the area will draw the number and type of guests that your business plan requires.

✔ **Critique the inn layout and furnishings.** Do all rooms have private, attached baths? Are the room appointments worn or outdated? Would you see a significant increase in revenues if you were to remodel one or more of the bathrooms or redecorate and refurbish guest rooms?

It's natural to think that you can do better, so be cautious about paying a premium for potential. Use care and good calculations when evaluating how much future investment and effort are needed in an existing property to bring the numbers up.

✔ **Review the marketing and publicity history of the inn.** Does the inn have a good Web site and a strong Internet presence? Is there a strong advertising campaign in place? (Refer to Chapters 8 and 15 to evaluate potential marketing strategies that you could implement.) You may be looking at a real opportunity if the current innkeepers haven't utilized every marketing and publicity opportunity to develop their business.

✔ **Determine the inn's reputation.** Type the name of the inn into your favorite Internet search engine and find out what guests are saying about the inn. Their reviews may be keeping potential guests away. These reviews give you a lot of information about what's wrong with the property and a clear picture of what needs to change in order to increase numbers.

Note: Some Web sites remove negative reviews for an inn when the ownership changes, something you should aggressively pursue if you become the owner. If negative reviews can't be removed, when you are the owner, see whether you can post a management response letting potential guests know that ownership has changed and telling them how you plan to address the problems that caused the negative review. Then provide outstanding service, and great reviews will come.

If the inn has a bad reputation in the neighborhood, you will need to work hard to change the perception local businesses and residents have of your inn. Here is another opportunity to increase business because locals can be a great source of referrals, so start by hosting a fabulous open house (Chapter 5 contains some great recommendations on this).

✔ **Analyze the current target market, if there is one.** How could you reposition the inn and improve its visibility?

✔ **Consider family or personal issues of the previous owners.** Have family or personal problems impeded the progress of the inn?

The answers to these questions will help you understand why an inn may not be operating at peak performance. Use this information to decide whether you've found a property that fits into the model and plan that you have set for your business.

Verifying zoning, permits, and codes

Just because you're buying an existing inn, don't assume that all the inn's zoning, permits, and codes are up-to-date. Oftentimes, existing inns have been grandfathered in for changes in codes and ordinances, but these exemptions may or may not carry over to you as a new owner, including requirements for guests with special needs (see Chapter 5 for more information). Sometimes, because the current innkeepers are well-known in the town, inspectors have looked the other way on issues that may be enforced now that the inn is under new ownership. Additionally, simply the change in ownership prompts inspectors, who may not have been making regular inspections, to pay a visit.

When it comes to zoning, permits, and codes, the more you know, the better. You need to either contact or meet with governing officials and agencies including, but not limited to, the

- ✔ Building and planning department (often through your local city hall or county building department in unincorporated areas)
- ✔ Fire department
- ✔ Health department

Ask to see the inspection files on the existing B&B so that you can view the inspectors' reports. Hiding from inspectors and regulations is a bad idea, and I strongly advise against it. To do so could put you out of business. The time to know the right way to do things is before you own the bed & breakfast, when you can factor in or negotiate any costs necessary to bring the property up to code and comply with regulations. Being current on federal, state, and local licenses, permits, codes, and regulations is not only required to do business and to keep your insurance in force, but it's also the way to keep your inn current on safety issues, making guests' stays at your inn safer.

In most areas, the Certificate of Occupancy (CO) transfers between owners, but you should verify that this is the case for an existing inn you're interested in purchasing. Insist on an inspection by the fire, health, and zoning authorities as a contingency of escrow so you know of issues that need correcting and can budget for them accordingly. If an on-site inspection by these agencies isn't possible as a contingency, you should still meet with the agencies specifically about the property you're buying to get their input. You want to know ahead of time about any renovations or changes that need to be made to be sure you're complying with all zoning and code requirements. After you own the inn, get to know these inspectors by inviting them over. They can educate you and help you stay up-to-date on codes and safety requirements. Some innkeepers know the inspectors so well that they visit more than necessary because of the delicious treats the innkeepers serve at each visit!

Regulations, local ordinances, and zoning requirements may prevent you from executing some of the plans that you envision. Carefully compare the existing use of properties you're considering with the uses you've incorporated into your business plan. For example, suppose that you anticipate hosting weddings at your bed & breakfast to bring in additional revenue. After looking at many inns, you're very excited about one in particular — it has beautiful architecture, beautiful gardens, and five guest rooms. The owners reside at the inn but don't rent the inn other than to lodging guests. For you to buy this inn and host weddings sounds easy enough, but consider that your intended use changes the current use of the property, which in all likelihood is fully permitted as it exists. In most areas, hosting even an occasional wedding requires special permits and zoning variances as well as renovations, such as additional parking and restroom facilities. (See Chapter 17 for additional information on codes and variances when adding additional services.)

Consider zoning ordinances and regulations in regards to expanding your business. Adding extra rooms or a gift shop may be the farthest thing from your mind right now, but knowing whether they're even a possibility under current zoning is smart business planning and can add value to the property.

Evaluating the added value of goodwill

Goodwill is an intangible asset from an accounting point of view. However, when buying an existing bed & breakfast, the business's reputation must be factored in because goodwill adds value. The easiest way to see the value of goodwill is through

- ✔ **Repeat business:** Returning guests are a ready source of business when you're starting out, especially if the transfer from your predecessors to you is handled well and your guests know who to expect at the front door (refer to the later section, "Transitioning an Existing B&B," for instructions). The more repeat business the inn receives, the higher the perceived goodwill.

- ✔ **Positive guest reviews:** Nearly every inn has online reviews. Do an Internet search to find guest reviews for the inn you're thinking of purchasing. Positive reviews add to the goodwill of the bed & breakfast, and negative reviews take away from the goodwill — and thus the value of the B&B. If an inn has a disproportionate number of negative reviews, this could be a bargaining point and an important aspect of your early marketing efforts if you buy the property. (You can find more information on updating your advertising at the end of this chapter.)

Considering lifestyle inns versus investment-grade inns

Bed & breakfasts can be either lifestyle inns or investment-grade inns. *Lifestyle inns* are priced more for the value of the real estate and the land than the value of the business. The gross revenue of a lifestyle inn would not, in itself, provide a good return on your investment. Although you are buying a business, the majority of the sales or list price of a lifestyle inn is for the real estate and land. *Investment-grade inns* are inns with very good cash flows and prices that are supported by their gross revenues. In the case of an investment-grade inn, the value of the business is realized because the cash flow it generates covers the investment. Both types of inns can make money and are run the same. They are both expected to show a profit at sale, but with lifestyle inns, a larger component of the sale price is real-estate-based versus business-based.

Most inns for sale are lifestyle inns, but that doesn't mean they don't make good business sense! The rise in real-estate prices has made the underlying asset — the property — more

valuable than the business that operates on it. The high price of real estate has made it more expensive to enter the bed & breakfast industry than it was years ago.

When considering a lifestyle inn, here are some questions to ask yourself:

- Is the bed & breakfast going to be your sole source of income? If so, will it be enough to sustain your style of living as well as cover the expenses of running a business?

- If it's an existing inn, have the current innkeepers operated it as a serious business, or are there things you can do to boost occupancy? For example, if the inn doesn't have a strong Internet presence, devoting resources to marketing could improve the numbers. (See Chapter 15 for help in finding ways to build on the existing business.)

- Does the business meet any other goals you may have, such as to be your own boss, live in a nice house, work with people, or provide a second income?

Making an Offer

Congratulations, you've found the inn that you hope to own! Now it's time to work with your team of experts (accountant, lawyer, inn broker, and inn consultant, ideally), along with the seller to make sure that you strike a fair deal and that it goes through. If there are problems, you want them caught early so that they can be worked out.

The procedures and requirements for the process from offer to closing differ among states. Some states require formal initial purchase agreement procedures. In other states, presenting your offer along with a letter of intent that spells out each party's intentions and responsibilities is common. When you're ready to make an offer, work closely with your broker and attorney to ensure it's in the correct format for your area and jurisdiction.

The ideal situation is for the buyer, the seller, and their respective brokers to work collectively to come to an agreement in the period between offer and closing. Maintaining cordial relations with the seller during the negotiation phase makes it easier to work together during the transition phase, which I cover at the end of this chapter. This is an emotional process for both sides, so you may want to negotiate only through your broker to keep things official and professional. Inevitably, you and the seller each want the best price and terms that you can negotiate. However, your goal from offer to close should be to try and avoid an "us versus them" mentality and remember you're working toward a common goal.

Outlining basic terms

Your first step in making an offer on an existing inn is to work with the seller and your brokers to negotiate the basic terms of the agreement. Establish at least the following terms:

- ✔ The purchase price, deposits, and contingencies
- ✔ A timeline for the sale process
- ✔ The major items included in and excluded from the sale

Part of the terms will come from the seller's *inclusion and exclusion lists.* These lists detail what the seller is and isn't including in the sale. For example, you should know ahead of time if the beautiful grandfather clock prominently pictured on the inn's Web site home page and incorporated into the inn's logo is really a family heirloom that the sellers have no intention of leaving. The same is true if the antique bedroom furniture in several of the guest rooms belonged to the seller's great-grandmother and he intends to take it with him. Sellers should have these lists already prepared as part of the listing process, but if they don't exist yet, they should be created early in your negotiations, and you should review them carefully with the seller and both your brokers.

With the basic terms set, you prepare either a letter of intent or comparable agreement to comply with local regulations and formally present to the seller with your offer. Your documents should clearly state the terms that you've negotiated with the seller. Use Figure 4-1 as a guideline because these are the basic terms all agreements must cover, and then work with your broker and attorney to construct your offer in the format required in your area.

Dear [name of the inn seller]:

This Letter of Intent confirms our interest in purchasing the [name of the Inn].

It is our intent to purchase the assets of the Inn, including but not limited to the real estate, furnishings, fixtures, equipment, contracts and contract rights, the name of the business, customer lists, business records, telephone number(s) and domain names, with all free and clear of liens, restrictions, or encumbrances.

The offer is made on the following terms and conditions:

1. The purchase price will be $2,000,000.00.

2. We shall present to the Seller, a Purchase and Sale Agreement with the usual provisions, including allocation of the assets to be sold and a non-compete agreement. The Purchase and Sale shall be executed within 30 days of the acceptance of this offer.

3. Upon acceptance of this offer, $5,000.00 will be deposited in the escrow account of the Seller's attorney as earnest money. An additional $45,000.00 will be deposited upon execution of the Purchase and Sale Agreement. All sums of money shall be released at closing, or in the event that the sale is not consummated through no fault of ours, the earnest monies shall be returned to us in full without recourse.

4. This offer is contingent upon:

   A. Our obtaining a first mortgage from a lending institution of $1,600,000.00 with terms acceptable to us. A commitment letter to be obtained within 30 days of the execution of the Purchase and Sale Agreement.

   B. An engineering inspection of the building and its systems to determine that there are no major problems with the building(s), systems, or equipment.

   C. An accounting examination by us and/or our agents including a review of all books, records and income tax returns of the business or the portion of the Sellers' individual returns that pertain to the business for the last three years.

   D. Our obtaining the necessary Federal, State and local licenses and permits to continue the present business.

   E. Our obtaining the necessary insurance at reasonable cost on the business and physical property.

5. It is understood that the Inn is to be conveyed as a "Turn Key" Bed and Breakfast business. The Seller shall provide an

Figure 4-1:
Sample letter of intent for the purchase of an existing B&B.

inventory of furniture, fixtures, equipment and supplies to be included in the sale price and a separate list of items not included in the sale.

6. The closing will take place no later than _____, 20XX.

7. Seller will continue to operate the business as it has been operated.

The foregoing paragraphs reflect our understanding of some of the principal terms of the Agreement but shall not constitute a complete statement of nor a legally binding or enforceable agreement or commitment with respect to the property or any other matters related to the sale until such time as the parties enter into a written Purchase and Sale Agreement, into which this Letter of Intent and all prior discussions of the parties shall merge.

This letter constitutes an expression of intent in good faith. It looks to the preparation and execution of a definitive Purchase and Sale Agreement that will contain the customary terms, agreements, reservations and warranties in a form satisfactory to all parties and their attorneys.

We look forward to your review of this letter. In the event that the terms are generally acceptable to you as outlined we would appreciate a timely reply.

Sincerely,

[Inn buyer, Date]

Courtesy of Bill Oates, Inn Consulting Partners

Checking the inn's condition with inspections

Be prepared for inspections to turn up problems. This isn't always a bad thing, however. You want to know about any issues before the deal is closed, because you become the not-so-proud owner of those problems and issues when you become the proud owner of the inn. At first, some problems may sound like deal-breakers (and some are, so don't be afraid to walk away). However, take time to look at each problem and probe for solutions.

The most common inspection is an engineering inspection, and this is the one where most problems are discovered. Before panicking, talk to the engineer about possible solutions — and the estimated costs of those solutions. Many times solutions and compromises can be made with the seller to accommodate these issue(s). Remember, the best compromises are when no one is happy because each side has had to give a little. Other inspections are covered in the previous "Verifying zoning, permits, and codes" section.

Preparing purchase and sale agreements

Depending on the regulations in your area, your lawyer, broker, and inn consultant (if you've engaged one) prepare the necessary documents that are required for the deal to close. You should expect these documents to include the following information:

- Terms of the deal
- Time frame for contingencies
- Everything outlined in the letter of intent and/or contract
- Whether training from the seller is included, and if so, the duration and terms (see the later section, "Working side by side with the current innkeeper")
- Supplies and inventories that have been negotiated into the sale and the purchase price
- Prepaid expenses for advertising, memberships, and so on, a schedule of which is usually prepared and attached as an addendum
- Allocation of assets to be sold

    The IRS treats the sale of business assets, such as real estate and personal property, differently depending on their particular value and classification. For tax purposes, be sure to get your accountant or consultant to advise you in this matter.
- Boilerplate legal requirements, such as damage to the property before closing, applicable law, and so on
- The procedure for handling outstanding gift certificates, advance deposits, and advance reservations

    The procedure for handling outstanding gift certificates is a frequent issue between buyers and sellers because some gift certificates go unused and you have to make good on others as the new owner. The question becomes how much of the existing gift certificate sale proceeds should be transferred to you. Some states require that the value of unused gift certificates be *escheated* to the state, which means the monies are turned over to the state as abandoned property after a specified time. To further complicate matters, some certificates may have been promotional gift certificates for which the seller received no money but which you'll have to honor when they're redeemed. Usually the buyer and seller do come to an agreement on outstanding gift certificates. For example, knowing that 20 to 40 percent of gift certificates sold are never redeemed, the seller could turn over to the buyer 100 percent of gift certificates sold within the last 12 months, 75 percent of gift certificates that are 1 to 2 years old, and keep or escheat the remainder, depending on state law. Certificates issued for promotional purposes are handled separately. Some inns have opted to hold monies in escrow with an attorney, but this incurs additional fees and may not be necessary.

Securing Financing

Expect this part of the sale process to take the longest. It's probably also the most nerve-racking part, so in this section I give you some tips on what to expect and how best to approach the bank or lender. Hugh Daniels of Ask Hugh Consulting (www.askhugh.com) advises clients to plan to shop a loan to at least six lenders. All will say they'll have an answer for you in 24 to 48 hours, but it often takes months to get the loan through, so be patient and responsive as you go through the process.

Often the purchase and sale (P&S) agreements don't allow sufficient time for you to get all the information you need to apply for the loan (including occupancies, average daily rates (ADRs), projections, business plan, and so on), get it to the bank, and get the loan approved. Twenty, even 30, days are often not enough, especially if a Small Business Administration (SBA) loan or guarantee is required. Inn consultant Hilary Jones (www.inngenium.com) advises clients to aim to set the contingency on their P&S for financing out at 45 days from the acceptance of the offer.

Working with a bank

In many places, the local community bank is your best source of financing. Before going to the bank, however, you should assemble all your financial information in a simple but complete format. When you approach the bank with your financial information in hand, remember that you're not asking for a loan. Rather, you're telling the bank what you need from a business point of view and why. The loan process should work something like this:

1. **Presentation of your plan to the bank.** Your plan includes the following:

   - The amount of the loan that you're applying for and the amount of your down payment (in most cases, expect to put 20 percent down)

   - Financial forecasts from your business plan

   - Analysis of the current business's performance for the past three years (primarily profit and loss statements and balance sheets from accounting software, such as QuickBooks)

   - Three years' worth of tax returns from the business

   - Reserves or secondary sources of payment (the lender wants to know how you'll repay the loan if the business can't)

   - Your resume with a listing of related activities indicating your experience related to innkeeping, including previous work experience, apprenticeships, training, and so on

The bank wants to see how much cash flow there will be to cover the debt service on your loan. It's not interested in your division of labor or your marketing strategy. Providing too much information with your loan application may actually cause confusion. On the other hand, you need to justify your projections, especially if the bank has never made a loan to a bed & breakfast; part of your job may be to educate the bank about what a bed & breakfast is in order to make everyone comfortable extending the loan to you. Your team of professionals can help you in this area, but you should be involved in every step of the process because the bank is making the loan to you.

2. **Title searches and other checks.** Who checks the real estate taxes and performs the other due diligence items, such as ordering a title search, varies by region, state, or local jurisdiction. In some areas or states, the bank does this, and in other areas, such as California, it's customary for a title insurance company (also called an *escrow company*) to be assigned these duties.

3. **Issuance of a terms letter.** The bank sends you a letter that outlines what the loan would look like if you were to get an offer.

4. **Issuance of a commitment.** The loan committee offers you the loan, usually subject to a property appraisal.

The entire inn-purchasing process doesn't come to a halt while you wait on financing. In the meantime, you and the seller can be working on issues and contingencies such as inventories and results of the engineering report.

Applying for an SBA loan

Many bed & breakfasts are wholly or partially financed with the help of a loan or guarantee from the SBA. You can read about the program on the SBA Web site at www.sba.gov. In the search box on the home page, enter "CDC/504 Program" (CDC stands for Certified Development Company) or "7a loan." The 504 program provides long-term financing for economic development within a community, and a 7a loan is a guarantee program whereby the SBA guarantees to repay your lender a portion of the loan if you default. Check with your lender to see which, if any, programs they offer.

Financing from the seller

In today's complex world of financing and mortgage loans, creativity can pay off. Seller financing is only an option for qualified buyers when the seller doesn't need the funds immediately. If the seller needs the proceeds from the sale of the inn to purchase another residence or another business, however, this arrangement isn't possible. Generally speaking, sellers are only interested in providing financing if they're reasonably assured that you'll be able to make payments. They have no interest in repossessing the inn if you default.

Transitioning an Existing B&B

While it's easy to pinpoint the exact date that you become the owner of your bed & breakfast (the day you close and finances change hands), there is no exact date when the transition process starts. There are also no set procedures that must be followed, and a big variable in the process is the seller's desired involvement in helping you through the transition phase.

Transition can be a frustrating time for you as the buyer. You're anxious to put on your innkeeper hat, but the inn isn't yours yet. I encourage you not to let this valuable time slip away. Instead, use it to prepare for the day that you welcome your first guests.

If you're relocating to a new area in order to operate your bed & breakfast, you may be tempted to stay in your current job as long as possible and earn as much money as possible before transitioning to innkeeper. Be mindful, though, of what you're giving up by continuing to work. The time before you take over your inn is the chance to get to know the area, your neighbors, other innkeepers in the area, and the sites and attractions that you'll recommend to guests. Additionally, you should use this time before you take over your inn to get your advertising and marketing in place (see Chapter 5 for more information on these elements). You can expect to be very busy once your inn is up and running under your management, so use this lead time wisely.

Working side by side with the current innkeeper

I'm sure you're anxious to roll up your sleeves and get started doing things your way, but in your excitement, don't skimp on learning everything you can about the inn, property, area, and experiences from the current innkeepers. Training is negotiable, but you should expect some sort of orientation as part of the transaction. When possible, aim for at least a week or two (depending on the size of the property and amount of business). If the seller isn't prepared to offer more than a basic orientation, you may be able to negotiate additional consultations for a fee. Some consultants advise that the training should take place before the closing, when it's clear who's in charge. Others have seen too many sales fall through and feel strongly that training should occur after the closing. This will be another point of negotiation between you and the seller.

No matter when it's conducted, on-site training is the best way for you to learn. Then, when it's your turn to be in charge, you can do things differently if you choose. You're taking over an existing inn, so learn as much as you can in order to harness the goodwill the inn has generated. Here are some suggestions for using your time with the current innkeepers wisely:

- **Learn software systems, and practice using them under the guidance of the current innkeeper.** What may seem simple may not be when you're on your own.

- **Walk through every inch of the inn and go over every appliance to be sure that you know how it works.** Pay close attention to any peculiarities and how to handle them.

- **Create folders with passwords, instructions, manuals, warranties, operating procedures, and so forth for everything at the inn.**

- **Make a complete list of all advertising, the expiration dates, and any passwords to manage it as well as a list of all current memberships and their expiration dates.**

- **Host a joint open house with the current innkeepers in order to meet the neighbors.** The open house can be a combination gathering for the current innkeepers to say goodbye to old friends and thank them for their support and for you to be introduced to your new neighbors and other local businesses, giving them a chance to meet you and see the inn if they haven't seen it in a while.

- **Meet and get to know the staff.** Find out about long-time staff members and everyone's duties, responsibilities, strengths, and weaknesses.

- **Jointly send out a letter to previous and future guests sharing the transition story.** Let guests know what the current innkeepers will be doing, and introduce yourself. Consider including a special offer for return guests who visit during a certain period.

Keeping the name

When you buy an existing inn, you're buying its goodwill, and this includes the name. If you change the inn name, you have to start from scratch to get your inn listed on Internet search engines (see Chapter 15 for information on search engines), in guidebooks, and so on. In general, you should keep the name unless it's a really bad one or the property has suffered from negative reviews and publicity, in which case you should definitely consider changing it and starting fresh.

If you decide that you must change the inn's name, work through the process outlined in Chapter 5 for naming your B&B. Then refer to Chapter 8 for important information on building your Web site and your brand, and getting your marketing started. Get everything ready to launch as soon as you leave the closing and are the innkeeper.

Reviewing your marketing presence

You can start to review and make plans for your marketing promotion before you close on the inn; however, you can't make changes without ownership and access. When you take ownership of the inn, you'll be very busy, and your marketing is likely to be neglected. Making plans ahead of time makes it easier for you to bring your advertising up-to-date once you close on the property. Analyze the inn's current marketing plan to see what's working and look for missing opportunities. (Review Chapters 8 and 15 for important marketing tips.)

Making your Web site current

Sometimes innkeepers trying to sell an inn let updates to their Web site slide. If you're planning on a complete redesign of the Web site, do it during the transition period. (See Chapter 8 for a list of Web site designers who specialize in the bed & breakfast industry.) Review the current Web site and make notes of sections and text that need updating, such as

- ✔ Your name(s) as innkeeper
- ✔ Specials and packages
- ✔ Keywords and area activities
- ✔ Pictures of the rooms and common areas
- ✔ Rates and policies

Updating your advertising

As you work on marketing during your transition period, you need to make sure that everything, everywhere about your B&B is correct, up-to-date, and presented in a good light. Although you should have performed an Internet search for the inn before you bought it, the transition period is the time to update any inaccuracies and to get any existing negative reviews and comments removed. Contact the review site and let them know about the change in ownership. Be persistent about getting old negative reviews taken down, because they'll hurt your business unnecessarily.

Make sure that all your advertising is up-to-date. Contact every directory that your inn is already listed on, and take advantage of the features included in the advertising package that the previous owners subscribed to. When that package expires, review its performance and determine its rate of return to see whether it warrants a continued investment. (Chapter 15 helps you evaluate your advertising results.)

Chapter 5

Starting a New Inn from Scratch

Chances are you have a picture in your mind of what your dream bed & breakfast looks like. You may have already performed an exhaustive search for an existing inn that matches this vision but come up empty-handed. As Plan B, you may have found the perfect piece of property with views so spectacular that it begs to be a bed & breakfast. Or maybe you've found a historic house that would be a perfect B&B, or you've decided to turn your own home into one. Perhaps you've simply always dreamed of building your own bed & breakfast. When you can't find an existing inn to take on, you turn to the idea of starting a new B&B from scratch.

In this chapter, I show you how to turn your B&B dreams into reality, but first I point out the pros, cons, and unique challenges of starting your own inn from scratch, either by building a new inn or converting your home or an existing property. Most importantly, I share the most common reasons that innkeepers run into problems when starting a new inn so that you can avoid them, and I help you get your new place up and running through the naming process and an open house.

Considering the New-Inn Option

Although not as common as purchasing an existing bed & breakfast, people build new inns and successfully convert properties into B&Bs for a variety of reasons. Creating a new inn is an exciting process, and when you start fresh you may have the advantage of new plumbing and electric, a new roof, new windows, new flooring, and new technology. Even better, you have easy access to the insulation in the walls to make sure it's adequate, which not only saves on heating costs but also gives your guests a level of privacy through soundproofing.

The biggest drawback of building an inn from the ground up or converting an existing property is cash flow, because you don't have the benefit of reservations on the books and past guests to contact you for future bookings, as you do when buying an existing inn. It may cost more to build or renovate and furnish a new inn than to buy an existing inn that's already furnished. On the other hand, you're able to decorate and furnish the inn over time in accordance with your tastes and with modern appliances and guest conveniences, such as jetted tubs. Equally as important to how the inn looks on the inside is how it looks on the outside. This means setting aside adequate funds to design a beautiful and comfortable interior as well as to cover landscaping costs, in order to create an inviting first impression when your guests arrive.

New innkeepers often underestimate the costs of landscaping. The outside is the first part of your inn that your guests see when they arrive, and they should see well-landscaped and appealing surroundings. Sparsely landscaped yards and gardens can look unfinished, and outdoor areas that still look like a construction zone are even worse. No matter how wonderful your B&B is on the inside, thanks to the service and hospitality that you offer, the exterior also must present a warm welcome. Mature trees and plants are the easiest way to create this image. Landscaping is expensive, so when carving out the footprint for the building, be mindful of existing trees and shrubs that you can preserve and reuse (a good architect can help you with this).

Early in the building process, designate a parking lot and staging area for your contractor and crew to use in order to avoid damage to outdoor areas.

It's Not Up to You: Zoning and Other Legalities

Many otherwise fabulous new B&B plans have stumbled because of one big problem — they can't be completed because of zoning restrictions. This is the area that causes new innkeepers the most headaches and is the reason many projects fail, often after the prospective innkeeper has spent a lot of money. In your excitement to build or to convert a property into your dream B&B, it's easy to become so passionate that you let your good business instincts relax. Doing your homework ahead of time to find out what a prospective property is or isn't zoned for and getting conditional use permit(s), if required, will prevent this from happening to you. Even if you think that the property you're considering would be the perfect place for a bed & breakfast, or if you strongly believe the town should embrace your inn because there's a need for such a business, don't proceed if you don't have the proper zoning and permits to build and run your dream inn.

The terms conditional use permit and variance are often used interchangeably. However, correctly used, a change in use for a single property is almost always called a *conditional use permit* (such as allowing a property to operate as a B&B in a residential area), whereas a *variance* is getting permission to make a change in the property, essentially allowing the property owner an exception to break the dimensional rules (such as setbacks or height limits) that would otherwise apply.

Zoning, permits, licenses, and restrictions vary greatly by area. Sometimes one county or town is particularly strict, but a location nearby may be very welcoming to your plans. Many states are strict on the number of rooms that you can have without building under commercial hotel guidelines. Some states and localities limit expansion, meaning you can't buy a four-room inn and renovate it to add three more rooms. This section outlines the major legal requirements and restrictions you face and must meet in order to get your new B&B up and running.

Getting to know state, county, and town zoning and building regulations

It would be great if common sense and persistence resolved all zoning issues, but this simply isn't the case. For the most part, you have no choice but to work with existing regulations. However, some zoning laws are open to exceptions and can reasonably be changed. If you do need a conditional use permit, it's important to get this commitment before you begin your project. Examples of zoning ordinances that have restricted prospective innkeepers' dreams include the following:

✔ **The number of rooms a B&B can have:** Local definitions of a bed & breakfast are often defined by the number of bedrooms. For instance, in some towns, anything more than four rooms is not considered a B&B and is either not permitted by zoning code or requires the inn to pay higher commercial property tax rates. Often the inclusion of more bedrooms brings additional requirements for the inn, such as a commercial kitchen (which involves expensive commercial equipment and a separate hand-washing sink, and therefore can cost ten times as much as a regular kitchen), a fire sprinkler system (which can cost as much as $50,000 depending on the size), large parking areas, additional taxes, and so on.

✔ **Outright denial to convert or build a bed & breakfast on a residential lot:** The town zoning commission may not allow a B&B on a residential lot, but neighborhood support sometimes helps in these instances. It certainly never hurts to have your neighbors on your side. I talk about educating and partnering with your neighbors later in this section.

✔ **The size of the septic system:** If your proposed property doesn't have access to a public sewage system, a percolation test must be performed to determine the sewage capacity of the soil and, therefore, the size of the septic system that the lot can accommodate. To adhere to zoning laws, you need to have a large enough septic system for the size of the inn that you're planning to build or convert.

In addition to building restrictions, there may be zoning and health department restrictions on meal preparation that limit your business. For example, even though it's your home, you may be surprised to find out that some departments don't allow the use of a range or oven to prepare breakfast, limiting your menu to continental breakfast. Many areas don't allow the preparation of dinner for B&B lodging guests without additional permits, inspections, and possibly a commercial kitchen. This is an important consideration if you're a rural property with limited nearby dining options, or if serving dinner is part of your future expansion plans.

To avoid any kind of zoning or permit problems, follow these steps:

1. **Research all the regulations and restrictions on new building design and construction that your zoning commission, building department, and fire and health departments have, to see which may affect the design of your property.**

2. **Work with an architect to design your building plans with these restrictions in mind.**

3. **Meet with the various departments to review your conceptual drawings prior to finalizing the architect's drawings.**

4. **Incorporate the departments' comments into your building plans and finalize your plans.**

If you don't yet own the property or if you're building your B&B from scratch, always get approval on your plans in writing from the various state, county, and town zoning and building boards before proceeding. If they won't put it in writing, there's a problem, and you need to find out what it is and deal with it before you start work on your inn.

Because many local zoning laws were written before B&Bs became popular, bed & breakfast zoning is often a gray area in zoning and building codes. If the land that you want to build on or the property that you want to convert isn't currently zoned for commercial use, you can apply for a conditional use permit in order to operate your B&B. Procedures, rules, and guidelines differ by area, and you need to do some investigating to find out the specifics for your situation. Here are some suggestions to help the process go more smoothly:

- ✔ **Educate your neighbors and local officials about what a B&B is.** Frequently, local concern and opposition stems from the fear that allowing one business to operate in a residential neighborhood opens the town up to numerous commercial business applications, causing increased traffic, overcrowded parking conditions, and other unpleasantries. By letting neighbors and local officials know the types of guests your inn will host (neighbors need to be assured that you're not running a boarding house) and the typical behavior of B&B guests (local officials will like hearing that they will patronize local restaurants and businesses, yet cause less traffic than a new dental practice) you can help to dispel the myths and fears about a new B&B in town. Find out what the local concern is, and contact state and local B&B associations for facts and figures that could help to alleviate these fears.

- ✔ **Be upfront with your neighbors, and listen to their concerns.** When people think that you're trying to pull something over on them, their suspicion makes them instinctively oppose your activity. Often local opposition is the biggest reason permits are denied, so the biggest mistake you can make is not obtaining your neighbors' support and excluding them from your plans. If you're upfront with them from the beginning, educate them about what you want to do and the effect it will have on them, listen to their objections, and so on, you'll have a better chance of engaging their support.

- ✔ **Talk to local innkeepers.** Don't be afraid to ask zoning or other permit questions of experienced B&B owners who have inns in the area you're considering. They can share their experiences with you and hopefully give advice for getting through rough patches.

Talking with your potential competition may seem uncomfortable for you, but it's the best way to introduce yourself, and it gives you a feel for the type of camaraderie that exists among other innkeepers. After you're open for business, you'll refer your overflow to these inns and vice versa.

Your attitude in approaching local seasoned innkeepers sets the tone for your relationships. Temper your enthusiasm with a willingness to listen and learn from them, because these people will more than likely become your best allies and your good friends.

Complying with codes for handicap accessibility

The Americans with Disabilities Act (ADA) establishes regulations that allow people with disabilities physical access to public buildings. These restrictions may impact the entrance to your facility (requiring a ramp), the width of hallways and doors, and the type of fixtures that you use. Generally speaking, new construction must meet stricter rules than conversions of existing or historical properties that are already serving the public. Licensed architects should be familiar with ADA code and able to help you determine what you must do to be in compliance on your project. The requirements of some states differ from the federal ADA requirements, but in general, properties that have five or fewer rooms to rent and where the proprietor lives in the same building are exempt from ADA compliance. If you're building a new inn, however, regardless of the size, you should plan to meet as many ADA requirements as you can. Being able to offer accommodations to those with special needs enables you to accommodate another group of guests, plus, although you would expect your inn to be grandfathered in to new regulations, you never know when laws may change.

When in doubt about the application of ADA law in your new building plans, contact the local building/planning department rather than going on hearsay from other inn owners.

At some point during your innkeeping career you may be contacted by a guest who needs to bring a service animal with him to your inn. Regardless of whether your inn has five rooms or less or you have a no-pet policy, you have no choice but to host the service animal under the ADA. For additional information on service animals and the ADA, visit www.ada.gov/svcanimb.htm.

Passing building inspections

A building inspector will make inspections at critical times throughout the building process to ensure that the structure is meeting all codes and matching the plans that you submitted. The number of inspections is up to the inspector in the jurisdiction where your property is located. Your general contractor and architect will work with the inspectors throughout the inspection process as your inn comes together. You have no involvement in the inspection process, other than to stay out of the way. In many cases, the contractor has a rapport with the inspector and interference from the building owner (asking questions) could impede the process. If you're curious, you can obtain a list of conditions for occupancy from your Department of Buildings or equivalent entity. However, any questions that you have should be directed to your contractor or architect. The critical inspection is the final one, giving you the Certificate of Occupancy (CO) that's necessary in order to greet your first guest — although it's not uncommon to get a temporary CO (TCO) while minor things are completed, such as painting, landscaping, and so on. A TCO may require an additional fee and is only issued for a limited period of time.

Earning the necessary licenses

In order to open and operate your B&B, you need to meet the requirements set by your city, county, and/or state for business licenses. Licensing needs and renewal requirements vary by location and by the activities that you conduct at your inn (such as selling retail items). Use the list below as a checklist; however, be sure to check with your lawyer, your state, city hall, and other innkeepers for information and requirements in your area.

- **Conditional use permit:** This gives you the authority to operate a B&B at your location (if necessary). (See "It's not up to you: Zoning and other legalities," earlier in this chapter.)

- **Employer Identification Number (EIN):** If you have at least one employee and/or your business structure is other than a sole proprietorship, you need to obtain a federal employer ID number. You also need to obtain a state employer ID number. For more information and to find out how to apply for an EIN online, visit the IRS Web site at www.irs.gov and enter "EIN" in the search box. For state ID numbers, check online for your state Web site and search for "starting a business." Before applying, you need to know the legal structure of your business (see Chapter 3, where I cover how to make these decisions with your accountant and attorney). If your legal structure is a sole proprietorship, you file your tax returns using your social security number. That may or may not be true for your state returns, and some states may require a different tax ID number from your employer ID number.

- **Business license:** This is the main document required for tax purposes and other business functions. To learn requirements in your area, contact the county clerk's office or city clerk's office.

- **DBA:** This is your "doing business as" or fictitious business name license. Having a DBA allows you to legally operate under your business name, so check with your attorney for help.

- **Certificate of Occupancy:** This authorizes your property for public occupancy. (I cover this information in the preceding section.)

- **Fire, building, and safety inspections:** Your local city hall can help you with this list so you know what to expect in your area.

- **Health department inspections and permit, food handler's license, and miscellaneous licenses:** In some areas, additional licenses are required, such as hot tub licenses.

Local health departments require training and certification for safe food handling in order to receive their licenses. Contact your local health department for information on training requirements. ServSafe (www. servsafe.com) is the most widely accepted food safety program and satisfies the requirements of most local, state, and federal health department standards. (They also have a program for responsible alcohol practices.)

✔ **Alcohol license or permit:** These are usually state-issued, and each state has its own regulations and requirements. In some areas, you may need to apply for a license from your town or city as well, so start with your county or town clerk's office to find out about requirements in your area.

✔ **Sign permit:** In many areas, in order to put a sign outside of your inn, you need to obtain a sign permit. Don't be surprised, however, if some areas don't allow this at all. Check with your local zoning office about restrictions and requirements in your area.

✔ **Seller's permit:** Sometimes called a certificate of resale, this permit is required when selling retail items or when sales tax is charged. The permit lets you collect required sales taxes from guests and turn these monies over to the state. Contact your state tax board, department of revenue, or similar entity for information.

A seller's permit is not the same as a transient tax or bed tax that most towns or counties also require you to collect. Typically, a transient or bed tax is collected monthly or quarterly by the town or county and is added to the sales tax amount that you charge guests for lodging. Where required, it's filed as a report and no additional license is required. Check with your county clerk's office for collection and filing requirements.

Funding Your Project

When building or renovating a new inn, you need to shop around for financing. Local, regional banks are your best source and the easiest to work with.

To avoid unnecessary fees, get a construction loan that later rolls into permanent financing after the construction phase is completed. This arrangement avoids the need to have two loans (a construction loan and then a conventional loan). Having one loan helps you know the amount of your debt service in order to set and stick to a budget, which therefore gives you a great deal of incentive to set a firm and fixed price with your contractor. After all, the bank isn't giving you an open-ended source of financing, and if you go over budget you have to go back to the bank to apply for additional financing.

Because you aren't able to show the bank current cash flow numbers as you would be able to when buying an existing inn, a well-written and well-presented business and financial plan is extremely important in securing financing. (Refer to Chapter 3 for help in writing a business plan.) Consider hiring an industry consultant for help and to add credibility to your plan.

Don't underestimate your participation in the process of securing a loan for the work on your new inn. Show bank representatives both your professionalism and your passion. Ask about the process for loan approval and find out how you can be involved. As you go through the process, continuously ask what else you need to provide so that the loan can be approved. If your lender is not familiar with the community your B&B will be located in or the B&B industry in general, then you need to educate the lender to help convince her that your project makes sense. One way to do this is to gather a team that might include an economic development person from the county and an inn consultant, plus industry statistics from the Professional Association of Innkeepers International (PAII) or your state or local B&B association to help the lender obtain the answers necessary to make the loan commitment.

Building from Scratch

When you build your inn from the ground up, you have a chance to give guests what they want and yourself what you need, after considering zoning and financial considerations of course. When you design your inn, you have the chance to influence guests' experiences at your inn by determining such things as the location and size of the guest rooms and big amenities like soaking tubs, fireplaces, or seating and dining areas. You also have the chance to build your own living quarters and work areas with the benefit of hindsight from seasoned innkeepers and information that you glean from this book. In order to make your dream B&B a reality, you need to hire an architect and a contractor. The following sections steer you in the right directions.

Designing the B&B of your dreams

Get out a piece of paper and draw a line down the center of it. On one side of the line, write down all the things you liked about previous B&B stays, and on the other side, jot down anything you disliked. Keep adding to this list every time you think of something. Before sitting down with the architect to begin designing your inn, look at the list of things you liked and circle all the structural things that should be added during the building stage. Cross off any that don't fit into your budget, those that fall outside the zoning laws, any that won't appeal to your target market, and those that aren't normally offered in B&Bs and rooms within your intended rate range.

Many of your design decisions are dictated by zoning code and local ordinances. However, all your decisions should keep the safety and comfort of your guests in mind.

Giving your guests what they want

When starting a new B&B project, one of the hardest things to understand and envision is the concept of space. Measure your own bedroom and bathroom at home, and measure guest rooms and bathrooms at every hotel and B&B you stay at as part of your research process. Which ones feel like a good size? As you get a feel for square footage in these spaces, you can figure out what is and what isn't enough for your own inn.

The size of guest rooms and bathrooms should match the price point — what you want to charge for your rooms. Also, when planning your guest rooms, consider the size of the beds and approximately where they'll be placed within the rooms. Then measure to be sure the planned room provides adequate space around all sides of the bed and space for other furniture in the room. When your inn opens, you'll be selling a room experience, which means you're selling space.

Here's a list of guest-friendly features that are guaranteed to be on the dream lists of seasoned innkeepers. You may want to include them in the plans for your own inn, particularly the spaces used by guests:

- ✔ Private en suite bath for each guest room
- ✔ Public half bath near common areas
- ✔ On-demand hot water to each guest bathroom
- ✔ Adequate hot water and water pressure
- ✔ Individual climate control for each guest room (sometimes required by code)
- ✔ Dual sinks in guest bathrooms
- ✔ At least one parking space per room
- ✔ Wet bar for guest refreshments
- ✔ Fireplaces and jetted tubs in guest rooms (depending on targeted clientele)
- ✔ Generator

  The value of a generator depends on your location. If you're in an area that frequently loses power or that has above-ground power lines, a generator is worth considering.

- ✔ Adequate electrical service (for the kitchen, laundry, and guest room whirlpools and spas, and also for lighting outdoor areas, such as walkways, patios, parking areas, signs, and recreational areas)
- ✔ Plenty of closet space

The design phase is the best time to decide what kind of furniture you want and where it will be placed in the guest rooms so you can be sure the rooms you design are big enough. You also need to plan for things such as soaking tubs and so on. (See Chapter 9 for ideas and considerations when furnishing your inn.) Remember to select features based on where your inn is located, your target market, the profile of the guests that you hope to attract, and the price of your rooms.

Giving yourself what you need

"You might be an innkeeper if you have a 5,000-square foot house and live in 500 square feet of it!" This quote from the humor section of the Florida B&B association newsletter isn't much of an exaggeration. If they had it to do over again, many innkeepers I've spoken with would have given more thought to the space they carved out for themselves when they set up their inns. If you plan to be an on-site innkeeper, you'll rarely get a second chance to extend your personal living quarters. In general, according to PAII's Industry Study of Operation and Finance, the average size of innkeeper's quarters is increasing, with about half of the participating inns having innkeeper's quarters of more than 1,000 square feet. Keep in mind this is an average — some innkeepers have just one room for themselves, which I don't recommend.

Some innkeepers decide to start out with smaller innkeeper's quarters so that in a few years they can move off-site and hire a night manager to occupy their former quarters. Less square footage for you can mean more square footage for bringing in revenue. It's important to strike a good balance that works for you, and these considerations should be part of your business planning process. The size of your living space and the privacy your quarters offer you will have an effect on your burnout rate, because you can easily become resentful of guests' spacious accommodations if you're feeling cramped and trapped in your own small quarters. So although guest rooms take priority, be sure not to neglect your own quarters in the planning of your bed & breakfast. (See Chapter 9 for information on furnishing your new home and tips for separating your personal space from the public areas of your inn.)

Although selling your inn is the farthest thing from your mind, buyers often choose an inn based on superior innkeeper's quarters. It doesn't hurt to keep this in mind as you plan your own place; more likely than not, the day will come when you're ready to put your place on the market. Why not give yourself a leg up on the competition?

Your private space needs to be comfortable for you and your family or partners. Planning ahead for your space, your privacy, and anything that makes the job of innkeeping easier is a benefit of building your inn from scratch, so take advantage of it! Following are some features and accommodations to give some serious thought to in different areas and aspects of the innkeeper's quarters:

✔ **Office:** You're running a business, so you need plenty of room for a desk, filing cabinets, and office equipment, such as a computer, printer, and so on.

✔ **Kitchen:** An efficient kitchen with room to work and good appliances makes your life easier. A commercial kitchen is ideal but very expensive. (Verify whether a commercial kitchen is required as part of your operating code.) When selecting appliances, purchase ones that will grow with your business, including a large enough refrigerator, stove, oven, and so on. (Refer to Chapter 13 for information on kitchen tools and equipment that can make your life easier.) Also, I recommend extra-deep (30-inch) counters and a three-bin kitchen sink.

✔ **Laundry room:** A lot of laundry will be done over the life of your inn, so set aside a large laundry area and stock it well. Factor in the size of the laundry room to not only hold the equipment that you buy now but also to add more equipment later on as the occupancy of the inn increases (for example, additional dryers are often on many innkeepers' wish lists). Refer to Chapter 13 for information on laundry tools and equipment that can make your life easier. Consider the amount of electrical service available in your laundry room as well as incoming water lines, the source and heat of the water, and the size of the wastewater drains.

It's ideal to have a water source for the laundry that's separate from the source of water for your guests. Then you can use higher water temperatures in the production areas (the laundry room and the kitchen) of your inn and you won't have to worry about water pressure for guests' showers.

✔ **Personal retreat:** Be sure to give yourself enough space to create your own haven: a place that you can retreat to with a feeling of "Ah, I'm home," when you're done with work or taking a break.

✔ **Private entrance:** Guests should know when you're away from the inn and how to reach you in the event of an emergency, but the ability to come and go via a private entrance to your quarters helps you run your business — from completing errands to being on time for appointments — without feeling like you have to cut guests off mid-conversation. Personal visitors also can use your private entrance to your guest quarters, allowing you to further separate business from pleasure.

✔ **Private outdoor space:** When possible, your B&B design should factor in outdoor areas that are private and preferably secluded so that you have a casual space to relax without being joined by guests.

✔ **Parking:** You should have separate innkeeper parking, or at least sufficient parking space in the guest parking area.

✔ **Workshop:** If you're handy and plan on repairing items, staining furniture, and so on, carve out space for a workshop so you can do these tasks away from your guests' view.

✔ **Storage space:** Plan for adequate storage space. You'll be amazed how much space you'll quickly use storing holiday decorations, bulk purchases, extra supplies, and so on.

Double the amount of storage that you think you need for general storage and in guest rooms.

Discuss with your accountant or consultant any tax implications involved if your residence is physically separated from the inn, such as a private apartment behind the main house.

Hiring a good architect and contractor

Hiring a good architect and contractor is the key to a smooth and successful project. Ideally, you should hire your architect first to design the plan for your inn, which you'll then put out to bid with various contractors. Additionally, the architect can often make recommendations for contractors whom you should consider. A big exception to the order in which you hire these key people is having a contractor who comes highly recommended to you — then he can make referrals for architects.

The best way to find a good contractor and a good architect is through first-hand referrals. All professionals can furnish you with references, but don't expect them to give you the names of dissatisfied customers. It's up to you to do your homework and get referrals from respected sources.

Consider going straight to the source: job sites the contractors and architects are currently working. When Dave Reusing began interviewing architects and contractors for the renovation of Town Hill Bed & Breakfast (`www.townhillbnb.com`) in Little Orleans, Maryland, he didn't ask them for references but rather what jobs they were currently working on. He then went to those job sites to see how the projects were going and spoke with the owners to find out whether they were happy with the process and progress of the work being done.

Working with an architect

You want an architect who can share your vision for your B&B. It's critical that the architect you hire is someone with whom you can communicate and work easily, because there will be a lot of communication and exchange of ideas surrounding the plans. Architects often specialize in particular types of projects — for example, designing homes, schools, or hospitals. Hiring a small firm with a focus on residential design but an understanding of commercial or hotel codes is a good choice because your architect needs to be sensitive to the needs of the lodging industry. For example, your architect needs to understand the importance of the building materials chosen, such as soundboard that provides another layer for soundproofing.

To avoid guesswork and save time in working with the architect you choose to design your inn, follow these tips:

- ✔ Be specific in all your communications. Rather than telling the architect that you want a large whirlpool in the Garden Room, clarify that you envision a 48-x-78-inch whirlpool with bubble jets in the bathroom of Guest Room One. Be ready to share images, brands, and model numbers of the equipment, fixtures, and appliances you want to use.

- ✔ Make a list of fixtures and appliances, room by room. Keep one copy on your computer and a hard copy at the construction site.

- ✔ Check stock and availability of fixtures and appliances when you make your selections during the design phase. I know of one innkeeper who wanted a specific bathtub that required an order to be placed six months in advance because the manufacturing plant was in South Africa. Many years later, this tub still looks great and the guests love it. But it's only there because of the advanced research that alerted the innkeeper to the lead time necessary for ordering it.

Working with a contractor

When hiring and working with your contractor, here are some things to know:

- ✔ **By law, contractors must be licensed, bonded, and insured. In addition to these protections, you need to purchase your own Builder's Risk insurance policy for the duration of the construction.** This is a temporary policy that provides another level of insurance coverage during the construction process. It protects you, the owner, and the contractor against loss, theft, or damage during the construction process. Ask your current home or auto insurance agent whether they provide this type of insurance, how much it costs, and what coverage it provides. If they don't offer it, they can usually make recommendations for agents who do, or you can ask other innkeepers who have built or renovated their inns for recommendations.

- ✔ **All prices are negotiable.** Do your homework on pricing so you have better leverage to negotiate.

- ✔ **You arrange to pay the contractor in stages.** The release of funds against your loan is commonly called a *draw* against the construction loan in that you are drawing down the funds from the total available. Most lenders have staff members who visit job sites to verify that the project is at the completion stage for the requested draw. For example, your contract with the contractor may request a 10 percent payment when the foundation is complete. While you may call the lender and authorize the release of the funds, the lender's inspector may visit to insure that the foundation is, in fact, complete. This insures that the funds will be there for the final phases of construction per the contract.

✔ **You specify all the materials to be used in your B&B project, unless you make other arrangements with the contractor.** For example, you choose kitchen appliances with model numbers and finishes, carpet, tile, window types, and so on.

✔ **The general contractor should be responsible for and should oversee the subcontractors.**

✔ **You should request a Release of Liens to ensure that you aren't responsible for any supplies, materials, or labor from the subcontractors.**

To keep costs down, help out. If your contractor is working for time and materials fees, anything that you can do to save some billable time will save you money. For example, you might pick up some supplies or help with cleanup around the job site. Just don't get in the way of work being done — that wastes just as much time as you're trying to save!

Keeping track of the building process

With your architect, contractor, permits, and funding in place, the building process begins! This will be your preoccupation for the foreseeable future. Although the process is different for the building of each inn, here are some of the main things you should expect during a typical building project:

✔ **A meeting with the HVAC installer.** You'll meet with the heating and a/c installer to discuss the location for the exterior and interior equipment, such as thermostats, a/c return, air grills, and a/c and heat controls for each room (which I recommend). Your job before this meeting is to plan where furniture will be located in the rooms — you don't want the floor grill to be covered later by an armoire.

✔ **A meeting with the electrician.** After all stud walls are in place, you'll meet with the electrician on-site with a floor plan to review the locations of all equipment requiring special electrical switches, plugs, speakers, telephones, and so on.

✔ **A meeting with other subcontractors.** Depending on your project, you may also meet with other subcontractors, such as the plumber or the person installing your Internet or sound system.

The electrician, HVAC installer and so on are subcontractors and employed by your contractor. While these people have building plans, they often don't read them closely and they don't know where you'll be placing appliances and furniture, so discuss with your architect and contractor when the best time is to set up a meeting with each subcontractor to review the key placement of outlets, controls, and the like. You should have already reviewed these decisions with your architect, who will help you make sure you aren't forgetting anything, and the architect may or may not be present at these meetings.

✔ **Weekly progress meetings.** You should have weekly meetings — ideally on the job site but some can be done by phone — with your contractor to review progress and obstacles. I encourage you to keep the tone of these weekly meetings or phone calls very friendly and professional. As the owner, you want to do everything you can to support the contractor in his efforts to build your inn on time and on budget. Don't get argumentative or create an adversarial relationship. Yes, he technically works for you, but treat him as you would a guest — it's good practice!

Converting an Existing Property into an Inn

The process of purchasing a property to convert into your bed & breakfast or turning your own home into a B&B is similar to building your inn from scratch. It's easy to get excited about a beautiful property or your desire to find a way to earn extra money from your existing home, but remember that this is a big business decision you're making. I outline the key considerations to help you through this process in the following sections.

The property on which a bed & breakfast resides is only a small part of its being. The majority of what makes a bed & breakfast comes from the guests' experiences. You can't simply convert a property or your home into a place where you rent rooms for extra income, magically open your doors to guests, and think you have a bed & breakfast. Without thought, planning, preparation, training, and commitment to the guest experience, you're merely running a boarding house.

Answering key questions

It's important that you take a good, hard look at the property and visualize it as a bed & breakfast. Analyze its possibilities and potential (both legal and practical) in the same ways you would if it were an existing B&B or if you were choosing a plot to build an inn from scratch. Key questions you'll need to answer are: Can I do this? Will guests come? Can I provide guests a comfortable lodging experience here so that they will return and refer others?

Getting a conditional use permit if you need it

The biggest obstacle to converting an existing property is zoning, no matter whether it's a property that you think would make a fabulous setting for a bed & breakfast or whether you're converting your own home into a B&B. If the property you want to convert is in a residential neighborhood (which most are) and not zoned for commercial use, you need to apply for a *conditional use permit.* In a residential neighborhood, your neighbors play a big role in whether you get approval or your plans and dreams end at the local zoning board office or planning commission. Refer to the earlier section, "Getting to know state, county, and town zoning and building regulations," for more information, and don't proceed with the conversion of the property until all permits and licenses are in place.

Confirming your location

Opening a B&B is a big commitment and a career decision, not something you should do because you're trying to achieve the objective of living somewhere that you can't afford otherwise (although this may be a nice side benefit). No matter how beautiful a property is, if it's not in a good location, guests won't visit. At a minimum, the property must be located in an area that offers popular attractions or it must be a convenient and frequent stopover point between two other popular locations. Chapter 2 helps you analyze potential B&B locations.

Carving out the space

When deciding whether it makes sense to convert an existing property into a bed & breakfast, it's important to consider the space and layout. Answer the following key questions to get a better feel for how the space will work for your needs:

- ✔ Are the guest rooms, common areas, and utility areas (including laundry and kitchen) large enough?
- ✔ Approximately how much will it cost to make renovations to bring the building up to code and to make the size of the rooms or the layout conducive to a bed & breakfast?
- ✔ Does the placement of the guest rooms and the innkeeper's quarters make sense? Can you create a true sense of privacy for your guests?
- ✔ Are there enough bathrooms? Are they private? If they're separate from the rooms, are they in good proximity to the rooms? Or are the bathrooms now — or will they be — en suite?
- ✔ Will you have sufficient private space in your innkeeper's quarters?

Restoring a historic or conventional property

If the property you're looking to convert into a B&B is officially on the National Register of Historic Places (www.nps.gov/nr), the property has been designated by the National Park Service as having significance to the history of the community, state, or nation. Before renovating such a property, consult with your State Historic Preservation Officer (SHPO) in addition to local authorities. You can find the contact information for your SHPO by visiting www.nps.gov/history/nr/shpolist.htm.

Compliance with ADA laws is more complicated for historic and existing conventional structures due to their exceptions. Neither type of property is exempt from ADA compliance unless it qualifies as having five rooms or less with the owner living within the building, as I discuss in the earlier section, "Complying with codes for handicap accessibility." There are some exceptions based on the ability to make changes and their financial impact. Exceptions generally have to be adjudicated if there's a complaint about the property, because sometimes the law can be vague. The law does allow you to make accommodations; for instance, if a guest can't get to your dining room for breakfast, you can serve it to her in her guest room.

Converting your home into a B&B

If you decide to turn your own home into a B&B, you need to follow all the considerations in the previous sections under this main topic of conversion. However, one additional big point that you must think long and hard about is this: You need to accept and understand that your home is no longer a private residence but rather a place of business where you, your family, and your guests must be comfortable. Plan the layout and the conversion of your home so that your guests don't feel that they're encroaching on your private living quarters. As guests paying to stay in your home, they don't want to hear your family discussions or TV noise coming from your private rooms.

Because renovations are nearly always required, owners tend to minimize the size of the job and underestimate the amount of time the renovations will take, so be sure to work out a time line with your architect and contractor before the project starts. Then factor in inevitable delays. Make good use of this time by getting your marketing ready (see Chapter 8).

Getting Ready to Open Your New Inn

So much is involved in getting a new inn ready for guests that you may be wondering when and where to begin. There is no magical day when a particular task should be done; however, it's best to make decisions long before the time to implement them arrives. In this section, I lead you through the important task of naming your B&B, and then I point out some other items that should be on your to-do list, including hosting a grand opening.

Naming your B&B

What's in a name? The simple answer is everything! It's your inn's identity, and just hearing it should evoke a positive image for potential guests and the media. Choosing a name for your B&B requires careful thought. In addition to sounding right and conveying the right meaning, the name should be easy to say, easy to remember, and, when it makes sense to do so, contain keywords that can help your Web site place highly in the results of Internet search engines such as Google and Yahoo! (See Chapter 8 for details on Web site designers who specialize in bed & breakfast Web site promotion and can help you select a name that will help your placement in the search engines.)

Picking your inn's name

Naming your inn is your single best chance to create an image of your B&B and to share that vision with guests. Things to consider when choosing the name for your bed & breakfast are

- ✔ **Making it easy to remember.** It's hard to get referrals if people can't remember the name of your inn.

- ✔ **Reflecting your geographic location.** Including your geographic location in your inn's name lets guests know where you're located and could give you an edge when guests do a search for bed & breakfasts in your area. A nice example is Hermann Hill Inn in Hermann, Missouri.

- ✔ **Using descriptive keywords that people may use in online searches.** *Keywords* are descriptive words that guests and media may use in Internet search engines when looking for a B&B. Including a keyword in your inn's name, such as Gettysburg Battlefield Bed & Breakfast Inn, tells potential guests something about your inn before they've even seen your Web site.

   Don't overlook the importance of the term "bed & breakfast" in your name, because many guests prefer to stay at B&Bs as opposed to hotels and use the term "bed & breakfast" in their Internet searches.

- ✔ **Appearing early in alphabetical listings.** Choosing a first word starting with a letter as early in the alphabet as possible is a good idea because phone books, many guidebooks, and some Internet sites still list properties alphabetically. Don't limit yourself by the alphabet, however. If you have an idea for a name that meets other favorable characteristics in this list, forego the alphabetical concern.

Get name suggestions from everyone you know and add them to your own list of favorites. Then try to picture your B&B with each name that you like. Imagine other people talking about your inn using the names you like best. You may be able to narrow down your list considerably with this exercise.

Remember, your B&B's name is a very important statement about your business and will be with you a long time, so take your time in deciding.

Practice saying each name candidate many times, over and over. How does it sound to you? "Good morning, the Winding Road End of Your Journey Bed & Breakfast Inn, this is Sue, how may I help you?" If you say it over and over and it's a mouthful, it's probably not a good name.

Protecting your identity

After you've narrowed down your choices and picked the name for your bed & breakfast, you need to be sure that no one else has rights to it and take steps to protect it before you start using it. As you build your business, you also build your brand and your reputation, so you want to be sure that you own this identity as securely as any other aspect of your business. Follow these steps for establishing and protecting your inn's name and identity:

1. **Perform an online search of your potential name.**

   Start by typing the name you've chosen into your favorite search engine and see whether other B&Bs come up. Are any nearby inns already using this name, or does anyone else's marketing use the terms in your potential inn name? As long as any inns that appear in the search results don't use the exact name, you can proceed. Don't skip this step. If you find another inn using the same name, even if it's located clear across the country, I strongly suggest that you start over and spend some time trying to find a more unique name for your bed & breakfast. True, many B&Bs have the same or similar names, but that always leads to confusion.

2. **Register your inn's name as a Web site address.**

   When you've settled on a name that you don't think anyone else is using, you need to immediately register it for your Web site address. (See Chapter 8 for information on Web sites and Internet terminology.) Domain registrars (such as www.godaddy.com and www.dotster.com) tell you whether the name you want to register is available, along with the extension options (.com, .net, .info, and so on). If your name is taken, the company offers suggestions of similar names. If you're still in contract on an existing inn, register the domain name under your current address. You can update it after closing.

   Don't settle for a domain name that's similar but has a hyphen or underscore, because guests won't remember to type these in and will end up visiting the other inn's Web site. Also, if you love the domain name and the .com extension is being used by another inn; don't settle for the .net name. If you do, chances are you'll end up helping to promote the other B&B instead of yours.

If you're unsure about which domain name and extension you want to use, spend the money to register several possible domains, and always register the .com extension as well as the .net and .info extensions to protect your identity.

When you decide on your inn name and register your domain name, register any common misspellings as well.

you'll be using the inn's name to run the business instead of your company name (for a limited liability company [LLC] or corporation) or your own name (if you're a sole proprietor), check with your state find out whether you have to register a DBA (doing business as).

For example, your B&B is the Grasshopper Inn, but your business may actually be Smith Hospitality LLC, or just John Smith.

ng care of important details

me leading up to opening day for tackling the following important

a food handler class. Complete any training and certification red for handling food and/or serving alcohol. ServSafe (www. safe.com) is the most popular program accepted by most health tments.

know your neighbors, the area, and contacts at city hall. Spend the area getting to know your neighborhood and area attracven if you already live in the area, look at it in a different light, to know other local businesses and attractions that you'll be referring guests to. Also visit the chamber of commerce and/or visitors bureau and become a member.

✔ **Start your marketing plan.** It's never too early to plan your advertising because with a new inn, you're starting at square one. You're building more than a physical property; you're building a business, and both processes should happen simultaneously. Work through all the advice in Chapter 8 so that you're building awareness and excitement about your inn while the inn itself is being built (or renovated).

✔ **Join your national, state, and local B&B associations.**

✔ **Choose and learn software programs.** Learn how to use your software programs, and train anyone else who may be using them as well. (Chapter 6 has information on accounting programs, reservations systems, and property management software.)

✔ **Plan your open house.** End every conversation with locals by getting their contact information so that you can invite them to your open house to celebrate your grand opening.

Showing off the place: Holding an open house

Opening your doors to guests is a big deal, and you should make the most of your first and biggest chance for publicity. Most innkeepers know to hold an open house, but the majority are surprised by the huge turnout they receive. Don't underestimate the local interest in touring the place. Here are some tips and guidelines for holding a successful open house and making the most of this promotional opportunity:

✔ **Planning and logistics**

- **There's no right or wrong time to hold your open house; however, Sunday from 1–5 p.m. is often a good choice in terms of guest and local availability.**

  Picking a date for an open house is tricky when you're not sure construction will be completed. In reality, construction runs late, and the time allocated to furnish and decorate the inn is compressed into a few days. If you've taken advance reservations, you're working hard to open those rooms in time for your guests. Waiting a few weeks until after you're open and a bit settled to host an open house ensures that the community sees the property complete and as you want them to see it.

- **Let the local newspapers, TV stations, and radio stations know about the event ahead of time.** As soon as you pick the date for your open house, get the word out by sending out invitations and/ or a press release (four to six weeks notice is ideal). Then make a personal call to follow up with the local media. This is a great way to introduce yourself to them, and it ensures that they have your open house information. Local media outlets often cover items of local interest for free. If you can get a local paper to cover the open house for a story before it takes place, you'll have a much better turnout at a much better price than placing an advertisement. (You can't beat the price of free publicity!)

- **Ask your local chamber of commerce and visitors bureau for assistance in promoting the event, and invite representatives to attend.** Introducing your inn to your local chamber of commerce and visitors bureau and engaging their help and support to promote your B&B early in the inn ownership process is a great practice. Your open house is a logical place to start if you're a member of these organizations.

✔ **Invitations**

- **Begin making your invite list as soon as you begin planning your bed & breakfast.** Keep the contact information for everyone you meet from the time you decide to open your bed & breakfast to when you send out the invitations.

waiting for the next tour or have completed a tour.

Don't let open house guests wander through the B&B unescorted, because things can easily disappear. Also, people tend to move things around, lay on the beds, and use the bathrooms, requiring them to be cleaned and straightened repeatedly. Affix ribbons across open doors to keep people out of rooms but still allow them to see inside. (You may have seen this done at historic homes or museums.)

- **If you have a gift shop, include it on the tour.** Make sure that items are prominently displayed so that local people know that they can shop for gifts at your B&B in the future.

- **Make sure your private innkeeper's quarters are locked and inaccessible.**

You may want to hold an "Open House Week" or an "Open House Weekend" with set hours rather than limit the event to just one day, so that people have more opportunities to visit your property and see what you have to offer. Your goal is to introduce your inn to as many people as possible and to get them inside your inn while you still have some free time before your business gets rolling along.

The most dangerous thing a
woman in Somaliland could do
was to get pregnant, and Edna
Adan Ismail couldn't accept tha
After she sold her car and used
her pension to build a Materni
and Teaching hospital in Harg
— based in a site where mass
killings had occurred during
civil war — we found out ab
mission. Linking up with Bo
for Africa, we sent 6,000 m
and other college-level bo
the nursing students there
Edna was able to train 22
students in Community M
a new category of schoo
the community, and a cr
toward tackling matern
mortality rates.

That's what happens w
or donate with Better \

In this part . . .

Opening your B&B for business requires some serious preparation. This part helps you to take your business through the process of getting ready to welcome guests, starting by establishing good record-keeping procedures from the start and setting your room rates and polices. You also find out how to attract guests by getting the word out through marketing, including your Web site, and tactics that improve your placement in search engine results. Comfortable, appropriate furnishings and good food help you to create a fabulous experience for your guests, so I cover them in this part as well. And throughout the part, I give you tips and secrets used by other successful innkeepers.

Chapter 6

Organizing Your Record-Keeping

. . . .

In This Chapter

▶ Understanding the business virtues of good record-keeping

▶ Establishing financial records

▶ Working with a property management software system

. . . .

Good records are the core of your business. They track your financial performance, and they're the information you use to analyze your successes and disappointments throughout the life of your bed & breakfast. Your financial records are the framework for the organization of the day-to-day running of your bed & breakfast, and they help you keep track of everything from guest reservations to housekeeping tasks.

In this chapter, you find out just how important good record-keeping is and how to set up organized and useful records from the start. I tell you how to set up your financial and accounting records to track revenue and expenses as well as how to pick property management software that tracks reservations, guest communications, and even inventory controls. Good records are invaluable, so the software packages that help you keep your information organized are some of the most important tools of your business and some of the most important investments you'll make in your business.

You Need Good Records, Plain and Simple

Setting up good record-keeping from the start is essential to the organization of your business and will save you valuable time in the future, so this is an area to give considerable thought to and a good time to draw upon the experiences of other innkeepers (see Chapter 1 for information on finding innkeeper resources). Think of your records as a snapshot of your business performance and an objective evaluation of how it's doing. You've heard the expression, "Numbers don't lie." Keep good records and you'll have strong, accurate tools to gauge your business's performance. More importantly, you'll have valuable information to help you plan your future.

Good records are an important part of your business for many reasons. Following is just a sampling:

- ✔ **Good records arm you with the necessary information to file your income taxes and required reports such as payroll taxes (FICA), unemployment taxes (FUTA and state), disability, workers compensation, and sales taxes.** Whether you prepare these reports and filings yourself or give the job to your CPA or accountant, you save yourself time and money if the financial information is organized and at your fingertips.

- ✔ **Good records allow you to see where your money goes and what areas it comes from.** When you keep good records you know what it costs to provide services and amenities to guests. You won't be profitable if you offer services and amenities that cost more than the revenue that they bring in. Knowing how much revenue each area of your business brings in helps you to plan accordingly so you can focus on the areas that bring in the most revenue. For example, it doesn't make financial sense to convert a guest room into a space for spa treatments if doing so would show less profit (revenue minus expenses) than using the space as a rentable guest room.

- ✔ **Your records contain the information needed to determine which marketing sources are paying for themselves, which helps you make informed decisions about which advertisements and memberships to renew.** (See Chapter 15 for more information on analyzing your advertising results.) You can track referrals in most property management software systems (for more information, see the section, "Choosing a Property Management System," later in this chapter) by recording the source of each guest referral (for example, the chamber of commerce, a specific online directory, past guest, repeat guest, direct mail, and so on). Then when it's time for renewal you can compare the renewal price with the amount of business the source has generated for you. The result tells you whether that marketing source warrants a future investment.

- ✔ **Looking at your revenue and expenses and comparing them to other periods helps you to predict future business and prepare for it.** For example, if you look back over last year's records and see that your revenue from small group meetings increased during the first three months of the year (typically a slow period for your B&B), you may proactively decide to advertise your business meeting facilities to local businesses in the coming year's first quarter. Your accounting software enables you to compare previous periods to current periods.

- ✔ **Buyers can't evaluate your business without good financial records, and they need reliable numbers to be able to make an educated decision and obtain financing to buy your inn.** Seeing as you're reading this book, selling your B&B is probably not even on your mind. However, the time may come or something unexpected (good or bad) may cause your plans to change and you may decide to sell your inn. Having kept consistently good and accurate records will make the whole process much easier.

Record everything accurately, and always put yourself in a buyer's shoes when considering your records. If you were to hear, "Our revenue is actually higher. We just didn't record everything for tax purposes" as a buyer, you would wonder what else wasn't recorded or what else the seller isn't being truthful about. And, by the way, understating revenue is against the law.

Setting Up Your Books

It's never too early to set up your books and keep track of expenses that you incur. No matter where you are in the process of starting your bed & breakfast, you're incurring expenses, so speak with your CPA or accountant about what business-related expenses you should be keeping track of and how to record them. It's tempting to throw your receipts into a box and think about dealing with them later, but with so many choices of easy-to-use accounting software on the market today, there's no excuse not to have an organized system from the start.

Opening a business checking account and credit card

If you haven't done so already, open a business checking account and apply for a business credit card — both in the name of your B&B. But how do you know what your B&B is called before you've either bought it or built it? Check with your attorney about setting up your legal entity first and using it as the holding company for the B&B. Then, when you open you can simply add the DBA (Doing Business As), which is the name of your B&B, to the account.

Use your business checking account and business credit card to begin a record of the start-up expenses associated with your business (seek the advice of your CPA or accountant to determine what qualifies as a business expense) and to begin establishing a credit rating. Most banks require evidence of a business before you can open a business account, including a FTIN (Federal Tax Identification Number) or your social security number if you're a sole proprietorship. (Chapter 3 has information on business structures.)

Picking an accounting software package

You don't need to have a financial or accounting background to keep good records. You have several popular software programs to choose from that are easy to use for small business owners such as yourself, regardless of whether you have a vast knowledge of bookkeeping and accounting or none at all.

Whatever software you choose, see if you can download a trial version from the company Web site before you buy. Trying out the trial versions will help you decide which program works best for you and your business. (Quick-Books Pro is by far the most popular software used by innkeepers.)

Don't buy home accounting or home business accounting software. It's not complete enough for your needs and doesn't have the ability to produce payroll. Make sure the software is for small businesses.

Your accounting software is an important tool that makes your life easier and saves you money. It gives you the ability to track revenues and expenses, produce payroll, and track and pay bills in a timely manner. It also simplifies matters at tax time. If you're called upon for an audit, your records are easy to pull together quickly. It saves you money because you're able to easily print or export your records to your CPA or accountant, saving you the hourly billing costs of having others pull this information together for you. For this reason, you may want to pick a program your CPA or accountant uses or is familiar with so you can easily send her your records at tax time.

Almost all accounting software offers more components than you need, but don't let that frighten you. Just make sure it has these features, and you'll be set:

- ✔ **Look for a program that's compatible with your bank and credit card statements.** Many programs automatically import your bank and credit card statements, making reconciliation a snap.

- ✔ **Choose a program that prints checks.** Being able to print and record checks directly from your accounting software is a serious time-saver.

- ✔ **Select a program that offers a payroll module.** This feature makes it easy for you to handle payroll on your own, saving the expense of a payroll service or having your CPA or accountant do it. Plus, you avoid the headaches of figuring payroll out on your own because the program does it for you.

Creating a chart of accounts

Your *chart of accounts* is the list of all the accounts for your business. An *account* is a category, such as interest expense, advertising, room sales, and so on, into or out of which money is paid. If you think of your bookkeeping system as a file cabinet, then each account or category is like a file folder. Every account is also allocated to one of five groups: revenues, expenses, assets, liabilities, and equity. Once you have your chart of accounts set up, you have more than just an organized system, you have easy access to all your financial information. You will use this information to compare how your business is doing from month to month and year to year, to know how much you've paid a particular vendor, to find out what services bring in the most revenue, to discover what you're spending the most money on, and so on.

Your chart of accounts is the foundation of your record-keeping so you want a good, strong base to work from. The set-up wizard in most accounting software recommends businesses or accounts that have to be adjusted later, and, depending on the software, once established, some accounts can be tricky or impossible to remove if you've entered data into them. Not only do you want them set up correctly from the start, but setting them up can also be an intimidating process. Getting help from an accountant or industry consultant (see Chapter 3 for help in finding a consultant) is recommended to get you started. It will save you significant tax return preparation costs by ensuring that the information for tax returns is readily available in your accounting system at year-end.

Table 6-1 shows the industry-recommended chart of accounts for a B&B prepared by the Professional Association of Innkeepers International (PAII; www.paii.com). You can use Table 6-1 as a guide in setting up the accounts that you'll use to generate your income statement (also called *profit and loss statement,* or P&L). This is a report that you should refer to often to gauge and monitor how your business is doing, so it's important that you're familiar with the accounts that generate this report. You should consult with your CPA or accountant for help in setting up other financial statements, such as your balance sheet (see Chapter 3), which includes your assets, liabilities, and equity.

Table 6-1	Sample Chart of Accounts for a Bed & Breakfast Inn
Revenue Accounts	*Descriptions*
Gross room rental	Rent received for guest rooms and suites, including allocation for complimentary breakfast, but not including any room or sales tax.
Gift shop sales	Retail sales such as cookbooks, mugs, toiletries, calling cards, souvenirs, and so on.
Food revenue	All food sales (a la carte and banquet), except breakfast when it is included in the room rate. This includes food included in packages and other food sales, such as picnic baskets.
Beverage revenue	All sales of beverages served on site, including a la carte and banquet beverage sales.
Meeting room rentals	Rent received for meeting rooms, banquet space, space for tented or outdoor functions, or other function space rentals.
Spa services	Sales of spa services performed on site, whether in a designated spa facility or en suite.

(continued)

Table 6-1 *(continued)*

Revenue Accounts	Descriptions
Other income	Any other revenue including commissions, interest, other sales, and so on.
Total Revenue	Inn revenue from all sources.

Expense Accounts	Descriptions
Inn Payroll and Related	
Salaries and wages	All pay to hourly and salaried employees.
Lodging benefits	Costs of benefits such as meals, insurance, vacation and sick days, car, retirement plan, and so on that are not included as wages or salary.
Lodging payroll taxes and related	FICA, FUTA, Medicare, Workers Compensation, and so on.
Other Operating Expenses	
Auto expenses	Automobile gas, repair, maintenance, lease, and related costs.
Bank fees	Bank service fees, check charges, credit card merchant fees.
Commissions	Travel agent and other referral feels; these are included as a rooms department expense in country inns and as an overhead expense for bed & breakfast inns.
Donations	Cash contributions, excluding in-kind and gift certificate donations.
Dues and subscriptions	Association dues, magazines, and other subscriptions to services.
Equipment rental	Rental of operating equipment, not land or building leases.
Cost of guest food and beverage	Cost of food and beverage included in room rate such as breakfast, tea, innkeeper's reception, and other food-related supplies for which guests are not charged.
Other food and beverage	Cost of food, beverage, and related supplies for events, banquets, and other revenue-generating purposes.

Expense Accounts	Descriptions
Gift shop	Cost of retail goods sold.
Insurance — property	Property, fire, theft, liability, and other insurance not related to payroll.
Interest — operating	Non-mortgage interest on business-related loans, credit cards, and so on.
Legal and accounting fees	Fees for legal and accounting services including bookkeeping and tax preparation.
Linens and terry	Terry and bedding including towels, linens, blankets, pillows, bathrobes, and so on (excluding restaurant linen, which is categorized as a restaurant other expense).
Marketing, ads, and promotion	Advertising, public relations (cash, not trade-outs), brochures, Web site, and other marketing expenses.
Maintenance, repairs, and fixtures	Materials for maintenance and repair, minor purchases for appliances, equipment, and furnishing replacements.
Office supplies	Paper, tape, pens, letterhead, computer supplies, and so on.
Outside services	Work contracted out, such as gardening, service calls (plumber, electrician), laundry sent out, and so on.
Room and housekeeping supplies	Soap, toilet paper, light bulbs, cleaning supplies, guest amenities (such as complimentary toiletries), and other guest and housekeeping items.
Telephone	Telephone, Internet access, and related expenses.
Training	Fees and expenses for professional workshops and conferences.
Travel and entertainment	Business trips and business entertainment
Utilities	Trash collection, gas, electric, water and sewer, cable TV, and so on.
Miscellaneous	Any other expenses.
Total Expenses	All inn expenses.
Net Operating Income/ Loss	Income before mortgage, depreciation, income taxes, and owner's draw

Courtesy of Professional Association of Innkeepers International (PAII)

Setting up your chart of accounts is an evolving process because you'll be continuously adding additional items that bring in revenue (for instance you may start selling mugs at your inn) and expenses (such as adding a new type of advertising). After setting up the basic accounts, you can fine-tune them by adding accounts, subtracting accounts, or establishing sub-accounts. For example, rather than booking all utilities under one utility expense account, you can break it into several sub-accounts, such as trash collection, gas, electric, water, sewer, and cable TV.

Breaking things down into customized sub-accounts may seem like a lot of work, but it's surprisingly simple, especially if you do it as you're paying bills. When your water bill comes in, create a water sub-account under utilities. When you pay the gas bill, create a separate gas sub-account under utilities. You only need to do this once, because you'll already have the sub-accounts set up when subsequent bills come in. When you want to see which utilities went up over the previous year, you have the information broken down by account, and you can tell if your utility expenses were higher this year because you were spending more on gas or electric than the year before. The more detailed information you put into your bookkeeping, the more detailed information you can take out of it.

If you only use a paper filing system for your accounts, which I definitely *don't* recommend, you have to sort through receipts manually and add them up in order to figure out how much you've spent during a given time period. On the other hand, if you use accounting software, you simply select the account that you want to calculate, enter the date range that you're analyzing, and let the software run a report for you. For example, if you want to figure out how much you spent on food and beverages for a specific period, you select the account where you post your food and beverage expenses and simply run a report for the dates that you choose.

Prepare year-to-date or month-to-date comparison reports from the same period last year to see whether you're on target to match or exceed the prior period's performance. For example, you can see if your reservations are behind or ahead for this year against prior years by running an advance deposits report and seeing if you have more or less money on hand than at the same time last year. If you see the numbers are sliding, it's time to take a closer look at why and maybe increase your marketing efforts to compensate or reduce expenses. (See Chapter 15 for tips on taking your marketing to the next level.)

Choosing a Property Management System

In addition to having your financial records in order, it's essential to keep good records of your reservations and the day-to-day operations at your inn. You use these records to prepare for your guests' arrivals and to analyze your business's performance from a different perspective. Your guests are counting on you to keep good records and be expecting them when they arrive; they don't want to hear that you made a mistake and booked them in the same room that's reserved for another guest.

Like hotel owners, most B&B owners use property management systems (PMS) software to manage their records and their reservations. You can get software versions tailored to the bed & breakfast industry. They take care of the reservations and all the record-keeping surrounding the guests' stays in addition to (as the name suggests) property management, which may include housekeeping schedules and rate management. Property management systems are so robust and can take care of so much of the organization of your inn that, if you're like most innkeepers, you'll find it's one of the best investments that you make.

Many innkeepers get confused between a property management system and an online availability program that manages rates, availability, and online reservations. Many PMSs serve both functions; however, a lot of innkeepers use two different systems that interface with each other. (See Chapter 11 for information on taking reservations online.)

Another option I discuss in this section is to keep records by hand without a computer. Although some innkeepers successfully keep their records by hand, I encourage you to thoroughly explore and pick from the myriad of software programs available. Maintaining good records not only helps you run the business, but if the day comes that you're ready to sell your bed & breakfast, these systems also provide the reports that interested buyers and lenders want and need to see.

Deciding between desktop and Web-based systems

Your first consideration in selecting PMS software is whether you prefer a desktop or Web-based system. Table 6-2 outlines the advantages and disadvantages of each system.

Table 6-2	Desktop versus Web-Based Systems		
System	*How It Works*	*Pros*	*Cons*
Desktop	All data is stored on your computer and you have complete control.	No one else has access to guest information.	The computer that's running your PMS software (usually the main computer at your inn) has to be running in order to access your data while traveling. Major problems occur if your computer crashes — you won't be able to access your data until the system is restored.
Web-based	All data is hosted on the software vendor's servers. If you choose this type of system, be sure you can always have access to download your information from the PMS's servers. That way, if you later want to switch PMS vendors, all your information is in your possession.	Your data is always backed up, and you can access your data from any computer. Server crashes are unlikely, but if they do occur, most vendors can have you up and running on a new server quickly.	You rely on your vendor to maintain its servers. If the servers are down, you can't access your data — but this would be a rare occurrence.

When you do your own homework on the desktop versus Web-based PMS debate, you'll probably develop your own opinion on which you prefer. However, features, functionality, marketing decisions, and ease of use will probably be the determining factors in selecting your program.

Narrowing your choices based on general factors

With the number of systems out there, choosing one can be a confusing process. Start by asking other B&B owners what system(s) they use and why they like them. Most innkeepers are happy to offer their opinions, so you may also ask what they would change about their systems. Head to online innkeeper forums (see Chapter 1) to connect with your peers, or contact your state and local B&B associations.

When faced with many options of PMS systems, you can narrow the list based on whether or not programs meet the following criteria:

- ✔ **Compatibility between your PMS and your online reservations and availability systems:** If you use a separate system to manage your online reservations, your property management system should be able to interface with this system. What this means is that when an update is made to one (such as an online reservation is made), the other should be seamlessly synchronized to avoid double work and double bookings.

- ✔ **Compatibility to your accounting software:** Nearly all property management systems that serve the B&B industry are compatible with QuickBooks Pro, and many also export data to Excel and Peachtree.

- ✔ **Compatibility with consolidated availability displays:** Many state and local B&B associations as well as online directories display availability and/or allow guests to make reservations. Although you don't have to use the same PMS as everyone else in your association, pick one that interfaces with the online availability system so that you're included when area availability is displayed or online reservations are offered.

- ✔ **Compatibility with mobile devices:** Many systems allow access from a cellphone or other mobile devices. This feature allows you to check availability and even manage your reservations from your cellphone when you're away from the inn. Even if you don't think you'll use it, check for the compatibility of the option — you just may change your mind.

- ✔ **Multi-user options:** Think ahead to when your inn business grows and you may need to have multiple users on the software. Find out what the costs are for additional users and licenses.

PMS and availability systems hold a lot of sensitive information. Ensure that others can work on your system, but keep sensitive information to yourself by creating access codes for different levels of usage. And don't forget to back up your data.

- ✔ **Cost:** As with everything, costs vary widely. Some PMS vendors charge one-time fees for their software with the option to purchase updates and upgrades down the road. Some charge monthly fees, some determine their fees based on transactions, and still others charge annual fees. As with any purchase, weigh the costs with the benefits to find a program that can grow with your business but that also fits within your budget.

- ✔ **Training, customer support, trial period, and charges for updates:** No matter how good the system is, if you can't use it or if it frustrates you and doesn't save you time, it's not for you. Find out how much training is provided for the initial set-up, the hours and cost for customer support, and the length of a trial period (if there is one) before you invest in the program. Because software is continuously upgraded, you also should know what to budget for upgrades. Ask about when the software was last updated and what enhancements are in development.

When choosing any software program, you need to think about who, in addition to yourself, will need to be trained to use the program. If you're the only person who knows how to use it, what happens if you have a personal emergency or are ill and can't use the program? How easy will it be for a partner, friend, relative, staff, or interim innkeeper to step in and learn the functionality of the program? You need to plan for the smooth operation of your inn, and part of that planning process is to determine how the inn — and the PMS software — will function in your absence. (See Chapter 14 for information on keeping the inn open when you're not there.)

Comparing property management system features

The features and functionality of innkeeping software are constantly being updated and improved. Property management systems are no exception. The following is a list of some of the robust features that the most popular PMS software tracks or maintains for you. Keep in mind that not all features are offered by all PMS providers.

- Arrival and departure lists
- Availability calendar
- Billing/invoicing
- Confirmation e-mails
- Confirmation letters
- Credit card entry
- Custom reporting
- Customizable reports
- Customized correspondence
- Data export
- Deposits
- Financial reports
- Gift certificate tracking

- Group bookings
- Guest history
- Guest invoices
- Housekeeping scheduling
- Inquiries
- Inventory control
- Marketing data
- Marketing e-mails
- Minimum stays
- Online backup
- Online reservations
- Packages
- Registration forms
- Reminders
- Reservation history

- ✔ Reservation requests
- ✔ Scheduling
- ✔ Seasonal pricing
- ✔ Taxes

- ✔ Thank-you e-mails
- ✔ Thank-you letters
- ✔ Yield management calculator

Because PMS software programs can have so many built-in features, in doing your research you may find a program that meets all your needs. Or you may discover that because many of the systems integrate with each other, you prefer to use one program for displaying your availability to guests and a different program as your property management system.

Finding software vendors who understand B&Bs

There are many hundreds of property management system vendors out there, most of whom cater to hotels and larger lodging properties. Therefore, their PMS software often is a bad fit for a small B&B or inn due to cost (it may cost many thousands of dollars, way outside the budget of most innkeepers!); room management (look for a system designed to manage approximately 50 rooms); and variations in room descriptions, room booking procedures, and deposit and cancellation policies. Whenever possible, you should choose a PMS software vendor who's familiar with the needs of bed & breakfasts and who devotes some or all of its efforts to serving the bed & breakfast industry in particular.

Good ways to find vendors who support the needs of the bed & breakfast industry are

- ✔ **Through the Vendor Marketplace maintained by the PAII (www. paii.org).**

- ✔ **By checking your state bed & breakfast association's Web site.** Many state B&B associations have preferred vendors who offer special deals to their members.

- ✔ **By attending an innkeeper trade show in your area.** (See Chapter 1 for information on innkeeper conferences where you can network, discover, learn, and teach about the business.) Numerous vendors attend these conferences, giving you the chance to take a test run of several programs in one spot. These events are excellent opportunities for you to test and compare several programs at once, talk to innkeepers who use the PMS software, and listen to the answers to questions other innkeepers ask that you may not have thought of.

TIP

Talk to the customer service department of each vendor you're considering buying PMS software from. This communication gives you a good idea of how supportive the company is and whether it's a good match for you based on your level of computer knowledge.

The following vendors currently work with hundreds of bed & breakfasts (some keep track of your availability and can be used alone or in conjunction with a PMS while others are complete property management systems, keeping track of everything including your availability):

- Availability Online (www.availabilityonline.com)
- Booking Center (www.bookingcenter.com)
- Convoyant Reservation Nexus (www.resnexus.com)
- RezOvation (www.rezovation.com)
- RezStream (www.rezstream.com)
- Super Inn (www.superinn.com)
- Webervations (www.webervations.com)

Keeping records without a computer

Although in a very small minority, you're not alone if you decide to bypass all software programs, or if you don't have a computer at your inn. Despite the variety of software programs available and the customization they offer, some existing innkeepers resist making the switch to computer software to help manage their financial and reservation information.

How you decide to keep track of your money and guests is your own personal preference, and even in the age of computers and rising technology, some innkeepers successfully and quite happily keep track of things using ledgers and a large calendar. Some established inns keep all their reservation information on large monthly calendars and guest phone sheets arranged monthly in three-ring binders. The binders hold all the guests' pertinent information, such as their names, contact numbers, number of nights they're visiting, why they're coming to the area, any food allergies, and so on. These inns consistently receive rave guest reviews for the personal attention that they offer to their guests.

Most innkeepers starting out, however, do choose a computer system, and each year a growing number of innkeepers who previously used the ledger system switch to some form of computer software to manage their financial records and reservations. If you decide to stick to the paper method, consult with your accountant to set up a system that includes all the information you need to pull together your figures at tax time. (See Chapter 3 for information on hiring an accountant who specializes in B&Bs.)

If you don't use technology effectively, you're at an increasing disadvantage to your competition — both other inns and hotels.

Chapter 7

Setting Rates and Establishing Policies

. . . .

In This Chapter

▶ Setting your rates to maximize your income

▶ Determining the types of payment to accept

▶ Setting fair and consistent policies

. . . .

*Y*our bed & breakfast is a special place, where you, as the innkeeper, strive to make sure that your guests feel at home. Although I hope you enjoy innkeeping so much that it doesn't seem like a job, it is a business, and you need to treat it like one. In this chapter, I give you tried-and-true advice for charging the appropriate rate and setting firm, fair, and consistent policies to help you maintain a full house of happy guests.

Setting Your Rates

Establishing and sticking to your room rates is an important aspect of running a B&B. *Rates* are simply what you charge to rent out a room. Pricing your rooms is a nuance that comes with experience. The rates that you set for your rooms are determined by what you can reasonably charge. That amount needs to enable you to cover your costs while keeping your rooms relatively full and leaving something left over for you.

Your rates are the income of your business and your rooms are the inventory, so setting rates has an immediate impact on your revenue and, thus, your paycheck. (See Chapter 3 for information on forecasting income.)

Setting appropriate rates is important to your profitability and your long-term success — set them too high, and you won't have the occupancy level that you need to succeed. Set them too low, and you may be leaving money on the table. Unfortunately, there is no exact formula that I can give you to plug in a few numbers and — voilà — tell you what to charge. Rather, setting your rates is a little like cooking — a pinch of this and a smidgen of that. The calculation of your rates depends on many factors, including what your competition is charging, your location, your amenities, the condition and size of your rooms, supply and demand, and, finally, your best guess.

Factoring in the basics

When setting your rates, you need to first establish your *base rate*. Think of your base rate as your break-even rate — the minimum rate that you need to charge in order to cover your costs. This isn't the rate that you publish, but it's one that's appropriate for the general experience you provide guests and one that should allow you to meet your target revenue projections.

To find your base rate, you need to figure out how much of your start-up costs (if any) to allocate to each year. Your CPA, accountant, or consultant can help with this. Then add your annual operating costs (food, amenities, advertising, insurance, licenses, taxes, staffing costs [including your income if you're paying yourself a salary], supplies, and so forth) and your yearly financing costs. Divide this figure by the number of room nights that you expect to book based on your estimated occupancy rate. This gives you the base — or average — rate you need to charge to cover your costs.

Once you've established your base rate, you can determine what adjustments to make based on the specific amenities each room offers and, to some extent, what the competition is charging. For example, you may decide to have three different rates for your rooms based on their individual amenities, with all of them hovering near the price of $225.

Rates generally vary based on a number of factors:

- ✔ **Day of the week:** Often, weekday rates are lower because fewer people stay at B&Bs during the week. Thus, having a lower weekday rate encourages business from Sunday through Thursday nights. Weekend and holiday rates are often higher because the demand for rooms is greater. Therefore, the market bears a higher price.

- ✔ **Time of the year:** Most areas have, at most, three seasons: a high season, a low season, and a *shoulder season*, which is the time between the low and high seasons. Many inns have only high and low seasons, and some innkeepers keep it simple with one rate all year for each room (which may be lower for weeknight bookings). During high season, when more guests are traveling, rates are usually set at their highest. This is followed by shoulder season, and then low season, when you offer your lowest rates to attract guests. There are no specific rules for setting the dates that define your seasons. My best advice is to keep them simple your first year, and keep your seasons in line with those of other lodging properties in the area. You can always tweak them the following year if you think they should be changed.

- ✓ **Room size and location:** The bigger the room and the better its location in the inn, the higher the rate guests expect to pay.

- ✓ **Type of breakfast you provide:** A full breakfast warrants higher rates than a simple continental breakfast. Some guests may not want the complimentary breakfast at all, so you may want to offer a lower rate for rooms that don't include breakfast, although in some areas separating the food from the lodging may cause your inn to lose the B&B classification.

- ✓ **Room amenities provided:** Rooms with upscale amenities, such as whirlpool tubs, fireplaces, and king-sized beds, are usually priced higher than rooms without these amenities.

- ✓ **Special circumstances:** Many inns offer a discount for extended stays, and larger inns may offer a discount for group bookings. During periods of special events, such as festivals, parents' visiting weekend at local colleges, and so forth, rates are often priced higher. This is a personal choice, however — many inns have numerous repeat guests during these events and choose not to raise their rates.

 If you're taking over an existing inn, you have the benefit of knowing what the previous owners charged and what their occupancy rate was, but you should still reevaluate those rates. If your goal is to increase occupancy, don't automatically assume you need to lower your rates.

 Start by setting your published rack rates high because with today's software, rates can be changed easily and quickly. Plus, it's always easier to lower rates or offer a discount than it is to raise rates.

Sizing up the competition

If you simply set your room rates based on what you would like to charge or what you think your rooms are worth, without doing any research, you won't be in business long. Guests have choices, and, to a large extent, your rates are dictated by what other lodging establishments in the area are charging.

 As a general rule, when you first set your rates, they should fall somewhere in the mid-range of what the established properties are charging. Be comparable, and don't be afraid to set the rate that reflects what you think your inn is worth relative to others. Remember, perception is everything.

Make your rates comparable

New innkeepers are often shy about charging a rate higher than they could afford to pay themselves. Just because you wouldn't eat at the most expensive restaurant in town doesn't mean that other people aren't willing to if they have disposable cash. These same guests will arrive at your bed & breakfast in expensive cars, wearing fancy clothes for their romantic weekend getaway. Guests look at quality lodging the same way they do other quality items in their lives. Guests want value and quality. When they receive it, they expect to pay for it, so your room rates should reflect the quality that you offer.

If you know without a doubt that your inn is one of the very best in your area, your service is excellent, and your food is heads above other local inns, don't hesitate to price your rooms at the high end of the market, even if you are the new kid on the block. If your prices are too low, potential guests will perceive your inn as being inferior to your competition.

To get a handle on what nearby bed & breakfasts are doing, you need to do some investigative work — yes, spy on them. It's public information, so there's nothing illicit here; it's just good business sense. Knowing what other B&Bs and hotels in your area offer and charge plays an important role in your decisions about what to offer your guests and how much to charge.

Avoid the temptation to discuss specific pricing structures with the competition. Discussing pricing with competitors could be considered "price fixing," which is a violation of the federal Sherman Anti-Trust Law.

To conduct your analysis:

1. **Select at least 5 lodging establishments in your area.**

   Your goal is to analyze what they offer guests, how much they charge, and how successful they appear to be. It's best to focus on B&Bs, but if you're in the fortunate position of being one of the first inns in your area, simply use some of the other lodging choices your guests have to conduct your analysis.

   Your competition may be not only surrounding inns but also those in another, comparable destination. Look at the rates these inns are charging, too.

   Don't worry if none of the properties is an exact match to yours — they shouldn't be. Remember, it's the uniqueness and personalization of bed & breakfasts that make them special.

2. **Visit each property's Web site.**

You should be able to get a good feel for a property from its Web site, which is something to keep in mind when you create your own site (see Chapter 8). Be sure to check the availability charts of other properties to see their occupancy.

3. **Make a chart of the inn's key features.**

   Using Table 7-1, note the number and size of rooms (whether they're small rooms, suites, large rooms with separate seating areas, and so on); rate each inn's location in relation to its convenience to town and major attractions on a scale of 1-5; record what type of breakfast they offer, if any; and note the most-requested amenities that they offer, such as private baths, whirlpool tubs, fireplaces, and free wireless Internet.

   Your chart should be tailored to your area, including things that your potential guests are likely to want. For example, if you're in an urban area, parking may not be important but proximity to public transportation may be.

4. **Evaluate the inn's parking situation.**

   At several different times during the day and evening, drive by each property and survey not only how busy they appear to be by the cars parked outside, but also note whether ample parking is available for guests. (For most urban inns, parking isn't a consideration.) Add that information to Table 7-1 as well.

5. **Complete the information in Table 7-1 for your own B&B as well.**

   Creating a sample chart like Table 7-1 can help you visualize where your bed & breakfast fits in as compared to other inns and lodging choices guests have in your area.

TIP

Evaluating the competition

You can glean information about your competitors in two ways: by freely sharing information with other innkeepers in your area, and by getting a leg up on information by doing your own investigative work.

✔ **Communicating openly:** In many communities, innkeepers join together to form local lodging associations (see Chapter 1). Seek out and join such a group, or, if none exists, start one of your own. The goal of these groups is usually to bring guests to the area, which benefits everyone. Innkeepers may also share their concerns and solutions with each other at these meetings. If a particular innkeeper offers to help you with something, express your appreciation with a thank-you note, cookies, or flowers.

✔ **Doing your homework:** Stay informed by signing up for all your competitors' newsletters (use a personal e-mail address that they won't recognize). This can allow you to find out about specials they offer, monitor how much discounting they do, get an idea of the packages they create, and basically get the gist of their marketing plans.

Table 7-1 **Analyzing the Competition's Amenities**

Feature	Property #1	Property #2	Property #3	Property #4	Property #5	Your B&B	Comments
Number of rooms							
Price range							
Location							
Full breakfast							
Continental breakfast							
No breakfast							
Whirlpool tubs							
Fireplaces							
Private baths							
Parking							
Wireless Internet							

Keep an eye on the competition, but don't become obsessed with them. Analyze, monitor, and get ideas from them, but don't follow them to the letter. Be unique and bring your new ideas to the area as a leader. Your success is defined by you, so don't be afraid to try what makes sense to you. You can always adjust your rates. Charging higher rates and having fewer guests could mean you make the same money without working as hard, plus, fewer guests reduce the wear and tear on the inn . . . and you.

Putting a value on what you offer

The only way to make money is by charging a fair price and maintaining a balance between what you charge, what you offer, and the cost to you of what you provide. (See Chapter 3 for help in forecasting your costs and expenses.) Charging a lower rate than your competition and offering high-end amenities may lead to a full house, but at what cost? You won't be in business very long if you serve an expensive gourmet breakfast but charge a very low rate for your rooms. High-end amenities cost money, so balancing the quality of the guest experience with the price of your rooms is part of setting your rates.

As you move through the process of setting your rates, you'll be adjusting your base rate to arrive at your *rack rate* per room or room type. Your rack rate is the official room price — one that keeps your rooms generally full and generates a profit. This is the rate you publish on your Web site, and the one on which all discounts are based.

Most likely each of your rooms, or room types, is unique. Depending on how you do your analysis, the price of each room or room type probably varies according to the season and day of the week. For example, your king room with a whirlpool and fireplace may be $325 in high season, $300 during your shoulder season, and $250 during your low season, whereas your smallest room might be $250 during high season, $225 during shoulder season, and $199 during your low season. Each of these rooms may also have a lower mid-week rate during each season.

Don't over-complicate your pricing and make it hard on you or your staff to clearly communicate your rates to guests. No matter how many different price levels you decide to have, make sure both you and your staff are clear on what the rates are.

In addition to season and day of the week, here are the most important factors that affect the rates you set for your rooms:

- ✔ **Size of the room:** The bigger the room, the more guests expect to pay for it. Size can be determined not just by square footage but also by the number of guests the room can sleep and whether it has a separate seating or dining area where guests can have breakfast delivered to their room and eat comfortably. So if you offer two rooms with king beds but one has a separate eating area where guests can enjoy breakfast, this room can be priced higher than the other king room.

✔ **Room location and view:** Guests are willing to pay more for rooms that are in the best location in your bed & breakfast. For example, guests are likely to pay a few dollars more for a king room where they only have to walk up one flight of steps as opposed to the same room on the third floor, which requires them to walk up two flights of steps. The same is true for rooms with a view. Guests are willing to pay more for rooms with a view or balcony, so you want to price these rooms higher than the same rooms without these features.

✔ **Amenities:** Analyze the amenities that your inn offers and compare them to what other accommodations in the area are offering. Today, the most requested amenity is a private bath, followed by fireplaces and two-person whirlpool tubs. The more amenities a room offers, the higher the price you should assign to it. Thus, a room with a fireplace should be priced higher than the same room with no fireplace.

While you don't want to price yourself out of the market, remember many amenities that B&B goers take for granted are things they would pay extra for at a hotel, for example, Internet access, local calls, movies (if you offer a DVD library) and room service (if you offer the option of having breakfast delivered to guests' rooms). Depending on your location, you may also offer the use of such things as beach chairs, umbrellas, bicycles, kayaks, and so forth (see Chapter 12 for information on consulting with your insurance agent if you plan to loan guests sporting equipment).

✔ **Breakfast:** As you calculate your rates, factor in the type of breakfast you serve. If you're serving a full, sit-down breakfast with homemade, hot entrées, your rates should be higher than if you're offering a light continental breakfast of pastries, juices, and coffee or tea.

✔ **Locale:** Many guests choose an inn specifically because of its location, so prime locations command a premium in pricing. If your guests can walk to the beach or into town, this adds value to their stay — and to your rooms — as compared to those of another inn further from the beach or town.

✔ **Guest services:** The higher your rates, the more guests will, and should, expect. The trick for you is to match guest expectations with your pricing. Do you offer concierge-type services, such as making reservations or providing wake-up calls or turndown service? If so, factor this into your rates. On the flip side, if you set your rates high, be prepared to offer the types of services guests expect from higher rates.

When setting your rates, start by setting the rate of your smallest room first. Determine a rack rate for this room based on your own expenses and what other inns in the area are charging for a room of this size with comparable amenities. Work your way up by room size. Look at each room in relation to your smallest room. As the size increases, so should the price. Increase the price a bit more if the room has additional amenities, such as a fireplace.

For example, if your smallest room has a queen bed and you determine the price to be $150 a night, you might set the rate for your next largest room, which also has a queen bed, a separate seating area, and a balcony, at $175 per night. Following this same logic, the next largest room, which has a king bed, separate seating area, fireplace, and two-person Jacuzzi, might go for $200 per night. If you offer the same king room with a balcony, the rate you set might be $215 per night.

Adjusting your rates

To tweak your income, maximize your revenue, and fill vacancies, factor in demand. Your business, like any other small business, is affected by supply and demand. Not just demand for your location and the amenities that you offer, but also demand based on when guests want to travel. Using the base rates that you set (see "Factoring in the basics," earlier in this chapter), you adjust your rates according to when you're most likely to be busy, charging more during peak times and setting lower rates during the week and off season, when fewer guests typically travel. This rate factoring technique is called *yield management* in the hospitality industry (see Chapter 15).

When posting your rates, always start with the lowest rate in off season and end with the highest rate in high season, for example, $129 to $195. By posting your rates in this manner, you're more likely to capture prospective guests who are rate-hunting.

Mid-week and extended stays

Whether to offer different rates during the week and for multiple-night stays depends on your market. In periods of high demand, this usually isn't necessary, but during slow periods, it can bring in additional guests. Weekday rates are priced lower because fewer people stay at B&Bs during the week.

Offering special pricing for corporate travelers is another great way to fill mid-week vacancies. To make the most of this strategy, contact the corporations in your area and let them know about your inn and the special rates you're offering for their visiting business colleagues. Find out the per diem rate typically allowed by corporations in your area and, if that rate is reasonable, offer an equal rate for their out-of-town employees.

Consider hosting an open house so companies can feel comfortable recommending your inn. See Chapter 5 for details.

Seasonal demand

Adjusting your rates according to the season is not only customary but also expected, so don't be afraid to do it. Think of it in terms of supply and demand. Remember, "high season" is called that for a reason. More potential guests are traveling and willing to pay a higher price for accommodations on valuable dates.

If you're just starting out, set higher rates for your peak season ahead of time. If you're rooms aren't being booked as the season approaches, you can experiment with lowering your rates. To do this, try lowering the price on one room and see whether bookings pick up for that room. If not, pricing probably isn't the issue, and you may want to reevaluate your marketing efforts. (See Chapters 8 and 15 for marketing techniques you may be missing out on.)

During peak season and on holiday weekends, consider adding a minimum- stay requirement. Then if your rooms aren't being booked as the season approaches, you can consider relaxing this policy before lowering your rates further.

When setting the dates for your seasons, avoid having the season end on a Friday. While August 15th may seem like a reasonable date for your high season to end as kids head back to school, if August 15th is a Friday, it means weekend guests will be staying one night in high season and one night in a slower season. In this instance, having your high season end on August 18th simplifies things, plus you earn the higher rate for the whole weekend.

Holidays and special events

Many inns raise their rates when they know they will be sold out no matter what. For example, you can raise your rates for college graduations, sporting events, Fourth of July weekend, festivals, and so on. These are your must-fill times, so at the very least, consider imposing minimum stays and stricter cancellation policies during these events. (For help setting policies, see the section "Setting reservation policies" later in this chapter.)

Knowing when to raise or lower rates

Your rooms are your inventory, so managing your rates is managing the inventory of your business. When your rates are too high, your rooms sit empty and don't earn income for you. When your rates are too low, you forgo the additional income that you could have earned by charging a higher rate that guests would have paid.

Be careful not to fall into the trap of being afraid to change your rates.

Just as there are no rigid standards for setting rates, knowing when to change them isn't an exact science either. A good way to determine when it's time to raise or lower your rates is to repeat the research you did when you first set your rates. As your business develops, you should perform this analysis at least once a year (see Chapter 15 for tips on how to compare your results with your expectations).

Your rates may be too high if your competition constantly seems busier than you are. However, lowering your rates isn't your only option. First, try increasing your marketing efforts (see Chapters 8 and 15 for valuable marketing techniques), adding more amenities, or relaxing your minimum-stay policies.

Conversely, your rates may be too low. The following are clues that this is the case:

- **Your rooms are booked far in advance.** If all your rooms are booked months in advance, experiment with raising your rates. Start by raising the rate of your most popular room by 5 to 10 percent. If the room continues to book far in advance, you're probably under-pricing your rooms and may want to bump them up a little.

- **You seem much busier than the competition.** If your parking lot is packed and the B&B across town seems to have plenty of extra space, or if you hear that you're busier than the other bed & breakfasts in the area, try raising the rates on your most popular rooms. If you find this has a negative effect on your occupancy, you can always lower them again.

- **Your occupancy rate is greater than 75 percent.** The most obvious clue that it's time to raise rates is a high occupancy rate. Don't be afraid to mess with success. Guests are telling you you're worth it, which means you're probably worth even more, and it's time to raise your rates.

No matter what rates you set, you can always change them, and you should as time goes on. When raising and lowering rates, you don't have to change the rates for all your rooms in all your seasons. Tweak only the ones that need it, and leave the rest alone.

Deciding What Types of Payment to Accept

Getting paid by guests who stay in your rooms is the main goal of your business, so you need to decide what forms of payment you'll accept. Your choices are cash, personal and corporate checks, traveler's checks, and credit cards. Some inns accept all of these payment types, while other inns choose not to accept certain forms of payment, such as personal checks or credit cards. Whatever you decide, you need to communicate the types of payment you accept clearly to guests before they arrive for their stay. Doing this avoids embarrassing situations for guests and uncomfortable situations for you when guests aren't able to settle their bill at the time of their stay because they don't have a form of payment that you accept.

Deciding which forms of payment to accept isn't difficult, but it's something you need to do before you can start accepting reservations. You can always change your mind later — it's not uncommon for an inn to add or drop a particular form of payment.

If you decide to change your policy regarding the forms of payment you accept, be sure to update your staff, all directories, all your advertising, your Web site, your brochure and rack cards, your reservation software, and anything else that lists the types of payment accepted.

Weighing the pros and cons of cash and checks

In an effort to avoid the fees associated with accepting credit cards, some innkeepers decide to limit the forms of payment they accept to personal checks, traveler's checks, and cash. Other innkeepers prefer not to accept cash or checks. To help you evaluate these types of payments, Table 7-2 lists some of the pros and cons of each.

Table 7-2	The Pros and Cons of Cash and Checks	
Form of Payment	*Pros*	*Cons*
Cash	Easy to accept	Must be able to make change
	No transaction costs	Risk of theft
		Guests may not travel with sufficient cash
Checks	Easy to accept	Risk of insufficient funds
	No transaction costs	Bank charges for returned checks
Traveler's Checks	Easy to accept	Must be sure guest signs in order to deposit
	No transaction costs	

Accepting credit cards

Most B&Bs today accept credit cards for guest convenience and to take deposits on future reservations. While you don't have to accept credit cards, you should be aware that most guests prefer to pay by credit card, and not giving them this option may result in lost business. Many innkeepers start out not accepting credit cards because they want to avoid paying the associated fees. You may be able to get away with this if your room rates are relatively inexpensive, if your market does not include business travelers, or if your typical guest books far enough in advance to have time to send in a check for a deposit. However, the higher the amount of the guests' bills, the more likely they are to want to charge it on their credit card, and corporate travelers almost always either prefer or are required to pay by credit card.

Becoming a merchant

In order to accept credit cards, you need to be set up as a *merchant*. Being a merchant means you are authorized to accept credit cards through a *credit card processor*, which is the entity that you submit your credit card transactions to in order to be paid. Here are some ways to find a credit card processor:

- ✔ **Go to your bank.** Most local banks can either be your credit card processor or help you set up a relationship with one.

- ✔ **Ask around.** Ask your local or state bed & breakfast association, local chamber of commerce, other innkeepers, or other small business owners for recommendations.

- ✔ **Check with your property management software provider.** The software you use may have the capability of processing credit cards. If not, the vendor may be able to help you set up an account with a processor that they use.

- ✔ **Look into wholesale warehouses.** Several of the wholesale warehouses that offer small business services, such as Costco, offer credit card processing services.

- ✔ **Contact the Professional Association of Innkeepers International (PAII).** The association maintains a list of credit card processors who specialize in providing services to bed & breakfasts. You can visit the association's Web site at www.paii.org, click Resources, then Vendor Marketplace, and then Credit Card Services.

Shop around and compare rates among processors. Ask each credit card processor you are considering for an itemized list of all fees, such as monthly maintenance fees and per-transaction fees. (Typically transaction fees are higher when you do not swipe the guest's credit card and on corporate cards.)

The credit card processor you ultimately choose will give you a merchant application to fill out. Don't be surprised if you're asked to provide a personal guarantee when filling out this application. In this case, your personal credit history is checked and you are guaranteeing that you will pay all outstanding fees when the account is closed. Some credit card processors may also require you to fill out a Lodging Addendum, which allows you to charge credit cards for advanced deposits. Questions on a typical merchant agreement include the average size of the transactions you will process, how many years you've been in business, the type of services you'll be providing, your cancellation policy, and so forth.

When you're approved as a merchant, you enter into a *merchant agreement* with the credit card processor. This document spells out all the terms of your agreement, such as fees (including any early termination fees) and when and how you will receive your money.

Processing guests' credit cards

A *terminal* is the mechanism used to process credit cards. If you have a physical terminal, which is the type used by most B&Bs, you process your guests' charges in one of two ways:

- **Swiped transactions:** You swipe the guest's card in the terminal to record the charge.

- **Keyed transactions:** You manually enter the guest's credit card numbers into the terminal.

If you have a physical terminal, swiped transactions are the way to go because these transactions usually result in lower processing charges. For this reason, some innkeepers take the guest's credit card number when making a reservation, but don't process the full amount until the time of the guest's stay, when they can swipe the card.

If you require your guests to make deposits in advance of their stays, you have no choice but to process these as keyed transactions or virtually through your reservation software. Innkeepers who require such prepayments consider the credit card merchant fees on these transactions as simply another cost of doing business.

Settling transactions and getting paid

When you run a guest's credit card through your system, you are usually receiving authorization for the transaction and the amount. You are not actually charging the guest's credit card. This is usually done at the end of each day, when all credit cards are settled at once. Settling your charges is a simple step in the credit card processing system — usually an automatic process or just the push of a button.

Settle all transactions each day to avoid additional surcharges. Most credit card processors charge a higher rate if you don't settle a transaction on the same day that you run it through your system.

Under most circumstances, you receive the money for a charge as a direct deposit into your bank account within 24 to 48 hours of settling the transaction. Visa, Mastercard, and Discover usually credit the full amount of the charge to you initially, and then automatically deduct the fees in one lump sum from your bank account (and send you an itemized statement) at the end of the month. Depending on your arrangement with American Express, their fees may be either deducted with each settlement batch or deducted as a lump sum at the end of the month.

Lowering your credit card fees

Accepting credit cards comes with a price, but it doesn't have to be an exorbitant one. Following are some tips to help you minimize the fees you pay for the privilege:

✔ **Consider buying rather than leasing your terminal.** This is generally a better deal, but do the math to be sure.

✔ **Ask questions about your statement.** Make time to call your credit card processor and ask them to explain any charges you don't understand.

✔ **Settle transactions daily.** Find out whether you can avoid surcharges by doing so.

✔ **Understand the difference between qualified and non-qualified rates.** Submitting a customer's address and the security code on his credit card usually qualifies you for the qualified rate, which is the lowest rate the credit card processor offers.

✔ **Know how to contest chargebacks.** A *chargeback* is when a guest disputes a charge on his credit card statement. Chargebacks are most common for no-show charges, cancellation fees, and damage charges. The credit card company investigates to determine whether the guest should receive his money back. Ask how chargebacks are handled and how to protect yourself from them. Knowing in advance the types of policies and documentation required can give you a stronger argument when contesting chargebacks.

Credit cards are a very effective way to take a deposit for future reservations. Guests often view having to mail a check in ahead of their stay as inconvenient and impractical.

Creating Clear Policies

Setting fair and consistent policies is good for you and all your guests. Such policies take away any uncertainty guests may have about what is acceptable, and policies help you ensure that no guests infringe on the rights of others during their stays.

Guests may want to live by the old adage that rules are meant to be broken, but it's your job to set and enforce policies that ensure your inn runs smoothly. Parents who are escaping for a romantic weekend may have specifically chosen your inn because of your policy that the inn is for adults only. If they have chosen to leave their kids at home to enjoy a child-free weekend, they won't appreciate your bending the rules to allow another couple to bring their baby. You may be tempted to try to make everyone happy, but consistently abiding by your policies is better.

Consider the following when setting your policies:

- ✔ Make a note of which policies you like and which ones you dislike when you stay at other inns.

- ✔ Look at the policies of other inns in your area on their Web sites or rack cards and brochures. Don't copy them, but use them as a guideline. Your inn is unique, so your policies should be too. However, it's okay to learn from others who may have thought of something that you didn't.

- ✔ Only institute policies that you are comfortable with.

- ✔ Make sure the wording of your policies doesn't discriminate against any individual or group and is clear, simple, concise, and consistent. Have your lawyer review your policies for these factors, as well as to be sure they don't discriminate against any individual or group.

- ✔ Consult your credit card processing company to determine ahead of time the steps you need to take in order to charge guests fees for late check-outs, no shows, cancellations, damages, and so forth.

- ✔ Include your policies in all written or published material about your inn. Post your policies on your Web site, on all your online directory advertisements, and on your rack cards or brochures. Relay important policies to guests when taking their reservations and include them in the confirmation letters you send. Giving guests a variety of places to refer to your policies helps to protect you from unhappy guests who would rather disregard your policies.

- ✔ Develop a room brochure outlining your inn's policies. You can do this by creating a guest directory which not only includes your inn's policies but also other information that guests will find useful during their stay, such as information about area activities, restaurants, and so on.

- ✔ State the consequences of willfully ignoring or breaking a policy in writing, where appropriate. For example, you might state, "We have a No Smoking policy. Guests who smoke in their rooms will be asked to check out immediately, and a $250 charge will be assessed to the credit card on file. This amount is to cover the cleaning charges incurred in rendering the room smoke-free for subsequent guests."

 Reading off your entire list of policies during the phone reservation process sounds militant. You should, however, mention any important or particularly relevant policies during the conversation. For example, you might say, "We're a non-smoking inn, and a full hot breakfast is served at 9 a.m." or "Your puppy sounds adorable, but I want to be sure you know that we're not able to accommodate pets."

Setting reservation policies

Reservation policies protect both your guests and your income. When you take reservations from guests, you are committing to having rooms for them and they are committing to come and pay for those rooms. The following sections give you some ideas about how to set and uphold deposit, cancellation, and minimum-stay policies.

Deposit policies

No standard deposit amount exists in the bed & breakfast industry. The deposit can vary from a dollar amount to a percentage of the reservation. Usually, the longer the reservation is for or the greater the number of rooms reserved, the greater the deposit. The deposit serves to solidify the commitment between you and the guest. When guests aren't willing to give you a deposit, it usually means they're not serious about their plans, and you're better off with a reservation from a guest you can rely on.

The following is an example of a well-written deposit policy:

> *To guarantee your reservation, a deposit of 50 percent is required for a stay of two or more nights, except for the months of July and August, when a 100 percent deposit is required. A 100 percent deposit is also required for one-night stays. The balance due at checkout may be paid by cash or credit card.*

Cancellation policies

These policies can vary depending on how far in advance the reservation is cancelled, how many nights the reservation was for, and the number of rooms it was for as well as the seasonal time of year. Your policy should allow you a reasonable period of time in which to re-rent the room.

Here is an example of a clearly written cancellation policy:

> *Should you wish to cancel or change your reservation for any reason, we require at least 14 days' advance notice (21 days during Tanglewood and Foliage Seasons and New Year's Eve for New Year's weekend when New Year's Eve falls on a Friday or Saturday night, and 28 days for groups of 3 or more rooms) by telephone. With at least 14 (21) days' notice, we will refund your deposit, less a service charge of 10 percent of your total reservation. Cancellations made within the 14-day (21-day) period will be charged for the full amount of the reserved stay unless we are able to rebook the room. If we are able to rebook the room, we will refund the rebooked portion, less the 10 percent service charge. We are a small inn, and cancellations affect us dramatically. If you have any concerns about possibly having to cancel, we recommend inexpensive trip cancellation insurance. This inn is in the Berkshires, the summer home of the Boston Symphony Orchestra, where Tanglewood and fall foliage are very popular attractions. We project and count on high occupancy during these periods.*

Minimum-stay requirements

Many innkeepers have a minimum stay requirement (remember, more cleaning is required when a guest checks out than on days the guest remains in the room). At the very least, you should be able to fill your rooms with two-night stays on weekends during periods of high demand. If you grant a Saturday-night-only reservation, you may find it difficult to fill the Friday-night-only vacancy, and in the meantime, you're likely to be turning away guests who would have booked the entire weekend. If you find you're not filling the rooms, you can always relax this policy.

A policy such as the following makes the minimum-stay requirements during periods of high demand clear to guests:

> *There is a three-night minimum stay on Tanglewood Season weekends as well as on most holiday weekends. There is a two-night minimum stay for midweek stays during Tanglewood and Foliage Seasons. Weekends during Tanglewood Season are Thursday, Friday, Saturday, and Sunday. There is a two-night minimum stay on weekends, excluding holiday weekends, from Labor Day through late June.*

Check-in and check-out policies

As excited as you are to welcome guests, waiting until 11 p.m. for them to check in when you have to get up at 6 a.m. to start breakfast isn't fair to you. It's also not fair to you or the next guests checking in for guests to stay past the check-out time, as this makes it difficult (if not impossible) for you to have the room ready for your arriving guests. Having clear check-in and check-out policies and sticking to them helps.

- ✔ **Setting a check-in policy:** Set a window of time for guest check-ins, and, when possible, have someone available to greet guests during this period. (See Chapter 12 for handling late arrivals). When you take reservations, ask your guests what time they plan to arrive. Ask them to kindly give you advance notice if their plans change and they find they won't be arriving at either the agreed-upon time or during your check-in period.

- ✔ **Setting your check-out policy:** Set a check-out time that allows you enough time to clean and ready the room for the next guest. Stick to this time. You may offer to hold guests' bags or, if the room is not being rented to a new guest, consider charging a half-day rate. While this may sound greedy, if a last-minute guest were to call needing a room, you'd have to turn her away, missing out on the full night's rate, so charging a half-day rate is a small consolation. When guests think there's a charge for late check-outs, they're more likely to take your policy seriously and stick to your check-out time.

One way to help ensure that guests remember the check-out time is to remind them of it upon their arrival. While this may seem inhospitable, many seasoned innkeepers make it a common practice to do so as they verify the rest of the reservation with the guest.

Establishing general policies

When you put together your general policies, consider the protection of your inn, the safety and comfort of your guests, and your sanity. You need to be sure your policies are fair and consistent, and don't discriminate against any individual or group.

Guidelines concerning children

We were all kids ourselves, but not all inns are appropriate for children. If your B&B is full of antiques, has a steep drop off a cliff in the backyard, or is known for romantic escapes, children are probably inappropriate, and this should be clearly stated in your policies. Policies regarding children range from excluding children of all ages to allowing only those over a certain age. Before crafting such policies, you should consult with your attorney, as specifically prohibiting children could be considered discrimination. A well-thought-out policy regarding children not only protects the inn but also helps both parents with children (how can anyone relax with priceless breakables within reach of little hands?), and guests looking for a romantic getaway.

Pet policies

Welcoming pets is not the norm at most B&Bs, so if you decide you can accommodate pets in some or all of your rooms, be sure to set clear policies for the guests who bring them and for the benefit of visitors who may not be fond of pets. Let everyone know what the policy is, including where pets are and are not allowed in the inn. Additionally, make guests aware of any extra cleaning fee, which is usually charged for accommodating pets.

If you have pets of your own and they interact with guests, this should be posted on your Web site. Many guests are allergic to or afraid of animals. Take the cue from the guest, and don't assume everyone loves friendly Fido as much as you do.

Alcohol considerations

Two issues arise with alcohol: serving it to guests and dealing with intoxicated guests. States have varying regulations regarding serving alcohol to guests. Small B&Bs are actually businesses in private homes, and some states allow serving complimentary alcohol to guests — but don't assume this is the case in your state. Check with your state B&B association or the ABC (Alcohol Beverage Control) board of your state. The logic of some states is that because you are charging for the room, some of those proceeds are used to purchase the liquor, so, in effect, you are charging for alcohol when you serve it, and therefore it is prohibited.

Making serious policies sound less harsh

Many of your guests will be first time B&B goers who aren't familiar with the necessity for different policies at a B&B versus a hotel. They look forward to the intimate atmosphere and personalization of the B&B lodging experience, but need to be educated on how you make this possible. You can begin the education process with a few words in your reservation policy. For example, an inn in the busy seaside town of Cape May, New Jersey, includes the following on their Web site:

Please be sure of your plans before booking! As a small inn dealing almost exclusively with advance reservations, date changes and cancellations affect us significantly. Consequently, we require a minimum of two weeks advance notice of any change to your reservation, including a change of dates, change in number of nights, or cancellation. As long as this notice is given, we will refund your deposit, less a $20 pro-

cessing fee per room. Without this notice, deposits are not returned. The only exception will occur if we are able to re-rent the room/s to fill the entire original booking, at which time we will make the same refund as described above.

We realize that life and the weather are unpredictable, but we do not assume responsibility for either! We ask that you carefully consider our policy before making a reservation.

Check-in time is between 2 p.m. and 8 p.m. Later arrivals can be arranged with prior notice. Check-out time is 11 a.m. Note that we are unable to accommodate early arrivals or late departures — this includes parking! Please be mindful of the clock. . . .

We regret that we cannot accommodate pets, and children under 10 years are generally happier elsewhere.

Group policies

It's wise to have separate and stringent cancellation and deposit policies when accommodating groups at your inn. For example, many innkeepers require that the group reserve the entire inn so that other guests don't feel overrun by the group. Cancellation policies help protect you and your income if the group decides to back out at the last minute, leaving you with an empty inn. Additionally, you need other policies and guidelines in place when hosting weddings and other group events.

Other house rules

Your insurance policy dictates additional house rules and policies that you need to enforce, not only to ensure coverage but also for the safety of your guests and your inn. You can find out about policies that you may not have thought of by reading innkeeper forums and by talking to other innkeepers (see Chapter 1 for information on how to find other successful innkeepers to talk to). You may want to consider the following policies for the safety and protection of your inn:

✔ **Candles:** Many inn fires have resulted from guests' use of candles. Some innkeepers ban candles completely; others allow only votive candles; and still others offer attractive, battery-operated candles as an alternative. It's okay to blame the insurance company or fire marshal for your restrictions on candles.

✔ **Incense:** Many innkeepers (and other guests) are bothered by the burning of incense and prohibit incense at the inn.

✔ **Eating in the room:** Some inns offer breakfast in bed while others discourage or prohibit food in the guest rooms. Don't put furniture in the rooms that accommodates in-room meals unless you're comfortable with guests eating in their rooms.

✔ **Bath oils in the hot tub:** Some inns don't allow bath oils or bubbles in their hot tubs and others provide them. If you have hot tubs or whirlpool tubs in your bed & breakfast, check with the manufacturer to find out what can harm the tubs.

You want to achieve a careful balance between policies and rules that protect your inn and those that ensure the rights of your guests, while not making so many rules that guests can't relax and enjoy their stay with you.

Chapter 8

B&B Marketing 101

Making people aware of your inn is the most important factor in your business's success. You may have the best breakfast recipes, the most gorgeous décor and the most luxurious guest rooms, but if potential guests don't know it, you'll have empty beds.

In this chapter, I show you how to spread the word about your bed & breakfast when it's new and keep the word spreading as your business grows. I share my favorite ideas to help you harness the power of marketing by creating an appealing image for your inn and promoting that image through the Internet, word-of-mouth, and print advertising.

Creating a Marketable Image

Marketing is just a fancy word for waving your own flag or tooting your own horn. There are many ways to get your message out, but before you can spread the word, you have to know what you want to say. Marketing is the art of portraying your B&B in the most favorable light possible and sharing that message with as many people as possible. Marketing is an ongoing process, which consists of advertising in print and on the Web, developing positive relationships with guests and businesses, and showing the media why your inn is wonderful. Filling your guest rooms is the most important aspect of your business, so how you market your inn determines the success of your B&B.

Deciding on your B&B's image is the first step in beginning to market your business. In simplest terms, your inn's image is how you want people to perceive your bed & breakfast. Your image can be summed up by asking yourself the question: "If a guest were describing my inn to a friend, what would I want them to say?"

Maybe this phantom conversation would be "It's a fantastic inn that's in the best spot on that beach" or "It's a wonderful B&B with the best pancakes I've ever tasted." You could solidify that image by marketing your inn as "The Best Spot on the Beach" or "Home of the World's Best Pancakes." Your bed & breakfast will succeed or fail on guests' perceptions of your image, so play to your strengths.

You can take one of many angles when developing your image. Your angle may be geographic, your theme, or it may be related to the food you serve, the history of your building, or a prominent feature in the area. For instance, The Songbird Prairie B&B is located on the edges of a very well-known bird sanctuary, so their image is "Where luxury and nature converse." Here are a few ideas to help you decide on a marketing angle for your B&B:

- ✔ If your inn is located in an area that is known for a specific attraction, like a beach, lake, grand architecture, or a famous museum, make this the focus of your image. Consider why guests typically visit the area. For example, if you're located in a town famous for its hot springs, your proximity to the springs may be a wonderful marketing tool.

- ✔ Make your message appeal to the type of guests you want to attract. If you're trying to attract couples on a romantic getaway, you'll be creating a different marketing image than if you want to focus on guests who are taking family vacations.

- ✔ Identify the characteristics of your inn that make guests want to stay with you, such as the fact that it's historic, rustic, or elegant. If your inn is in a Second Empire home, you may want to expound on the view from the top of your turret or your porches that "Go on forever."

Indentifying what makes you unique

B&B guests are looking for a unique experience, not a cookie-cutter place to sleep. The goal of marketing your inn is to make it stand out and appeal to guests so that they choose you over the many alternatives available to them. Accentuate what makes your inn unique, and elaborate on the features, services, and amenities that only your B&B provides.

Of the many things that may make your inn unique, some of the most popular to feature in your marketing message are:

> ✔ **Your inn's personality:** Historic, Victorian, modern, and so on
>
> ✔ **Your inn's guest list:** The type of guests you're trying to attract
>
> ✔ **Your inn's location:** Proximity to attractions

The Gettysburg Battlefield Bed & Breakfast has nicely combined several unique attributes into a successful marketing plan. It's a historic inn, which attracts history buffs as well as families interested in an educational trip. The inn is located right on the Gettysburg battlefield, so its proprietors discuss this unique attribute in all their marketing literature. By discerning what makes their B&B unique, the innkeepers are able to create an environment where guests don't just learn history, they see, feel, smell, and sense the history around them. That's their marketing angle, and because it's unique, they have a very successful inn.

Be honest in all of your advertising! For instance, be straightforward about where your inn is located. You may be able to trick guests into making a reservation by letting them think you're in a popular tourist destination when, in fact, you're 15 minutes outside of it. Once they arrive, however, you'll have unhappy guests who'll know they've been lied to. State how close you are to the destination. Many guests will be fine with the location, as long as they're aware of it in advance.

Don't forget popular tourist destinations are important search keywords that should be prominent in the text of your Web site.

Creating a marketing image is an ongoing process. Begin identifying the key parts of your message as soon as you start the planning process for your bed & breakfast.

Building a brand

Deciding on your brand and your inn's message in the beginning is as important as mapping out a long trip before your departure. Branding is creating and choosing the best verbal, visual, and intangible symbols to represent your inn's message. Think of your inn's brand as its personality or attitude. Continue to ask yourself, "What message do I want to send?" Is your B&B the closest one to the Grand Canyon? The one with the oceanfront location, or historical significance, or world-famous muffins (at least they should be)? Integrating these kinds of messages in all your communications is branding.

Start developing your brand by creating a tagline that incorporates your message, and use it on business cards, stationary, rack cards, and your Web site. Your tagline should be simple and descriptive. A good tagline is "The closest inn to the Grand Canyon." "The best B&B in St. Louis" is a weak example because it doesn't convey anything special or unique about your inn — any number of bed & breakfasts could claim it. Stay away from anything generic or hackneyed.

For more ideas on branding, see *Branding For Dummies* by Bill Chiaravalle and Barbara Findlay Schenck (Wiley).

Developing a logo

Golden arches for McDonalds, a red check mark for Verizon Wireless, and the swoosh for Nike all represent logos which immediately bring to mind the brand they represent. While it would be great to have a logo equally as recognizable, the main purpose of the logo for your B&B is to communicate the image you want to convey about your bed & breakfast. A Web site designer may be willing to help with this, or you can hire an online company like Logoworks (www.logoworks.com) to develop a logo for your inn.

Creating the right graphic image to symbolize your brand is a process that can be very time consuming, but it's extremely important and will have a lasting effect on your business. A good way to get started is to sketch out numerous logo designs and solicit as many opinions as possible. An effective logo is one that's

- **Communicative:** Your logo should communicate and reinforce your brand image and marketing message.

- **Simple:** The simpler the logo is, the easier it is for the brain to process and remember it.

- **Inspirational:** You want the logo to produce a good feeling when viewed by potential guests.

- **Memorable:** Your logo should help guests remember the name of your inn.

- **Reproducible:** Pick a design that will look good on your Web site, your stationary, clothing and gift items (shirts and mugs), and in print. A good logo can be scaled to many different sizes and reproduced without color for black-and-white printing.

Marketing on the Internet

Show me a successful new inn and I'll show you a strong Internet presence. Marketing on the Internet is essential when you're starting a new inn, and it's probably the single easiest way to build your business if you're taking over an established B&B. Nowhere will you get a bigger bang for your buck or your effort than on the Internet. The Internet puts small properties on a level playing field with larger accommodations, making it one of the best things to happen to the bed & breakfast industry.

Working with a Web site

Web sites are a must-have in the lodging industry. Your Web site is your online brochure, potentially delivered to millions of prospective guests around the world 24 hours a day, 7 days a week, 365 days a year. The cost is nominal in comparison to the benefits it provides.

Whether you decide to have your site professionally designed or create it yourself, the best way to get started is to spend time researching other Web sites and compiling a list of sites you like and why. Your Web site should be easy to use, informative, attractive, and, most importantly, place high in the search engines. It doesn't have to be fancy, complicated, or expensive. It's easy to fall for flash over functionality, but I encourage you to have an attractive, clean-looking Web site that represents the personality of your inn. Most travelers research lodging choices on the Web, so your Web site may create a guest's first impression.

Brushing up on Internet lingo

Internet jargon can be confusing, so here are a few key terms to help you become familiar with Web site lingo:

- **Web site address:** People often use the terms *domain name* and *URL* to refer to Web site addresses.

  - **Domain Name:** This is the part of your Web site address after the www. For example, in `www.journeyinn.com`, journeyinn.com is the domain name.

  - **URL:** This stands for Universal Resource Locator, and it refers to the full Web site address of a particular page. For example, `www.journeyinn.com` is the URL for Journey Inn's home page, `www.journeyinn.com/rooms-suites.php` is the URL for their rooms page, and `www.journeyinn.com/breakfast.php` is the URL for their breakfast page.

- **Domain Registrar:** You register your domain name with a domain registrar. Just as two people can't have the same phone number, domain registrars keep track of domain ownership to prevent two people or companies from registering the same domain name. You can register your domain name with established domain registrars like Network Solutions (`www.networksolutions.com`), GoDaddy (`www.godaddy.com`) or Dotster (`www.dotster.com`). The fees to register a domain name vary by company, but should not exceed $35 per year. Domain registrations are for a period of one to ten years. Registering your domain for a longer term means you don't need to worry about renewing it every year, and some think that Google gives a slight preference to domains that are registered for longer periods.

Most registrars offer the option of having your domain name automatically renewed, which is a good idea. Always mark the renewal dates of your domains on your calendar so you can verify that the renewal has been completed, even if you sign up for automatic renewals.

Many unethical domain registrars send innkeepers false e-mail renewal notices, and many busy innkeepers pay them thinking they are renewing their domain. It's important to make sure you know who you are registered with and when your renewal is due.

✔ **Hosting company:** A *hosting company* is a company you pay to make your Web site available to online users 24 hours a day via a *server,* or large computer. Just as dialing a phone number connects a caller to a particular location, entering a URL in a browser connects an online user to your Web site via your hosting company's server. Your hosting company can also help you set up your e-mail and get rid of *spam,* or unsolicited junk e-mail. To pick a hosting company, ask other innkeepers or the person who helps you design your Web site for referrals.

✔ **Keywords:** These are simply the words that prospective guests are most likely to use when searching online for a bed & breakfast. Many guests looking for an oceanfront bed & breakfast in Cape May, New Jersey, type the keywords "oceanfront," "bed," "breakfast," "cape may," and/or "new jersey" into Google or another search engine to begin their search. Good Web sites include keywords in their text not only because that's what guests are looking for, but also because keywords are one of the ways search engines match guest requests with the results that they display.

Optimizing your site's chances of being found

Professional strategies known as *Search Engine Optimization (SEO)* should be implemented on your Web site to ensure that prospective guests who are using search engines to look for lodging will find your inn. Before you begin to design your site — or even choose a domain name — you should either find out about SEO or consult a professional. (See the "Hiring a Web site designer" section later in this chapter). Making wise design and domain name choices can boost your placement by the search engines.

Many companies offer SEO services, some good and some bad. Stay on the safe side — stick with those who are familiar with the bed & breakfast industry, and be sure to check their references.

If you're opening a new inn, you should begin designing your Web site and register your domain name as soon as possible. You should have your Web site or a "coming soon" page, with a brief introduction about your inn, online three to six months before opening. This gets you in front of the search engines sooner and lets guests planning ahead know you'll be opening and when. Start by picking a domain name that's easy for guests to remember, closely matches your inn name, and contains keywords guests are likely to use when searching for an inn like yours. (See Chapter 5 for information on picking a name for your inn.) Registering common misspellings for your inn name is also a good idea. For example, if your inn name includes "Harbor," consider registering the same domain with the spelling "Harbour."

Choose one primary domain name and have any others set as secondary names, which point to the primary domain name. Otherwise, the search engines may think you're trying to cheat with multiple listings, and your Web site may be penalized.

If you're buying an existing inn, you may be thinking about changing the inn's name or Web site address. You shouldn't feel compelled to live with an inn name or domain name you're not happy with, but you should be aware of the ramifications of making a change. The longer a Web site is online, the higher — and more frequently — search engines are likely to display it when users type in relevant keywords, and the more likely guests are to visit your site. Changing domain names puts you back at square one in terms of establishing your site in the search engines.

For more information about getting your Web site displayed in search results, check out *Search Engine Optimization For Dummies,* 3rd Edition, by Peter Kent (Wiley).

Knowing what makes a good Web site

Think of your Web site as an extension of your inn's personality. It's like a calling card with your inn's marketing message. It's also the first thing many guests see about your inn. You don't get a second chance to make a first impression, so make sure your Web site greets your potential guests in a style that reflects what you have to offer.

Professional photography

Pictures say a thousand words when promoting your bed & breakfast, and the quality of your photos has an enormous effect on how people view your inn. A good-quality digital camera is a versatile tool that every innkeeper should have. In addition to taking photos of your inn when initially setting up your Web site, it can come in handy in dozens of other ways. Having a camera on hand to snap photos of memorable guests, wonderful dishes you've cooked, or other noteworthy events enables you to continually update your Web site and blog with new material.

You can't compete in today's "eye candy" society with amateurish photos. The most stunning inn can look like a fleabag motel on the Web if the photos of it aren't done well. If your own photography skills aren't up to snuff, you may want to hire a professional photographer. Professional photos are expensive, but easily worth their cost in reservations.

If you have your Web site professionally designed, the designer may recommend specific professional photographers. Some companies, like Jumping Rocks Photography (www.jumpingrocks.com), Acorn Internet Services (www.acorn-is.com) and George Gardner Associates (www.marketing forinns.com) specialize in photographing bed & breakfasts. They can help you spread your message by creating images that appeal specifically to the clientele you are trying to attract.

If your inn is known for its mountain views and you offer guests the opportunity to have breakfast on a deck overlooking the mountains, experienced photographers can capture the essence of this guest experience in their photos. To get inspiration for how a setting can sell your property, take a look at the opening shots and views captured on Inn at Riverbend's Web site (www.innatriverbend.com).

If you don't have photographs on your Web site, guests will wonder what you're hiding. Even if it's just a few good shots, start your Web site with pictures.

Take numerous shots until you achieve the look that you want to portray to guests. Experiment with different angles. Try pushing the furniture a little closer together to improve your photos. You can also rent lighting equipment, which can improve photos a great deal. It's important to get your Web site online as soon as possible, so don't wait until you've finished renovating or building to take pictures.

You can take pictures of your inn's views right away to get a jump-start on your Web site. And after you've purchased a few pieces of furniture, you can stage even more photos. I know of some innkeepers who staged a photo shoot in their apartment with an antique bed that would be in one of the guest rooms. They made the bed, placed a tray of delectable goodies on it and flowers alongside it, and shot some close-ups. The beautiful, antique, four-poster bed was intended to be the focus of the guest room, so it made sense to feature it in pictures. This allowed them to start their Web site with pictures even before construction of the B&B was complete.

It's so important to start your Web site early in the planning process of your B&B that some inns have successfully used stock photos for outdoor and food shots.

Compelling text

The text on your Web site should be descriptive, compelling, and easy to read. The goal is to immediately convey your marketing message, your inn's best features and location, and what your inn is known for. Your Web site will be useful to guests and generate many reservations if you make this information prominent on the home page of your Web site.

Be sure to include the keywords that you think guests will search for when looking for accommodations such as yours. Whispering Pines in Dellroy, Ohio, does a nice job of this in their Web site's opening paragraph:

> *Welcome to the gently rolling hills of the Atwood Lake Region. Whispering Pines, an Ohio bed and breakfast, sits on a hill overlooking the picturesque and lush landscape of Atwood Lake where the views are breathtaking and the surroundings are indescribably tranquil. Atwood Lake's 28 miles of scenic shoreline is the perfect setting for picnics, hiking, and water activities.*

This creates an image of an idyllic setting in the viewer's mind. It also includes many keywords, such as "Ohio," "bed and breakfast," "Atwood Lake," and "hiking." Text is a huge contributor to search engine placement, and the appropriate use of keywords in the first paragraph is the most important placement factor.

Easy navigation

Think about the frustration you experience when you find a Web site but you're not able to find the information you need. This is exactly what you want to avoid. Make it simple for guests to find your contact information, room pictures, rates, availability, information about the local area, and details about your inn, including what type of breakfast you serve, the amenities you offer, and your policies. Most importantly, make it obvious and easy for guests to see how to make a reservation.

Your *home page* is the main page on your site, and it's of utmost importance because it's usually the first page guests see. Ask yourself the following questions about your home page:

- ✔ Is it appealing?

- ✔ Does it capture prospective guests' attention?

- ✔ Does it convey the image I want to about my inn?

- ✔ Is it easy for guests to find critical contact information? (Without this, they can't make a reservation.)

Guests should be able to do everything quickly and easily from your home page — and every page — on your site. To accomplish this, you need tabs or links that are easy to find on each page of your Web site. These links serve as connections to the various sections (or pages) of your site, such as Home, Rooms, Area Attractions, Specials, Make a Reservation, Contact Us, and so forth. These links should be *above the fold* (meaning they're visible without a guest having to scroll down) and in the same place on every page, so guests don't have to spend time figuring out how to go from one page to another.

One-page Web sites are as outdated as the Model T. Multiple pages not only make it easier to organize and categorize information, but they also increase your chances of high placement with search engines. Search engines count the number of pages on your Web site, and more is better — as long as they have good content.

Fast loading

A quick-loading home page is essential. If a page takes more than a few seconds to load, viewers are likely to give up on it, and you lose the possibility of that guest making a reservation at your inn. High-speed Internet is common in most places, but some people still access the Web via slower dial-up connections, so be sure to keep this in mind if you design your own Web site.

If your Web site is slow to load, compress any digital pictures on the site to no more than 72 dpi. Photo editing software makes this easy to do. If your site still loads slowly, the problem may be with your Web hosting company. Talk to them, and stay on top of the issue until you're satisfied with the speed at which your site loads.

Creating the site yourself

If you have a background in programming, you may want to try creating your Web site yourself. Web page editing software, such as Front Page or Dreamweaver, can guide you through the process. (For help using these programs, see *Front Page 2003 All-in-One Desk Reference For Dummies* by John Paul Mueller or *Dreamweaver CS4 For Dummies* by Janine C. Warner [both published by Wiley].) Another alternative is to check with domain registrars and hosting companies, many of which have online templates and other resources available to help you build a simple Web site.

Designing and maintaining a Web site can require a tremendous amount of time and effort, which may take you away from the many other things that need to be done to get your inn ready for guests. Although experimenting with Web design may be fun, if this is a new area for you, you may be foregoing some great features and a professional look because you don't have the necessary skills or aren't aware of the newest Web technologies that could benefit your business.

You're investing a lot of money and resources into your B&B. Your Web site is the most important tool you have to bring guests to your inn, so consider carefully before deciding to design the site yourself. Being able to update your rates and packages is a nice feature that many professional designers can set up for you.

Hiring a Web site designer

Hiring a Web site designer is no different than hiring a contractor to perform physical work at your inn. It requires a careful selection process and a clear vision of the finished product you want. Don't try to cut corners here. Remember, you're hiring someone to create your most valuable marketing tool and the public online presence of your B&B.

Here are some things to consider when hiring — and ultimately working with — a Web site designer:

✔ **Look for a designer who's open to your input.** You may not be a Web design expert, but only you can describe the personal vision you have for your inn. The designer you hire should ask a lot of questions about the marketing messages you're trying to convey.

You should have a strong vision of what you want your Web site to look like. You probably have a file of pictures torn from magazines of decorating ideas that you like. Create a similar file of Web sites with features you like, and share them with designers. No one can read your mind.

✔ **Look for a Web site designer who knows the bed & breakfast industry.** The following designers have specialized in the B&B industry for years, are familiar with SEO, and have created hundreds of successful bed & breakfast Web sites:

- Acorn Internet Services (www.acorn-is.com)

- InsideOut Solutions (www.savvyinnkeeper.com)

- Rare Brick (www.rarebrick.com)

- Whitestone Marketing (www.whitestonemarketing.com)

✔ **Find out who designed other B&B Web sites you like.** Pretend you're a guest looking for a bed & breakfast, and search for inns as a guest would. Visit the Web sites that come up first in the search engines. If you like the design of a particular site, look at the bottom of the home page to see who designed it. (This is usually listed under Hosting/Design or Marketing/Promotion.)

It's a good idea to look in nearby towns and not just your own. Using a designer who has already worked successfully with one or more inns in your town has both pros and cons. On the one hand, your site may not be as original as you'd like; on the other hand, the designer has a proven track record.

Repeat your search in other geographic areas to find inns that are branded the way you'd like yours to be. For example, you might search using the keywords "mountain getaway, Colorado" and "mountain getaway, Montana."

✔ **Request and check references.** Talk to other innkeepers who have used the designer that you're considering. Ask around at conferences and in innkeeper forums for advice. (See Chapter 1 for resources you can draw upon). Ask for examples of the designers' work.

✔ **Ask about getting mockups of your site.** After you find a designer you like and sign on with them, you'll want to get mockups of their ideas for your site. A *mockup* is a picture of what some of the pages on your site might look like. It's a non-functional but graphically pleasing way to get a feel for the type of work this designer is capable of. Creating mockups gives both you and the designer something to look at when talking about your future Web site to be sure you both have the same vision and message in mind. Make sure the mockups match the look and feel of your marketing image in terms of style, color, layout, and features. Examining mockups together makes it easier to enact the changes you want by having a concrete example to modify and improve.

✔ **Find out whether you'll be able to edit pages yourself.** Many designers can create pages on your Web site that you can edit and update yourself. This gives you the flexibility to change your rates and add packages and specials as often as you like. Being able to adjust rates by season and demand gives you more flexibility to manage the inventory of your business (your rooms). Having the ability to add specials anytime allows you to take advantage of special events, holidays, or activities in your area. Without the ability to make frequent updates, you may miss out on opportunities to get bookings.

✔ **Ask whether the designer is willing to accept payment in phases.** You should never pay a designer everything up front. Paying a Web designer in phases, just as you would a contractor, is customary.

If your Web designer registers your domain name, be sure you are listed as the registrant (owner). You domain name is a valuable asset, just like the physical building of your B&B. You don't want there to be any doubt as to who owns your domain, in case you decide not to work with a particular designer or Web host in the future.

Getting guests to your Web site

Having a fabulous Web site that no one knows about is like having an unlisted phone number and not giving it out to anyone. Links from other quality Web sites to yours are essential. As an added benefit, sites that are linked to other quality sites are ranked higher by search engines. Once you get guests to your Web site, they'll be focused on your inn only. Here are some tips for making that happen:

✔ Anytime your inn is mentioned in an article, either online or in print, ask the author to include a link to your Web site, and offer to give them a link in return.

Try to get them to link to the page on your site that's most relevant to the article. For example, if the article is about weddings that you host, ask them to link to your wedding page rather than your home page. This is better for both you and their readers.

✔ Submit your site to the major search engines — Google, Yahoo!, and MSN — by using the following links:

  • **Google:** www.google.com/addurl/

  • **Yahoo!:** https://siteexplorer.search.yahoo.com/submit

  • **MSN/Live Search:** http://search.msn.com/docs/submit.aspx

While it doesn't hurt to submit your site to the search engines, it's not strictly necessary. As long as other sites are linking to your site, search engines will find you. But if you're eager to get started and don't have anyone linking to you yet, submitting your site to the major search engines will get things rolling. Make sure you read each search engine's Webmaster rules and don't hire anyone to do "automatic" submissions of your Web site to hundreds of search engines at once.

✔ When evaluating advertising opportunities, verify that the ad will include a link to your Web site.

✔ Include your Web site address on all business cards, stationery, and rack cards or brochures.

✔ Always have a supply of business cards, brochures, or rack cards with you to give to anyone you meet who expresses interest in your inn.

Listing in online directories

You've probably used online directories to find some of the bed & breakfasts you've visited, but you may not have known you were on a B&B directory. An *online directory* is a Web site that lists numerous bed & breakfasts by posting their advertisements, which are usually paid for by the innkeepers. A directory may list anywhere from a dozen to a several thousand bed & breakfasts. At last count, over 150 online directories existed with new ones starting up all the time. Their names are often similar and their promises may sound the same, but their results can be very different. More inns spend money on online B&B directories than any other form of advertising. Most innkeepers are listed in several directories, and many attribute a significant percentage of their reservations to a few online B&B directories.

Understanding what a directory is

A directory is a combination of an online guidebook and a search engine. Directories have surpassed guidebooks in popularity by providing potential guests with an easy way to find and compare hundreds of B&Bs in one place. Unlike guidebooks, good online directories are constantly being updated with new rates, pictures, and bed & breakfasts for guests to choose from.

When your inn is listed in a directory, the listing is an advertisement for your inn. Because most directory listings are comprehensive in the coverage of the inns they list, guests usually don't realize the listings are paid advertisements. Directories come in all shapes and sizes, so investigate sites that mesh with your geographic area and the types of guests you want to attract to your B&B. There are worldwide directories, local and regional directories, and directories that cater to special interests (such as gay & lesbian travel, traveling with pets, Christian travel, and so on).

Online bed & breakfast directories offer guests a variety of useful features to search for an inn, and they offer you an easy way to quickly gain an Internet presence with very little effort or expense. Most directories have simple online registration forms, whereby you can upload information and pictures through a template to create a listing. Some directory listings contain as much information as most inns' Web sites, and guests frequently cannot differentiate between the two. Many directories have staff available to help you create your listing if you're not comfortable using a computer.

Choosing the right directories

Sorting through the huge number of directory prospects that are available is a difficult task for anyone, especially a busy innkeeper. Many directories are extremely aggressive in contacting inns with special offers and promotions. If you haven't already, you'll soon be receiving numerous unsolicited e-mails, which you should evaluate carefully before pulling out your credit card. Although the cost to join the top directories is reasonable and an excellent use of your marketing budget, be cautious when making your choices. Bargains are tempting, but remember that putting together a quality product costs money. Many free or low-cost directories are not actively managed because they don't have the budget for a full-time staff. When you're unsure, pick up the phone. If you can't reach the directory's staff when you want to join, it's a pretty sure bet that this directory will be difficult to keep up-to-date.

You want to be sure that anything you publish on the Internet stays current and brings results, and updating dozens of free directories each time you change rates or add amenities requires a tremendous time commitment. Fast-forward three years: You don't want a potential guest calling and arguing for an old rate. That guest won't care that the site was free and you couldn't spare the time to update it, and if you don't grant the guest's request, you'll create the impression that your business doesn't honor its posted prices.

On the other side of the coin, if a lower-cost directory is working better than a higher priced one, you can certainly save some money by dropping the higher-priced directory. (See Chapter 15 for help in determining which advertising is working.)

There are no absolute guarantees when picking a directory, but here are some tips to help you sort through the vast array of choices:

> ✔ **Perform several Internet searches as a guest would to see which directories are listed first.** You should be listed in any directory that comes up on the first results page of the most popular guest searches. Think of the keywords that guests might enter to find inns in your area or inns that offer what you do. There are many search engines that guests may use, but Google is the most popular. Start by doing the following searches on Google, and later you can drill down further and repeat the same searches on Yahoo!, AOL, MSN, and so on. You probably won't find

any directory that comes up on every search, but keep track of the ones you see most often — these are the ones you should consider first. Here are some common searches you should perform:

- Bed and Breakfast
- Your State Bed and Breakfast (for example, New York Bed and Breakfast)
- Your City, State Bed and Breakfast (for example, Hyde Park, New York Bed and Breakfast)
- Abbreviations for your state bed and breakfast (for example, NY bed and breakfast)
- Popular tourist locations, Your state Bed and Breakfast (for example, Wine Country, California Bed and Breakfast)

Repeat the above searches using "B&B" and "bed & breakfast" in place of "bed and breakfast."

Do not use this method as the only way to choose a directory. If a particular directory doesn't currently have any listings in your city, it won't come up in your searches. If you later decide this is a good directory to advertise in, you'll have the advantage of being the only one listed in your locale.

✔ **Ask advice from other innkeepers.** Ask other innkeepers which directories are effective for them by asking questions in innkeeper forums and association meetings and by speaking with other B&B owners you've met (see Chapter 1 for help locating innkeeper resources).

✔ **Keep in mind that geography plays a large role in the effectiveness of directories.** A directory that has better results on the West Coast is great if your bed & breakfast is in Oregon, but not so hot if you're in Vermont.

✔ **Remember which directories you see mentioned in magazines, newspapers, and on TV.** Often prospective guests tear out magazine and newspaper articles to save for future reference. Pay attention to which directories are quoted as resources by the media. Directories that frequently appear in the media usually have aggressive PR efforts that can help your inn gain good press.

✔ **Look for niche directories.** If you have a special niche, like being pet-friendly or Christian-oriented, refine your Google search to seek out directories that promote these niches (for examples, check out www.petswelcome.com and www.icbbn.com).

✔ **Determine whether the directory is well organized.** Guests should be able to easily find your bed & breakfast on the directory, so pretend you're using the directory as a guest, and see how many clicks it takes to find your B&B on the site. Also check to see whether a lot of outside advertisements have the potential to lure prospective guests away from the site (and your inn).

 ✔ **Look for directories that represent the personality of your inn.** Ask yourself whether your B&B is a good fit. If your bed & breakfast is a Victorian inn with four guest rooms, a directory of small hotels and large inns probably isn't going to attract the type of B&B guests you're looking for.

To get you started, Table 8-1 lists some of the most popular online directories in alphabetical order.

Table 8-1	Popular Online B&B Directories	
Name of Directory	*URL of Directory*	*Listing Costs*
BBOnline.com	`www.bbonline.com`	Packages range from $169–$515 and include a link to your Web site.
BedandBreakfast.com	`www.bedandbreak fast.com`	Packages range from $240 with no link to your Web site to $420–$900 with a link to your Web site.
BnBFinder.com	`www.bnbfinder.com`	Packages range from $129–$299 and include a link to your Web site.
ILoveInns.com	`www.iloveinns.com`	Packages range from $135 with no link to your Web site to $195–$295 with a link to your Web site.
Lanier Publishing	`www.lanierbb.com`	Packages are $159 plus a $40 set-up fee and include a link to your Web site.

Ask about special offers for members of any B&B associations that you belong to. Also, some directories have special offers for new innkeepers, so be sure to tell them you're new to the business.

No matter which directories you start out with, you'll want to track their performance before renewing with them. (See Chapter 15 for help in analyzing your advertising results.)

Many new directories pick a name similar to established directories and then send innkeepers e-mail renewal notices. Many busy innkeepers pay them, thinking they're renewing one of their existing directory listings. Don't fall into that trap.

Featuring your B&B on state, local, and association Web sites

Taking advantage of the extensive advertising campaigns of your local, regional, and state tourism boards is an excellent opportunity to get the word out about your inn. The job of these organizations is to "sell" travelers on your area and provide tourists with comprehensive information. Tourism organizations provide information on many topics, including local activities, restaurants, festivals, and places to stay.

Not all sites are created equal in terms of their adverting value to you. Some states and chambers of commerce or visitors bureaus are more devoted to promoting travel and tourism than others. To determine which groups to join, look for signs that the organization is actively promoting travel and tourism in your area. The best way to find this out is to look for prominent links to lodging options right on the organization's home page.

State tourism Web sites

If you're in a state that devotes a lot of resources to promoting tourism — and most do — check out the official state tourism Web site and see whether lodging is listed and easy to find. If so, find out how you can get your B&B listed, especially if the site includes a category for bed & breakfasts. Some states, such as Arkansas, partner with the state bed & breakfast association so when visitors call looking for lodging information, they're offered a free book that lists bed & breakfasts in the state. This is a very targeted way to let potential guests know about your inn. Links between state promotions and local bed & breakfast associations make the association membership that much more valuable. Guests tend to remember finding you in the book the state sent them, so the effectiveness of this type of advertising is easy to track.

Chamber of commerce Web sites

One benefit of being a member of your local chamber of commerce is being listed on their Web site. The value of this from a marketing perspective depends on how actively the chamber promotes their Web site, how organized the site is, and how many people use it to find lodging. Some chambers provide innkeepers with many reservation referrals, while others provide little or no help in advertising because other organizations, such as convention and visitors bureaus, provide the marketing function for lodging. Research your local chamber of commerce, tourism board, and visitors bureau to find out which organizations handle lodging referrals.

Surprisingly, some large chambers that offer lodging resources in well-known tourist destinations are not a big source of reservations for their member inns, while some inns in lesser-known areas with smaller chambers report great success from their memberships. Evaluating all the benefits the membership offers and asking other innkeepers what works for them can help you make informed decisions about which organizations to join. Carefully tracking where guests tell you they found your inn can help you determine whether the membership is worth maintaining after the first year.

You can belong to more than one chamber of commerce. For example, if you have a bed & breakfast in Lenox, Massachusetts, you may be able to join the Berkshires Visitors Bureau, the Lenox Chamber of Commerce, and nearby town chambers, such as the Stockbridge Chamber of Commerce.

Local Web sites

Taking the time to seek out local Web sites can pay big rewards when it comes to promoting your inn. Local businesses may be willing to exchange links from their Web site to yours. This means they're referring their customers to you — for free. For example, a local winery might have a section about lodging on their Web site. If so, contact them to request that your inn be listed; if such a section doesn't exist, suggest that they create one. In return, you could have a section on your Web site for area activities, and include a link to the winery. Doing this with several Web sites provides your guests with resources about area activities, and gets other sites to link to yours in the process. Not only does this strategy have the potential to bring new guests to your inn, but it usually improves your ranking by search engines, which consider linked sites a plus.

Beware of having too much of a good thing. Links that don't make sense may actually hurt you. Search engines use algorithms that make them suspicious of too many inbound and outbound links (links coming into your Web site or links to other Web sites from yours). People used to abuse this technique, and the search engines caught on. Stick with partnerships and link exchanges that provide information and resources for your guests, and don't add too many links at once.

B&B association Web sites

Belonging to local and state B&B associations can provide you with a wealth of information and resources, and many associations are organized to provide specific marketing assistance to their members. Strong B&B associations can also drive a significant amount of guest traffic to your Web site. When you contact the associations, ask about the benefits of membership and the marketing efforts of the association.

Organized advertising campaigns are often coordinated by local, regional, and state bed & breakfast associations. Inn tours, frequent stay programs and gift certificates may further enhance the advertising reach of these associations.

If the association's Web site places high in a Google search, be sure your inn is listed on their site, with a link back to your site.

Generating Word-of-Mouth Promotion

Word-of-mouth promotion is great for two reasons: It doesn't cost anything, and potential guests view it as more genuine than viewing an advertisement. Don't be shy about trying to generate recommendations and word-of-mouth promotion for your inn. This is a time to toot your own horn and get others to toot it for you as well.

Getting guest referrals

Guest referrals are like found treasure and should be rewarded. There is no greater compliment a guest can give you than to vouch for your inn and recommend it to a friend, colleague, or family member.

Be sure to treat referrals as a gift and thank the referrer. A short personal note or e-mail is a perfect way to say thanks for the referral. Some innkeepers also send the referrer a small discount certificate to be used on their next visit within a given period of time (approximately 10 percent is appreciated and appropriate).

Think of clever and unobtrusive ways to ask for referrals. If you're having trouble thinking of ideas, here are a few to get you started:

- **Mail or e-mail a thank you.** After each stay, send guests a thank-you telling them that you hope they enjoyed their stay. This is a good time to tell them you value their feedback and ask them to post a review. The addition of a simple statement like, "The greatest compliment is your guest referrals" is a low-key way to remind guests that you appreciate their referrals.

- **Ask for referrals.** When guests compliment you about their stay, tell them you hope they will tell their friends and family so that you may have the privilege of hosting them in the future. If you publish a newsletter (see Chapter 15), include a section about appreciating the many referrals you've received from previous guests and add that you look forward to welcoming them to your inn.

Seeing everyone as a potential guest

Whether you think of yourself as a salesperson or not, you are. Everyone, everywhere is a potential guest. You have the nonstop job of selling your inn to everyone you come in contact with. Here are some ways to constantly be ready to promote your inn:

✔ Always carry a supply of business or rack cards/brochures with you.

✔ Have shirts made with your inn's name and logo, and wear them.

✔ Include an e-mail signature with your inn information on all your e-mails — business-related and otherwise.

✔ Offer to host meetings at your inn for clubs or organizations you belong to. By impressing members with your wonderful hospitality, you encourage them to recommend your B&B to visiting family and friends.

Handling online guest reviews

The jury is out amongst innkeepers about whether to embrace or reject online reviews, but like it or not, they're here to stay and their popularity is growing. While you might not be comfortable asking guests to post reviews, finding out what they are and how to use them to your benefit is another marketing strategy. *Guest reviews* are comments (both positive and negative) from previous guests about your inn. They're considered word-of-mouth advertising because they tell future guests what they liked and disliked about your inn. Managing your online review image is a part of managing your brand and your inn's identity.

Harnessing the power of positive reviews

Guests are more likely to believe something another guest says about your inn than an advertisement you write, so managing the impression guests get about your inn from reviews is important. Guests know the difference between a Holiday Inn and a Four Seasons. In the case of your B&B, however, they have only your word and the Web — your site and those of online directories — to try and figure out the difference between you and the B&B across town. Having many reviews from guests who have enjoyed their stays at your B&B is a great testimonial about your inn, and often the reason a future guest chooses your inn over the competition.

Positive reviews are free advertising, so here are some tips on how to encourage satisfied guests to share their reviews with others:

✔ **Ask guests to write a review.** When guests compliment you about some aspect of their stay, encourage them to share their views online. Guests often feel they want to do something for you after you've helped them have an enjoyable getaway, so asking them to share a review with future guests is perfectly fine.

✔ **Include a link to sites that maintain reviews for your inn in thank you e-mails and notes to your guests.** This makes posting reviews easier for your guests, and allows you to direct their reviews to the sites you prefer.

- ✔ **Rotate the sites you ask guests to post reviews on monthly.** You can't expect each guest to post reviews on multiple sites, but you don't want all the reviews to end up on one site at the expense of another.

- ✔ **To help guests remember to post reviews, some inns distribute guest comment cards.** Some directories have premade cards or you can prepare your own. You can leave them on an information table or in the guest's room, or include them in thank-you notes. The cards may serve as reminders for the guests to post a review on a given site, or they may be cards that the guests fill out and mail to the site directly.

- ✔ **Offer to let guests use a computer to post reviews.** Some inns have a guest computer in the common area with links to sites that maintain reviews listed under favorites. Be aware, however, that asking guests to post reviews on the spot may make them uncomfortable, and some review sites can filter reviews coming from the same IP address.

Managing bad reviews

Negative reviews give you a chance to show potential guests the true extent of your hospitality. All reputable review sites give you the opportunity to respond to a reviewer's comments. Savvy innkeepers take this opportunity to "talk" to future guests by letting their concern for their guests' experiences shine through.

Following are two examples in which innkeepers used negative comments to show their hospitality and their desire to make each guest's stay wonderful:

- ✔ One guest gave an inn a negative review because the breakfast was not as advertised. The innkeeper politely responded by explaining that *"at the last minute, this guest told us she was checking out at 7 a.m. for a business meeting, although the posted time for breakfast was 8:30 a.m. I didn't have time to create the planned dish, which takes an hour in the oven, so I quickly whipped up an omelet using the same ingredients as those in the casserole."*

- ✔ An innkeeper responded to a guest who complained about the guest rooms this way: *"It is our wonderful guests who help to make us better hosts by letting us know of issues that many times we are just not aware of. For those who have allergies, special needs, or prefer more open space, please let us know when making your reservation. We can remove many items from your room if needed. Thank you for your input; we wish you had told us during your visit so we could have accommodated you better."*

Keep in mind that most reasonable people understand that you can't fully please every single guest all the time. Bad news can even be good news, because when potential guests see a full list of glowing, positive reviews, they tend to wonder whether they're authentic or written solely by the innkeepers and their friends. Having a few less-glowing reviews mixed in with many positive ones makes your good reviews seem more legitimate.

Networking for fun and profit

You've chosen the profession of innkeeping, so use your love of people and your social skills to promote your bed & breakfast. Networking takes a variety of forms. In its simplest terms, it's meeting people, getting to know them, and finding out what they can do to help your business and what you can do to help theirs.

Meeting your new neighbors

Getting to know your neighbors early in the planning process of your B&B can prove to be part of your business's success. Generating goodwill among your neighbors can have many tangible and intangible benefits. Whether you're taking over an existing inn or opening a new one, having the neighborhood on your team is always a positive thing. Neighbors can be a source of referrals. They can also support — or oppose — your expansion plans or any zoning-related issues, including parking, what type of sign you have out front, and how many guests you can accommodate. Here are some suggestions for being neighborly:

- Invite neighbors in for a tour of your inn.

- If you host bridal showers and other get-togethers, make sure your neighbors know your inn is available as a venue for their special gatherings.

- Consider offering a local discount to your neighbors' visiting family and friends if they stay with you.

Getting to know city hall

Getting to know your local officials can never start too early in the planning process of your bed & breakfast. Like your neighbors, local officials can be a great source of referrals and can help or hinder zoning decisions regarding your B&B. Many successful innkeepers are actively involved in their communities, which helps their businesses and gives them input and first-hand information about local happenings.

Get to know city hall by:

- **Visiting and passing out your rack cards or brochures.** Accompanying them with a sampling of your baked goods makes your inn more memorable.

- **Attending chamber meetings.** Take a supply of brochures and rack cards with you.

- **Offering to host meetings at your inn.** This gives you the opportunity to showcase your hospitality.

Connecting with other local businesses

You're probably not the only small business in your town, and many other local businesses face the same challenges and issues you do. From hiring employees to zoning issues, you have a lot in common. Seek out other small businesses to exchange information and resources with.

Get to know other local businesses by:

- ✔ **Creating a mailing** that introduces your inn to other local businesses.

- ✔ **Visiting local businesses** with rack cards and brochures to introduce yourself and your B&B. Bringing muffins or cookies will ensure that they remember you.

- ✔ **Visiting gas stations** with rack cards, brochures, preprinted directions to your inn, and baked goods is a great way to spread the word about your inn because many visitors inquire about local lodging when they stop for gas. You need to make these visits frequently because gas stations have a high turnover of personnel.

- ✔ **Hosting an open house (see Chapter 5)** and inviting neighbors, local officials, and other local businesses. Not only is this a great way to network, but it also allows others to see your B&B and hospitality in action, so they're comfortable referring guests to you.

Partnering with local businesses can be mutually beneficial. For example, you could create a golf package with a local golf course, secure the freshest produce for your inn by getting to know and ordering from a local grower, or reach out to businesses that have colleagues or customers in need of accommodations.

Reconnecting with old friends

Connecting with old friends can be fun, and it's also a way to build your business. A new innkeeper I know recently attended her college reunion and reconnected with a friend who writes the college newsletter. Through this connection, her bed & breakfast was prominently featured in the newsletter, resulting in many guest bookings.

New innkeepers often wonder about charging friends for staying at their inns. While this is a personal decision, remember your inn is your business. If you're going to give friends rooms that could be taken by paying guests — not to mention working for and serving them — you should charge them. It is also a good idea to convey the importance of letting you know in advance if they can't come so you can make the rooms available for other paying guests. Having the luxury to close the inn to other guests and invite old friends to your inn for a reunion where everyone chips in on the work is another story.

Print Advertising

Seeing your name in print is always good, but the question to ask yourself is, "What's it worth?" No discussion on marketing is complete without a discussion of paid print advertisements. As guests move toward the Internet for instant information and newspaper and magazine circulation plummets, print advertising becomes less and less effective. Having your inn mentioned or featured in a print *article*, on the other hand, is priceless.

Newspapers and magazines: A thing of the past?

Surprisingly, newspaper and magazine advertising in any publication with a large distribution is usually a waste of money. Because inns themselves are not a destination, it's unlikely that someone reading a well-known travel magazine will call you as the result of a small ad placed in the classified section. These ads fail to produce results, and when you combine this with the high cost of even the smallest ads, it rarely makes sense to even experiment.

Local newspapers and publications may be a different story, and the cost is usually low enough to allow experimentation. Many innkeepers find that these publications are not successful in attracting locals; however, placing an ad in a local paper that tourists read may result in guest inquiries. If you're going to experiment with local newspapers, try a paper from a nearby town. Guests who may not take a quick getaway in their own town may consider one 30 to 60 miles away.

If you do experiment with print advertising, have your Webmaster set up a separate URL so you can track the results.

If you're fortunate enough to have your bed & breakfast featured in a published article, you can expect your phone to ring. A mention in an article or a write-up about a special event at your inn will get better results than a paid advertisement. Therefore, when you're holding an open house, be sure to put local editors and journalists on your guest list. (See Chapter 15 for more suggestions on how to get your B&B featured by travel writers and the media.)

Getting into guidebooks

Don't write off the guidebooks yet! While online Internet directories have replaced guidebooks in popularity, savvy innkeepers still seek out listings in the top guidebooks. Sometimes you're lucky enough to get a call from an editor creating or updating a guidebook who wants to include your B&B. Because such editors often contact the local chamber of commerce or convention and visitors bureau for recommendations, your networking and friendships there could get you a referral for inclusion. However, don't sit back and wait for the top guidebooks to find you. Here are some tips for submitting your info to them:

- ✔ **Frommer's:** Frommer's accepts submissions by e-mail from their Web site at `www.frommers.com` (click on FAQ at the bottom of the home page).

- ✔ **Fodor's:** Fodor's accepts submissions by e-mail from their Web site at `www.fodors.com` (click on About Us at the bottom of the home page, and then select Contact Us from the menu on the left-hand side of the resulting page).

- ✔ **Mobil Travel Guide:** Mobil Travel Guide covers many areas, and if your B&B is in an area they cover, you could receive a surprise knock at your door for an immediate inspection. If they don't come to you and you'd like your inn to be considered, you can fill out an application (which includes a fee). Information can be found on their Web site at `www.mobiletravelguide.howstuffworks.com` (click on About Star Ratings).

- ✔ **AAA:** AAA has an application process and fees. Before filing the application, make sure your B&B meets the basic guidelines for inspected properties. The guidelines and application can be found at `www.aaa.biz/approved` (click on Evaluations/Ratings).

Don't overlook regional and niche guides! (See Chapter 15 for tips on niche marketing).

Visit a large bookstore or search online for bed & breakfast guidebooks that your inn would be a good fit with. Contact the publisher and ask them for their submission policies.

Utilizing the Yellow Pages

Simply having a business phone line with AT&T entitles your B&B to a courtesy listing in the local print edition of their _Yellow Pages_. As with everything, take advantage of anything you're entitled to. If your business line is with another carrier, you can pay to be listed. (Some inns try it for a year because results are easy to track; guests know if they found you in the phone book.) Yellowpages.com requires a separate fee for advertising. Contact information can be found for both print and online ads at `www.yellowpages.com`.

Evaluating rack cards and brochures

Is less more? Brochures look wonderful and contain lots of space for photos and information, but their cost can be prohibitive. Rack cards are less expensive to produce, but have about 70 percent less space for photos and text. There are pros and cons to both methods of advertising, and, of course, some innkeepers choose to use both brochures and rack cards. When deciding what's best for your inn, ask yourself the following questions:

- ✔ **Do you have enough professional images and well-written copy for a brochure?** If not, rack cards are the better choice. Having a rack card with one or two perfect images is much smarter than having a brochure with 8 or 10 mediocre images.

- ✔ **Is the view at your inn simply stunning, and a big part of your image?** If so, creating a brochure that opens up to an oversize photo of your view is the way to go.

- ✔ **How do your guests find you?** Ask them, and keep track of their responses. Many inns report that they religiously place rack cards (or brochures) at the local visitors center, but doing so rarely results in bookings. However, rack cards left in the guest rooms or on their information table are taken and given to friends.

Make sure that whatever you choose conveys the brand of your inn. Your rack card and/or brochure should match your Web site and other marketing materials in look, feel, tone, and color. Rack cards should be printed on quality card stock so they stand up well in display racks. And both rack cards and brochures should fit in a standard, #10 envelope for ease of mailing.

Chapter 9

Furnishing Your Inn

If you're like many innkeepers, you've fantasized about how you're going to furnish your B&B and you're thinking, "Now comes one of the fun parts!" Everyone enjoys certain aspects of their job more than others, so it's okay if furnishing is one of your favorite parts of getting your inn ready for guests. It's important to remember, though, that the furnishings you choose determine the comfort of your guests, the image of your inn, and even the price you can charge for your rooms. Practical, comfortable, sensible, appealing, inviting, and durable are all furnishing buzzwords in this chapter, and you should keep them in mind as you shop.

This chapter guides you in choosing a décor that defines your inn's personality and shapes your guests' experiences. You find out what to include when furnishing your inn and also the important considerations to make when furnishing your own private accommodations. I tell you what practical and legal considerations to make regarding furnishings, and then you get to put all this information to work so your guests can't help but say "Wow!" as they enter your inn.

Periodically stay at your inn as a guest. Pack a suitcase, and spread out everything as a guest would. This is the best way to check for any amenities that you think you should add; find out if anything is missing, broken, or uncomfortable; determine whether you're providing guests with adequate space; and assess the lighting and level of darkness in the guest rooms at night. When friends or family stay at the inn, take advantage of a fresh set of eyes and ask them to provide you with a critical review of their stay.

Decorating Your Inn: Choosing Practical but Tasteful Décor

It's often said that the little things in life count and add up to something sensational, and this concept applies to each choice you make in choosing the furnishings for your inn. The detail and thought you put into your choices add up to a sensational guest experience. As you go through the process of choosing the décor for your inn, keep the following things in mind:

- ✔ **Guests choose your inn over a hotel, so they don't want a sterile, cookie-cutter hotel guest room experience.**

- ✔ **Don't be afraid to get help if you need it.** If you really don't think you have what it takes to pick out the furnishings for your rooms, consider talking to a design consultant. Get recommendations and be clear about your decorating budget. It doesn't cost anything to talk to a designer until you hire him. Designers usually can buy things at a lower price than you can, so hiring one may not cost you much more than doing the job yourself.

- ✔ **Don't be afraid to ask for advice from other innkeepers whose styles you like.** They'll be flattered as long as you don't copy anything exactly without their permission.

- ✔ **Make sure your furnishings fit the look and feel of your B&B and its surroundings.** Before choosing furnishings and accessories, evaluate your market, define your inn's personality and theme, and set aside your personal taste. For example, a Southwestern look and feel isn't a good match for a historic Victorian B&B, and a mountain ranch inn should have different furnishings than a gourmet inn in wine country.

- ✔ **Use color to accent your rooms and complement the personality of your inn.** For example, beautiful earth tones complement the splendid wilderness setting at The Prairie Creek Inn in Alberta, Canada (www.theprairiecreekinn.com), and bold, vivid colors accentuate the Southwestern motif at the Chocolate Turtle in Corrales, New Mexico, (www.chocolateturtlebb.com).

- ✔ **Initial perception and presentation prevail.** If guests think your rooms are tastefully decorated and they have a good first impression of your inn, the rest of their experiences will usually start out positive. Studies have shown guests with positive first impressions are more satisfied customers and often overlook little things (such as an errant dust bunny or stray hair on the bathroom floor).

Walk through every inch of your inn just as a guest would, and make notes of what you want the guest to see and feel at each turn. Follow the guest's typical route from entering the inn to seeing a room, to relaxing in the common areas, to strolling any outdoor space, and finally to enjoying the breakfast area. Does each furnished area convey the look, feel, and perception that you want guests to have about your inn, and do the areas come together as a whole?

Creating Comfortable Guest Rooms

Welcoming, comfortable, well-appointed guest rooms turn a happy guest into a repeat guest who refers others to your inn. The décor that achieves this mix is different at every inn and may even be different in each of the rooms at your own inn. For example, you may have a few pet-friendly rooms with less fancy appointments than the rooms booked by guests on a romantic getaway; similarly, rooms that accommodate children shouldn't contain precious and breakable antiques.

Don't put anything in your rooms that you can't bear to part with if it gets broken or goes missing.

Key factors that influence the décor of your guest rooms in particular include

- ✔ **The price of your guest rooms.** Guests expect more expensive guest rooms to be larger with bigger beds and bathrooms and to have more luxurious amenities.

- ✔ **The purpose of your guests' visits.** Tourists, vacationers, honeymooners, business travelers, and other categories of guests have different needs. For example, business travelers need a table or desk large enough for a laptop and space to spread out their papers.

This section helps you manage all decorative elements of your guest rooms, from general amenities and guidelines to beds, furnishings, and lighting.

Offering the most requested guest room amenities

Amenities are a big part of what separates the bed & breakfast experience from a typical hotel stay because you, the innkeeper and host, choose the amenities carefully and personally based on your guests needs and the experience you're creating for them.

The amenities that you offer in guest rooms should fit the style and mood of your inn, support the price of your rooms, and create a desirable impression of your inn with guests. The more popular a feature or amenity, the more guests are willing to pay for it, and rooms with these amenities are often the first ones booked. While there are thousands of different extras offered by B&Bs, some popular and requested guest room amenities and features are

- ✔ Private bathroom
- ✔ Whirlpool tub or soaker tub (room for two is best)
- ✔ Fireplace
- ✔ Wireless Internet access
- ✔ Bottled water or water carafe
- ✔ Robes and slippers
- ✔ Ice bucket and glassware
- ✔ Luggage racks (two per room)
- ✔ Flowers
- ✔ Alarm clock (perhaps with a combined MP3 player and CD player)
- ✔ Magazines
- ✔ Stationery
- ✔ Docking station for MP3 players
- ✔ Iron and ironing board
- ✔ Turndown chocolates
- ✔ TV
- ✔ In-room coffee maker

In reality, guests rarely use telephones in their rooms or in the common area but before deciding not to have them you should consider the following:

- ✔ **Incoming guest calls:** Typically leisure travelers don't receive many calls but your business travelers might, and you need to decide how to handle messages and incoming calls. Remember, they will tie up your business line when friends, family, and colleagues call the inn directly, unless the inn has an incoming guest telephone line.

- ✔ **Cellphone coverage:** If your area has poor cellphone reception, you should have in-room phones or a phone in the common area for guests to use. Also, international travelers frequently don't have cellphone coverage while traveling.

- ✔ **Wake up calls:** If you plan to offer wake-up service, you need to have in-room phones to perform this service.

- ✔ **Emergencies:** If your system for guests to reach you after hours is by phone, you need to provide them with a phone to call you (either in their room or in the hallway).

Before picking amenities, create a budget and stick to it. Your guest rooms are a main feature of your B&B, and it's easy to go overboard and overspend in your desire to provide the guest with a fabulous experience. You can start with the basics and add items as you go along. Make sure you've budgeted for all required code work and renovations before you shop for extra nice-to-have features.

General guest room décor

You can scour decorating magazines to find out what styles are in and out for your guest rooms, but many professional designers recommend sticking to classic looks, which are always in style. Use trends sparingly to keep the room from looking dated too soon. Also, steer clear of wallpaper borders, dried flowers, knickknacks, faux finishes, and frilly window valances. Many people persist in decorating with these things, but the look tends to be dated.

Even if they fit the theme and personality of your B&B, don't overdo the use of antiques and Victorian furniture and accessories in guest rooms, which shouldn't feel like museums. The look can be busy, heavy, and fussy in a space that should be comfortable and restful.

Here are some tips on handling two significant elements of guest rooms:

- **Artwork:** If possible, display good-quality artwork — it doesn't necessarily have to be original art (if it's a special piece, make sure it can't be easily removed). Also consider the scale of artwork in the room: One or two larger pieces have much more impact and appeal than a lot of smaller, less expensive artwork (avoid small flowery prints in general). Many people make the mistake of hanging their artwork too high or placing a small, framed picture on a large wall or above the bed. Again, the scale and placement of art must balance with the setting.

- **Accessories:** A few well-chosen accessories are the key to making your rooms unique. The accessories you choose should add interest and color and accentuate the theme of the room or inn. For example, an interesting vase with flowers (choose pottery, china, or glass to fit your room décor), a coffee table book of the area, a tray or platter, and so on.

Don't go overboard with accessories. Too many accessories appear cluttered, and too much of a theme can look kitschy. Also, steer clear of shiny gold metal on picture frames, lamps, and other accessories; brushed or polished silver and bronze give things a newer look.

Consider your male guests when decorating guest rooms. Many men (especially business travelers) don't feel particularly comfortable in rooms that are overly feminine. They prefer more neutral decorating styles with a polished, professional look.

Making your beds

The bed is the focal point of the guest room and should make a statement by always being meticulously made. Hospital corners are the standard for making a bed. At the very least, each guest room should have the following bed-related items to ensure your guests get a good night's sleep:

- ✔ **A good quality mattress made for lodging:** A mattress made for the lodging industry has a built-up edge spring to account for guests sitting on the edge of the bed. The mattress should be medium to firm (definitely not too soft or too hard), and it should feel lush with a solid foundation. Try out mattresses before buying, and ask for referrals from other innkeepers about which mattresses their guests like. (Turn to Chapter 1 for information on innkeeper forums and resources.)

    Consider setting up an account with the lodging department of a mattress company and buying your mattresses wholesale. You usually save up to 50 percent of the purchase price, with delivery included.

- ✔ **A waterproof mattress cover:** The best choice is a zippered one that encases the mattress entirely.

- ✔ **A cover for the box spring:** A bare box spring is unsightly and easily concealed. A bed skirt that coordinates with the linens does the job, or you can use a fitted sheet if you have a bed frame that you prefer to leave exposed.

- ✔ **Three sets of sheets and pillowcases for each bed:** You need one set for the bed, one for the laundry, and one for the closet. I get into the specifics of bed linen quality later in this section.

- ✔ **At least four pillows (two soft and two firm) per bed:** Offering both soft and firm bed pillows accounts for guest preferences.

- ✔ **Pillow protectors:** This extra casing helps to protect your pillows from dust mites and allergens. (See www.innstyle.com for a selection.) Some are also waterproof.

- ✔ **A headboard:** The size of the headboard should be in balance with the bed, and proportionate to the size to the room. Headboards must be securely fastened to prevent wobbling as well as comfortable when guests prop themselves up in bed.

Consider the placement of the bed in the room. Set it up not only where it looks best when guests enter the room but also where it gives guests the best view in the room when they're laying in bed. Also be sure not to place the bed where it blocks an air-conditioning or heating unit or where these may blow directly on the guests while they're sleeping.

When you know what you must have regarding a guest bed, you can move on to making your selections and considering what, if any, luxuries you can afford. Keep in mind that many innkeepers start out with the essentials and add luxuries such as down comforters or higher-quality linens after they've been up and running for a while. The following points help guide your bed and linen decisions.

- ✔ **Bed size:** Even though you should definitely consider the size of the room when selecting a bed, king- and queen-size beds are by far the most popular.

  Two twin beds that can be made into a king bed allow you the extra flexibility of creating a room with two beds. To do this, you must have two extra-long twin beds and use a mattress connecting kit. Innstyle (www.innstyle.com) offers a Create-a-King kit that works well.

  King beds come in two sizes: A standard king bed is 76 inches wide by 80 inches long, and a California king is 72 inches wide by 84 inches long. Bed linen choices are limited for California king beds, so get one only if it's the only way to fit a king bed in the room.

- ✔ **Size and design of bed linens:** Before purchasing bed linens, make sure they will fit your mattress. Some pillow-top mattresses are thicker and may require special bedding (particularly fitted bed sheets). As for comforters and duvet covers, some manufacturers don't take into account the added thickness of pillow-top mattresses, so look for oversized queen or king duvet covers and comforters so that the sides of your bedding aren't visible when guests walk in the room.

  Choose bed coverings not only for their design but also their feel, durability, and washability. Soft, textured fabrics create a warm, cozy feel, whereas smooth, satiny fabrics produce a cooler sensation. You want the bed coverings to look coordinated, but don't overdo it. Steer away from a bed-in-a-bag, in which you get a lot of pieces that all match — even window treatments! A few shams, decorative pillows, and/or bolsters are a nice luxurious touch and help to provide accents in the room; however, keep in mind that too many can crowd the bed and usually end up on the floor.

- ✔ **Quality of bed linens:** Bed linens can have a significant impact on the quality of a guest's experience; the higher your room price, the more luxurious your sheets should feel. White, 100-percent-cotton sheets are the most common. Fine linens begin with fine cotton and linen quality is based on thread count (the number of threads per square inch) and the length of the fibers. The minimum thread count that you should consider is 300. Egyptian and Pima cotton plants grow the longest fibers, so these sheets with high thread counts are considered the best quality. In addition to selecting sheets made with high-quality cotton, you need to consider the feel. Cotton sateen sheets are softer than those with a crisp, classic linen weave.

✔ **Down (feather) comforter:** This is definitely a luxury item because of the cost, but you're likely to find a deal if you look hard enough. The higher the percentage of down, the lighter and warmer the comforter is. Protect your investment with a washable comforter cover called a *duvet*; it's like a big pillowcase for the comforter, and you can get duvets in all sorts of colors and patterns — just like other bed coverings.

Some guests may be allergic to down, so you should have several comforters in a down alternative, which look and feel like the real thing. Having a few sets (depending on the size of your inn) of hypo-allergenic pillows and down-alternative comforters on hand is recommended. Your reservation procedures should include asking guests about allergies (and not just food allergies) so that you can be prepared. Some inns make all their beds with down-alternative products just to be safe.

Always have extra blankets, duvets, comforters, pillow protectors, mattress covers, and pillows on hand in case of accidents or last-minute housekeeping needs. One set of extras per room is an investment you'll be thankful for.

Finding functional furnishings

The furniture in your guest rooms must not only look good and fit your overall décor, but it also must be comfortable, functional, and sturdy.

An ideal guest room has

✔ A bedside table on each side of the bed.

✔ Reading lamps on the bedside tables (see the next section for more on guest room lighting).

✔ Ample closet space with hangers and/or a dresser or wardrobe.

✔ Two chairs and a table.

✔ A desk, table or workspace if you're catering to business travelers. Finding tasteful but functional guest room desks that fit your décor can be a challenge. The key is to achieve a balance between appearance and functionality. For example, a guest may have trouble spreading out work papers and using a laptop on a Victorian roll-top desk.

When deciding on guest room furnishings, check for minimum requirements of rating and inspection agencies. For example, most require each guest room to have a nightstand or equivalent by each bed. Also, stop and think about whether your future goal is to obtain a AAA four- or five-diamond or other rating, such as Canada Select, membership in Select Registry, or a state association. All rating agencies have published guidelines. Perform a Web search to find their contact information and request an application and a list of their inspection and rating requirements for furnishings, lighting, and so on.

Your guest room furniture choices are determined by your target market, your budget, and the size and price of your rooms. Furnishing guest rooms is an ongoing process for most inns, and it's important to remember that something doesn't have to be expensive to look good.

Getting the lighting just right

Lighting can make a room, and a well-lit guest room makes the best first impression. Inadequate guest room lighting is an issue that many guests complain about, so it's best to over-light a room with plenty of lamps and overhead light fixtures than to under-light it. Each room should contain general lighting (an overhead fixture), task lighting (table and desk lamps), and mood lighting (small lamps or any other type of lighting) to create ambiance. Bedside lamps can be attached to the wall if space is limited, and must provide at least 60-watt lighting. They should be of a size that creates balance with the bed and bedside table and be at a comfortable height for reading in bed.

Candles in guest rooms can be a fire hazard and violate most insurance policies. (Check with your insurance company for specifics.) A great alternative to this kind of mood lighting is attractive battery-operated candles. A variety of these flameless candles is on the market. Type "battery-operated candle" into your favorite Internet search engine if you're not familiar with them.

Equally as important to adequate lighting is darkness to ensure a restful sleep. Whatever you use as window treatments should keep the light out. For example, draperies should be lined and to the floor. If guests are meant to pull them closed at night, they should be on rings or a mechanism that's easily drawn.

Planning Great Bathrooms

Many people overlook bathrooms as a great place to wow guests. After all, guests spend a fair amount of time in their bathrooms. The amenities, furnishings, and décor of your guest bathrooms go a long way toward making guests feel pampered at your inn.

Traditionally, B&Bs offer three types of bathroom settings: private in-room bathrooms, private baths (reserved just for one room) in the hallway, and shared bathrooms. Guests strongly prefer rooms with private in-room baths, and this is the most popular arrangement.

Stocking bathroom amenities

You have some flexibility in the presentation of your guest bathrooms, but some amenities are simply necessities. Following are the most common bathroom must-haves:

- Cotton balls and swabs: Consider presentation in attractive, covered glassware, baskets, or antique containers
- Tissues
- Mouthwash
- Soap and/or bath gel
- Makeup-remover pads
- Lotion
- Shampoo and conditioner
- Shower cap
- Hairdryer
- Individually wrapped rolls of quality two-ply toilet paper
- At least two bath towels, one hand towel, and one washcloth per guest
- Bathmat
- At least two sterilized drinking glasses in each bathroom

Many innkeepers place the clean glasses upside down on nice paper doilies instead of wrapping them in paper wrappers that have an industrial, hotel look.

Bathroom furnishings and décor

Avoid look-alike bathrooms. Instead, when possible, match the décor of your bathrooms to your rooms (which I assume will all look different). Let the expression of your room's personality extend into your bathrooms by using pictures or accessories in the same theme as the room.

Here are some guidelines and recommendations for bathroom furnishings and décor that not only make great impressions on your guests but also, in some cases, help you maintain clean, quality bathrooms in your inn:

- **Provide adequate lighting for shaving and applying makeup.**
- **Install large mirrors and makeup mirrors in the bathroom.** An added bonus is that large mirrors help create the illusion of a bigger bathroom.

✔ **Offer the most plush, absorbent towels your budget can afford.**

The towel color is up to you. However, white is considered luxurious. It's also the easiest to maintain because you can bleach white towels when needed. If you choose other colors, beware of laundry issues such as fading and spotting. (I discuss laundry and other cleaning concerns in Chapter 13.)

Avoid makeup stains on your towels by offering makeup remover pads or by placing dark-colored washcloths in bathrooms. The Inn at Riverbend (www.innatriverbend.com) in Pearisburg, Virginia, has had the word "Makeup" attractively embroidered on dark washcloths that compliment the color schemes of its bathrooms. Housekeeping staff places the washcloths on top of the towels, letting guests know not to use the white towels for makeup removal.

✔ **Provide adequate hooks for guests to hang their towels on.**

✔ **Stock each bathroom with an amenities basket with common toiletry items guests may have forgotten,** such as a toothbrush, toothpaste, disposable razor, and the like.

You'll quickly find out whether the bathroom amenities basket works for your clientele and is appreciated or if guests simply take the items with them. If you find that guests take advantage of complimentary toiletries in the bathroom, you can opt to keep the items on hand and let guests know during their welcome tour that you have some of the most frequently forgotten items if they're needed.

✔ **Use double-sided bath rugs and flip them over to cut washing in half.** However, you must balance this convenience with safety; to prevent slipping, you may need to use mats with rubber backing. Unfortunately, rubber-backed mats need to be replaced more often than double-sided ones because the rubber wears off with frequent washings.

✔ **Protect guests from slipping in the tub by providing rubber tub mats or applying grip strips to the tub.**

Bradford Place Inn and Gardens (www.bradfordplaceinn.com) in Sonora, California, creates a nice presentation by rolling up white bubble tub mats and tying them with raffia. Tub mats are placed so that, if guests choose not to use the mats, they must move them in order to get into showers or tubs. The mats are sprayed with a bleach cleaner, then rinsed and air-dried.

✔ **Install anti-scald valves on all guest showers.**

If you're not able to offer in-room bathrooms, in addition to offering clean bathrobes and slippers in guest rooms, prepare a basket with personal items that guests can easily carry to the bathroom. Be sure to leave room in the basket so they can add some of their own toiletries.

Considerations for bathrooms under construction

If you're in the planning stage of your bed & breakfast and are either constructing bathrooms or simply renovating them, consider these tips for creating fabulous bathrooms:

- **Flooring:** Pick a color or design that doesn't show every little hair. If you choose a tile floor, choose a good-quality, non-porous tile with an interesting but classic design. Lighter, neutral colors stand the test of time and match almost any décor.

  Larger tiles mean less grout to keep clean. And textured tiles help keep bath rugs and guests from skidding, although they may be harder to keep clean.

  You may also want to consider linoleum for flooring material, because it's softer and warmer than tile, and if a guest drops something breakable, the item isn't likely to break on linoleum.

- **Tubs:** Double whirlpool tubs (either in guest rooms or in bathrooms) are the most requested amenities, but soaker tubs without the water movement are becoming a popular, quieter, and more sanitary alternative. Many come in double sizes that appeal to the romantic getaway market.

  To be greener, choose compact model tubs that use less water.

  Whirlpool tubs are popular with guests, but they're not right for every inn. Consider the type of guest you're trying to attract, and then get advice from innkeepers with similar inns and weigh the decision for yourself. You need to consider that they do have the potential to cause a lot of plumbing and leaking problems. They also can be noisy, so locate them accordingly and plan for extra insulation in and around the tubs and in the walls to avoid disturbing other guests in the rooms below or next door. When shopping for whirlpool tubs, check with other innkeepers in the innkeeper forums (see Chapter 1 for help in finding an innkeeper forum) about the different types of tubs, some of which are easier to clean than others. If you opt for whirlpool tubs, read the manufacturer's instructions to find out what products are safe for the tubs (such as bath oils), and set your policies accordingly. Also follow the manufacturer's instructions for cleaning and maintenance of the tubs, and check with your health department for specific cleaning standards that you must follow.

- **Fixtures:** Avoid ordinary-looking fixtures. Selecting interesting fixtures, possibly even something dramatic, depending on the size of the bathroom, is an inexpensive way to dress up the appearance of your bathrooms.

Select the same style of faucets, showerheads, toilets, doorknobs, locks, toilet seats, emergency lighting, smoke detectors, and other smaller hardware and accessories. If you can't get multiples of the same item, opt for similar styles because consistency lets you stockpile repair and replacement parts and supplies.

✔ **Vanities:** If you use lovely pedestal-style sinks in your guest rooms, you have to provide other shelf space for the guests' use. Remember, guests need countertop space for their cosmetic and toiletry bags; a minimum 4-foot space is recommended for vanities or alternate counter space in the case of pedestal sinks.

Making Guests at Home in Common Areas

Creating an inviting and comfortable place for your guests to gather or relax on their own is a distinguishing feature that bed & breakfasts offer over traditional hotels. For many guests, it's one of the nice extras that compel them to choose your inn again or become devoted B&B travelers. Your common areas are the places to let your hospitality skills shine by anticipating guest needs and wants. Choose the furnishings and amenities accordingly. For example, if your inn is in a remote area where guests come to relax, unplug, and get away, think carefully before putting a flat screen TV in your common area. Additionally, consider whether guests even want to watch TV together, given their different preferences.

Your common areas may also include dining areas, particularly if your inn is smaller and you need to take advantage of the extra space. For example, you may encourage guests to enjoy card games or board games at the cleared dining table. You can find out more about setting up dining areas (particularly the breakfast setting) in Chapter 10.

Your service, architecture, and décor are the most distinguishing features of your B&B, so choose amenities and furnishings that fit with these features and contribute to the personality and experience you're trying to create for your guests. Here are some tips for furnishing your common areas:

✔ **Consider the purpose of each room or outdoor space.** Choose durable furnishings that look inviting yet fit the ambiance of the area.

✔ **Arrange furniture groupings based on your target market.** Furniture can be placed to encourage either group interaction or more private settings.

✔ **Provide adequate lighting with overhead fixtures and individual lamps.** Lighting should reflect the time of day: brighter during the day and more subdued at night when you want the space to look more calming and relaxing. Be sure outdoor areas that are used by guests in the evening are adequately lit and provide umbrellas or awnings so that they are properly shaded during the day.

✔ **Keep a fire going to add warmth (both literally and figuratively) to a common space if you have a fireplace.** Of course, whether or not you use a fireplace depends on your location and the time of year.

✔ **Stock up on cards and board games, and set out up-to-date magazines and newspapers.**

✔ **Start with a phone in the common area if you don't provide phones in the guest rooms.** (See the earlier section, "Offering the most requested amenities," for help in deciding about telephones in guest rooms.) After you've been open for a short time, you can assess your guests' telephone needs and add in-room phones or remove the one in the common area accordingly.

✔ **Offer complimentary refreshments.** Guests appreciate hot and cold beverages and snacks available 24 hours a day. Afternoon refreshments, after-dinner drinks, and/or desserts are also common offerings at B&Bs, and they encourage social interaction between your guests in common spaces.

Research local liquor laws and licensing requirements when deciding what to serve.

✔ **Offer your guests the use of a microwave and a small guest refrigerator in a common area.** This discourages them from asking to use yours and alleviates the mess of cooking and eating in guest rooms (which many innkeepers discourage). Guests often enjoy a place to heat up snacks or light meals and a place to keep beverages cold. These common area amenities are particularly helpful if there are limited eating establishments nearby or if guests stay for more than a few days at a time.

✔ **Create a lending library for guests to borrow and recycle books.** You may want to invite guests to take a book and leave a book. Begin your collection with your own books and build it by visiting public library sales and used book stores.

✔ **Establish a video/DVD library if you have VCR or DVD players for guests to watch movies in their rooms.**

✔ **Display maps and local brochures, and keep plenty of copies on hand for guests.**

✔ **Create and display a book of menus from nearby restaurants.**

Only include restaurants that you've been to or that other guests have recommended. Sharing the menus with guests serves as an indirect, but still personal, recommendation and factors into guests' experiences at your inn.

✔ **Make wireless Internet access available throughout the inn (including in guest rooms), but if possible, set up at least one guest computer with Internet access in your common area.**

✔ **Install umbrellas to add a nice touch.** They not only provide comfort but they also give an upscale first impression to arriving guests. Solid colored umbrellas seem more high-end than patterned ones.

Safety Considerations

As an innkeeper, making your bed & breakfast safe for all guests is a primary and ongoing concern. Some precautions taken to keep guests safe and comfortable are practical considerations such as adequate lighting, tucked-away cords, nailed-down floorboards, sturdy railings, and so on, and others are mandated by law. Your goal should be to know fire, health, and zoning requirements even better than the inspectors so that you can provide comfortable and safe accommodations for your guests and avoid hassles and headaches when the inspectors come calling.

In addition to meeting local ordinances, be familiar with your insurance policies and their safety requirements in order to be sure you're covered in the event a guest is injured at your inn. (Chapter 3 has information on protecting your business with insurance.)

This section explores safety elements with regard to lighting and posting notices for guests.

Proper lighting

Even seemingly safe areas can be dangerous if they're poorly lit. Proper lighting not only shows your inn in a better light (no pun intended), but it also keeps your guests safe.

Assess the practicality of your lighting. Conduct thorough walk-throughs of your inn at all hours of the day and night to check lighting. For safety, you should answer "yes" to all the following questions regarding safe lighting:

✔ Do each guest room and each bathroom have a nightlight?

✔ Is there adequate lighting for guests who are coming and going late at night and for those who depart early in the morning (before sunrise)?

✔ Do guests using hall bathrooms during the night have enough light to safely find them?

✔ Are electric cords to table and floor lamps neatly coiled and out of the way?

✔ Are light switches easy to find in guest rooms?

Point out light switches during your walk-through with guests when they check in.

✔ If you offer 24-hour snacks, is there adequate lighting for guests to safely get to them?

✔ If you have an outdoor area that guests can enjoy in the evening, are the path to it and the space itself adequately lit?

It's important to know and follow local ordinances and requirements regarding lighting in your inn. Contact your city hall to see which agency is responsible for your licensing. It may be the fire department, the board of health, the zoning board, or some combination. Also check for additional state or federal requirements.

Certain lighting is required to obtain your certificate of occupancy, and lighting requirements may be determined by square footage of your rooms. Also, emergency lighting may be required in guest rooms, hallways, staircases, and at exits.

Required notices

Many required notices definitely don't fit in with the look and feel of the bed & breakfast environment. Putting up a big red EXIT sign may conflict with your decorating plans, but complying with the law and keeping guests safe is a necessary part of the business — and it makes guests feel that the inn takes their safety seriously. In addition to lighted exit signs, fire extinguishers need to be clearly visible — check with your local fire inspector for requirements in your area.

In many areas, you're required to post a map of exits on the backs of guest room doors. You can soften the look slightly by putting these in attractive frames that hang on the backs of the doors.

Shopping for Your Inn

As you get ready to make the purchases you've planned for, I caution you to keep your budget in mind and encourage you to consult other innkeepers so that you can learn from their experiences.

Finding suppliers who understand the needs of B&Bs

Numerous suppliers specifically cater to the bed & breakfast industry. They understand the needs of your guests and the size of your orders, and they make a conscious effort to support you, the innkeeper, as their customer.

Don't overlook the value of a great deal by shopping in discount stores and bargain hunting. However, sometimes it makes sense to buy from vendors who understand and support the industry. Following are some ways to find industry vendors who are knowledgeable about your needs:

- ✔ Ask your local and state B&B associations for a list of vendors who may offer a discount to members of your association.

- ✔ Consult the list provided by the Professional Association of Innkeepers International at www.paii.org: Click Resources, then Vendor Marketplace, and then select a vendor category. If you're a member of the association, be sure to ask for the PAII (pronounced "pie") discount if you purchase from any of the vendors listed on the site.

- ✔ Ask other innkeepers and search industry forums (see Chapter 1 for information on finding these forums) for information on vendors that other innkeepers have ordered from.

Creating your shopping list for appliances, furniture, and supplies

It's important to distinguish your shopping list from your wish list in order to stay on budget (see Chapter 3 for help in budgeting for purchases). It's okay to maintain a wish list, but be realistic about when and which furnishing purchases make sense based on the plan you created for your business. Your shopping list should include priority appliances and furniture that make your life easier and the guest experience better as well as essential supplies to have on hand. Keep an ongoing shopping list (and a separate wish list) to write down things as you think of them, not just in the planning process but also in the day-to-day operation of your B&B.

Choosing appliances that make your life easier

When choosing appliances for your bed & breakfast,

- ✔ Choose good-quality, easy-to-use appliances that will stand up to constant use (more use than in a typical household). Paying more for quality pays off in the long run.
- ✔ Choose appliances that are quiet so there's less disturbance to guests.

Following is a list of many common appliances in B&Bs — some more common than others. Note that some of the appliances listed, such as warming drawers and convection ovens, are expensive. Only you can determine how important they are to your operation and whether they fit into your budget.

- ✔ Blender
- ✔ Bread maker
- ✔ Coffee grinder
- ✔ Coffee maker
- ✔ Convection oven
- ✔ Corkscrew(s)
- ✔ Electric can opener
- ✔ Electric mixer
- ✔ Electric skillet
- ✔ Electric water kettle
- ✔ Fans
- ✔ Food processor

- ✔ Freezer
- ✔ Juice extractor
- ✔ Microwave
- ✔ Refrigerator
- ✔ Stove/oven/grill
- ✔ Toaster oven
- ✔ Toaster(s)
- ✔ Waffle iron
- ✔ Warming drawer (for keeping food warm without overcooking it while you're preparing other items)

Consult several of the resources for buying furniture later in this chapter, as these outlets also carry appliances at reasonable prices.

Buying furniture

You can save a great deal of money (and maybe buy more with the money you save) if you're patient and creative about where you shop for furniture. The key considerations when buying furniture for your inn are

- Price
- Quality
- Buying only what fits the look and feel of your inn
- Functionality

Purchase a good selection of quality furniture pieces, particularly wood furniture, sofas, and chairs. You can mix in antiques and used shabby chic finds for a great eclectic look, but you shouldn't rely solely on used and old-looking items if you want a quality B&B that guests will rave about.

No matter the style of your inn, your furniture doesn't have to be expensive to serve its function and make a good impression on guests. Here are some ideas about where to get started:

- **Check local thrift and antique shops.** Stop in often to see what they have, and make friends with the owners and employees, who can be great resources for inside information. I recommend that you stop in when you're looking for something in particular and say, "I'm on the lookout for . . . let me know if you see something."

- **Enter "hotel liquidators" into your favorite Internet search engine, and investigate the results.** These companies handle the liquidation of top-quality hotel furnishings when hotels remodel. If you're lucky, you'll find one within driving distance. Call ahead to inquire about any minimum purchase restrictions so that, for example, you don't have to buy identical mirrors for all your rooms but rather can mix and match pieces.

  No matter how good of a deal you find on furnishings, you should only buy individual pieces that fit the style of your inn. Don't be tempted by a bargain and end up with a corporate, hotel look!

- **Search for items on eBay** (www.ebay.com). You can narrow your search field to items available for pickup in your local area in order to save on shipping if you're looking at large pieces of furniture.

- **Look into Habitat for Humanity ReStores** (search for locations near you at www.habitat.org/env/restores). They sell appliances, furniture, plumbing and electric fixtures, and more quality used and surplus building materials at a fraction of normal prices. Proceeds from ReStores help local affiliates fund the construction of Habitat houses within the community. (I found out about this resource from an innkeeper when I was searching the PAII members' forum — see, it pays off!)

If you scrimp on too many furnishings, your inn will reflect it. Your furniture is a necessary part of your business, and it needs to be viewed as a good investment. Instead, save money on accessories; you can get plenty of less expensive ones that still look great.

Keeping essential supplies on hand

It's impossible to be prepared for everything, but part of the job of innkeeper is anticipating guests' needs and requests. The following list gets you started thinking about additional supplies to have on hand to keep your B&B well-stocked and properly furnished.

- Air freshener
- Batteries
- Cleaning supplies
- Extension cords
- Extra amenities
- First-aid supplies
- Flashlights
- Insect repellant
- Light bulbs
- Memo pads and pens or pencils for guest use
- Scissors
- Sunscreen
- Tape
- Tissues
- Toilet paper
- Toilet plungers

Making the Innkeepers' Quarters Cozy and Private

In setting up your B&B, the bulk of your resources will go to furnishing the areas that guests see and occupy. Despite this, I encourage you to give serious thought to your private quarters. If you're buying a new inn, carefully consider the size and layout of your quarters. If you're already an innkeeper, pull back and reevaluate your quarters. Ask yourself what you can do to make your area better and more comfortable. Perhaps a fresh coat of paint or some new bedding will be the little change that makes a big difference in the feeling you get when you enter your home.

It's also very important that guests know where the inn starts and where it ends and where your personal space begins. In order to communicate this, the boundaries first must be clearly defined in your mind. Natural physical boundaries such as doors that you can lock are a step in the right direction, but oftentimes they're not enough. Here are some ideas to create further separation for your personal space in the kitchen and in your personal quarters:

- **The kitchen:** Your personal space can include the kitchen, where you're likely to spend a fair amount of time prepping and fixing meals. True, some innkeepers enjoy guests visiting the kitchen, but for most it's a distraction and guests are only in the way. Here are some suggestions for keeping the kitchen off-limits to guests:

- **Close the door.** If your kitchen doesn't have a door, install one. A Dutch door is effective at closing off the space but still allowing limited interactions with the innkeeper.

- **Post a sign on the door or explain the restriction to guests.** Many innkeepers simply post a sign that says "Private." Other innkeepers politely tell guests, "The health department doesn't allow guests in the kitchen." Innkeepers who have used the line, "Anyone who comes in the kitchen is put to work" have found it ineffective because many guests don't mind helping.

- **Lock the door from the inside.** A lock on the inside of the kitchen door helps to close the kitchen to guests while you're cooking as well as prevents the refrigerator from being raided by snackers throughout the day and during the night.

✔ **Innkeeper's quarters:** This area is your home, and only those who are invited should enter, but sometimes guests need reminding. Here are some suggestions for drawing the line:

- Use locks on the doors and post a notice or sign that reads "Private Innkeeper's Quarters."

- When practical and tasteful, use shrubbery, fences or gates to create a physical barrier so that guests are prevented from easily encroaching onto your private patio or other outdoor areas that are strictly for you and your family.

- If possible, establish a private entrance to your quarters (as well as access through the inn) so that you can come and go without walking in the common areas of the inn. A secret way of escape allows you to get away from the inn for errands, appointments, and meetings without being seen and stopped by guests — or you can just escape to enjoy an evening out.

Because you'll be spending time in your private quarters, separate from your guests, and away from the inn, make sure that guests know how to reach you. Tell guests when they check in how to reach you (cellphone, private phone number, intercom, and so on) and make sure this information is available to them. Some ways to do this are by making cards for the guest rooms, including the information in a welcome letter or in guest information booklets in their rooms, posting your number beside telephones, and so on.

Put yourself in the mindset of wanting guests to feel comfortable at your B&B — your business — rather than comfortable in your home. This slight distinction can help you separate the business space of the B&B from the personal space of your home.

Chapter 10

Making Breakfast a Memorable Meal

In This Chapter

▶ Creating the perfect breakfast setting

▶ Choosing a breakfast style

▶ Planning and shopping for your breakfasts

▶ Sampling some popular breakfast menus and recipes

The breakfast that you serve your guests is just as important as the bed you provide them. After all, breakfast is half of the bed & breakfast experience! In the B&B world, creating fabulous, memorable breakfasts for your guests is imperative.

In this chapter, I help you pick a breakfast setting and style that fits your inn's image and appeals to the type of guests your inn caters to. I give you tips on menu planning and food preparation, and I share some menus and recipes that are proven guest favorites.

Setting the Breakfast Scene

When your guests tell friends about their stay at your bed & breakfast, no doubt their impressions and memories of the morning meal will be included. Breakfast is an opportunity to let your hospitality shine through by creating a comfortable and inviting breakfast setting. The style of breakfast you choose to serve also influences your guests' experiences. You have several choices with regard to both setting and style.

Creating an appealing breakfast setting

One of the decisions you need to make regarding the breakfast setting is whether you want to offer it only in your inn's dining room or give guests the option of having breakfast privately in their own rooms. In the dining room setting, you need to choose between individual party seating and group seating. Descriptions of these options follow:

- ✔ **Individual party seating:** Many inns offer tables for two which can be easily combined to accommodate groups traveling together. This type of seating is more private than group seating arrangements.

- ✔ **Group seating:** In a group seating arrangement, guests are seated together at one table in the dining room. This type of seating is common at many B&Bs. In fact, for many guests a popular aspect of the bed & breakfast experience is interacting with other interesting people over breakfast. Group seating encourages conversation and provides a more family-like atmosphere.

- ✔ **In-room service:** While some innkeepers offer breakfast in bed, you need to remember that when guests eat in bed, food will be spilled on sheets, blankets, comforters, and pillows. Instead, when designing or decorating your inn, you may want to consider adding space for in-room dining. This usually consists of a seating area with a table and two chairs. Some innkeepers find that in-room service is actually easier on them because once the guests are served, they're taken care of.

Several factors contribute to your setting choices. Consider the following as they apply to your inn:

- ✔ **Space:** The amount of space you have may determine the type of setting you opt for. If your space is limited, you may be confined to a group seating arrangement because one large table requires less space than multiple, individual-party tables.

- ✔ **Inn design:** If your inn has areas that are appropriate for outdoor seating, such as porches or patios, these venues may make comfortable and relaxing settings for breakfast, weather permitting. However, be sure to factor in extra efforts on your part that serving breakfast outside may entail. Things to consider are:

  - • Keeping food warm

  - • Serving guests together

  - • Providing shade for guests

  - • Keeping chairs and tables clean

  - • Finding space for tray stands that don't interfere with normal traffic patterns

- • Being organized to avoid needless trips back and forth for forgotten items if the space is not near the kitchen

✔ **Types of guests:** Your guests' purpose in coming to your inn may determine the type of setting they're likely to enjoy most. For example, couples on a romantic getaway often prefer individual party seating or in-room service to group seating arrangements. Guests traveling on business or those wanting to get a jump-start on the day may prefer to forgo a formal breakfast in favor of an early, quick continental breakfast or in-room service.

Selecting a style of breakfast to offer

According to the Professional Association of Innkeepers International's Industry Study of Operations and Finance, over 70 percent of inns offer a full breakfast with a set menu, but this doesn't mean that *you* have to. You may choose to offer a continental breakfast, breakfast cooked to order, or a buffet instead. You may even decide to vary the style of breakfast you serve: full breakfast on weekends and holidays and a continental breakfast during the week, for example. The choice is up to you — as long as you abide by local zoning laws and make sure your guests know what to expect by describing breakfast on your Web site and in your advertising.

✔ **Continental breakfast:** Innkeepers use a variety of definitions to define continental breakfasts, which can range from a very simple selection of juice, muffins, and coffee to more elaborate offerings such as hot oatmeal, a selection of cereals, pastries, coffees, and teas. Some innkeepers offer a *continental plus,* or *extended continental,* breakfast which includes all the previously named selections and one hot item, such as a tray of French toast. Typically, a continental breakfast would be self-serve, buffet style. Continental breakfast is often preferred by those who want to be up and out early, such as business travelers, skiers, golfers, and so on.

✔ **Full breakfast with a set menu:** This breakfast style allows you the most flexibility to exercise your creativity and presentation skills and offers the added benefit of being adaptable for advance planning and preparation on your part! A full breakfast menu typically consists of a fruit course, a main course, and fresh baked goods along with a selection of coffees, teas, and juices. A variety of cereals, granola, and yogurt are also usually available. Many innkeepers rotate daily between sweet and savory menu themes. On the plus side, guests enjoy the upscale feeling of being served; however, vivacious as well as picky eaters often prefer a bountiful buffet.

✔ **Full breakfast cooked to order:** Some innkeepers give guests a choice of breakfast selections (within reason). For example, a combination of custom-made omelets, various styles of egg preparation, pancakes, French toast, bacon, or sausage are popular choices guests can choose from when ordering. The bigger your inn is and the more guests you need to serve at once, the more difficult this becomes.

- **Buffet:** Breakfast buffets can be as simple as the continental breakfast previously described or elaborate spreads with several entrée choices. Offering breakfast buffet-style makes it easier to offer guests flexible breakfast times; however, see cost and space considerations later in this chapter.

- **Cook your own breakfast:** Some properties offer a cook-your-own breakfast where the innkeeper provides kitchen facilities and the ingredients for breakfast. These properties are generally vacation rentals and are not usually considered bed & breakfasts. It is not uncommon, however, for a B&B to offer a variety of accommodations, for example, B&B rooms inside the main house where the innkeeper prepares and serves breakfast and cabins or cottages on the grounds where guests can prepare their own breakfast as well as other meals.

Before you decide what style of breakfast to serve, know your guests. Ask yourself why guests are visiting your inn. Are guests primarily coming to your inn for business purposes, for an active vacation, for sightseeing, or for a relaxing getaway? Are they coming for a romantic getaway or will they want to chat with you and other guests? The answers to these questions will help you to pick the style that best suits your guests. Those who need to get up and out prefer continental and early buffet breakfasts, while guests looking for relaxation savor the feeling of being served. When romance is in the air, individual seating is preferred, whereas guests who enjoy meeting other guests prefer group seating arrangements. Here are some other things to keep in mind when choosing the type and style of breakfast to serve to your guests:

- **Zoning and health department codes:** Some areas prohibit cooking for guests and only a continental breakfast of prepared foods may be served. Local innkeepers are usually knowledgeable on zoning regulations; however, you shouldn't rely on them. Check with city hall for direction. You'll usually be dealing with a zoning or planning board along with the local health department. You'll also need to check for state conformance policies, although zoning issues are normally handled at the local level.

- **Space:** Guests' comfort and safety play a major role in determining your breakfast setting. Guests must have enough room to move around. For example, maneuvering a buffet may be difficult in smaller spaces. You don't want your guests squeezing between tables and pieces of furniture to get to and around the buffet.

- **Room rates:** Generally, the higher your room rates are, the more elaborate of a breakfast your guests will expect.

- **Cost:** Naturally, the more food you prepare the greater the cost. For example, when serving a buffet breakfast, you need to prepare a sufficient amount of every item to ensure that guests who take generous servings leave enough for your other guests. Leftovers, however, are typically wasted, and this is something you don't have much control over. With a plated breakfast, you control the serving sizes.

Designating breakfast times

There is no right or wrong time to serve breakfast to your guests. The only rule is to designate the time (or times) when breakfast will be served, so that you can prepare accordingly and your guests know what to expect. Figuring out breakfast times is a blend between what works for you and what your typical guests want. Here are some popular choices:

✔ **A set breakfast time:** If you plan to serve a sit-down, plated breakfast, one set breakfast time usually works best. Typically, innkeepers pick a set time to serve breakfast between 8:30 a.m. and 10 a.m. At check-in they remind guests that breakfast will be served in the dining room at 9 a.m., for example. Be sure to allow enough time between breakfast and check-out.

✔ **A flexible breakfast time:** You may decide to offer guests a flexible time period during which to have breakfast (for example, between 8:30 and 9:30 a.m. or 9 and 10 a.m., again, being mindful of your check-out time). This creates more work for you, but some innkeepers find that this flexibility distinguishes their inn from other B&Bs in the area.

If you want to give guests a choice of breakfast times, consider limiting your menu to a few choices that you serve on a daily basis. Bradford Place Inn and Gardens (www.bradfordplaceinn.com), a four-room B&B in Sonora, California, offers the same three breakfast entrees daily — two are savory and one is sweet. The breakfast menu is posted on the inn's Web site and guests are given the printed menu upon arrival to indicate where, when, and what they would like to eat. Entrees are built individually at the time of cooking, so it's easy to accommodate virtually any type of diet or whim with little or no advance notice. This menu style works well for guests who are early breakfast eaters, light eaters, picky eaters, and late-morning eaters, as well as those who have health, social, or religious dietary restrictions because guests always get what they want. The innkeeper is happy because individual dietary issues are automatically handled, menu planning is eliminated, and food shopping requires less planning.

✔ **Light early breakfast:** For business travelers or guests departing early, you may want to offer a lighter option such as juice, coffee, cereal, and muffins. You can make guests who need to depart very early very happy with only a little bit of advance preparation on your part. The night before:

- Set up a coffeepot on a timer.

- Set out a hot pot for boiling water.

- Put out cereal, tea selections, and condiments.

- Set out dishes, mugs, glasses, utensils, and napkins.

- Arrange non-perishable, wrapped baked goods in a basket.

- Pour juices and milk into covered pitchers and leave in guest refrigerator.

✔ **Different times on weekends and mid-week:** You may decide to offer a later breakfast on weekends if you find this is what your guests prefer.

It's a good idea to post the breakfast time or time period on your Web site (flexible breakfast times are used by some inns as a marketing tool). Also mention the breakfast time in the reservation process and in the confirmation letter: for example, "A full breakfast is served in our dining room daily at 9 a.m." Show guests where breakfast is served during your welcome tour of the inn, and remind them of breakfast times. Some inns also include it in the guest room welcome letter and state it in a nicely framed sign in the dining parlor or hospitality room.

If you offer in-room dining as a breakfast option, be clear about the times it is available, and when guests' orders must be placed by.

How you handle the guest who slides in just as you've finished serving breakfast is your decision, and may differ based on circumstances. Many innkeepers don't wait for guests and give a gentle knock on the door when a guest doesn't show up for breakfast at the set time. Others prepare the guest's breakfast and keep it warm. Many anticipate this (as it is guaranteed to happen) and plan to close the kitchen "officially" a half hour after the stated breakfast time so they can accommodate late arrivals and still stay on schedule. Depending on the situation, some innkeepers forgo the preparation of any hot entree and offer a simpler breakfast or pack a breakfast to go if the time is approaching check-out.

No matter what time you decide to serve breakfast, set up coffee and tea the night before to accommodate early risers.

Attending to the daily details

Presentation is a key ingredient to meeting guests' expectations, and this is where every detail that goes into the table preparation, the ambiance, and serving techniques is critical. Here are some tips for daily finishing touches that ensure breakfast is served in the atmosphere that you want to create for your guests:

✔ **Table settings and placement are key, so have everything on the table that you will need,** including salt and pepper shakers, a basket or attractive container of sugar and sweeteners and cream for at least every two or three guests, utensils, plates, glasses, mugs, napkins, juice and water pitchers, and so on.

✔ **Practice serving guests.** Guests are impressed when you serve without wasting a motion. Practice ahead of time how you will bring hot entrees to the table, which side of the guest you'll place the food from, and which side you'll remove their plates from. If you are serving more than one course, decide ahead of time how you'll remove the first-course dishes and where you'll stack them. Will you bring the dirty dishes into the kitchen before bringing the next course to guests?

It's a good idea to have a hostess staging area, such as a rolling tea cart or a tray stand, next to the table so that you can temporarily stack dirty dishes and utensils away from food that has not yet been served.

Soft background music can set the mood and also entertain guests who may be enjoying a cup of coffee or tea if you are still in the kitchen doing final breakfast preparations.

Music played in a commercial establishment must be licensed. An economical way to offer music is to subscribe to the commercial version of Sirius satellite radio.

Serving up something special

Breakfast is one of the many features that makes a bed & breakfast more than just a place to sleep and separates B&Bs from hotels. When guests wake up and smell your coffee brewing and your breads baking, they know they are waking up someplace special and have made the right choice in choosing your inn.

The ambiance that you create around the breakfast setting adds to your guests' experience. Subtle touches can make your breakfast presentation special. For example, you might

✔ Offer a gourmet breakfast on china, sometimes even by candlelight.

✔ Garnish plates with fresh fruit, edible flowers, and sauces.

✔ Accessorize with fun and interesting table and glassware.

✔ Create menus around regional and local themes, such as southwestern cuisine or, if your inn is located on a farm or in a rural area, full country breakfasts.

Planning the Big Meal

Breakfast is an opportunity for you to wow your guests with your sensational recipes and culinary skills (don't worry; you don't have to be a master chef to serve an impressive breakfast). What you serve for breakfast impacts you, in terms of how much work it is, as well as your guests, in terms of how good it is and the degree to which it entices them to make a return visit or recommend your inn to others. Guest referrals naturally affect your business, as do the ingredients, the cost of which have an immediate impact on your bottom line.

You're likely to have a variety of favorite recipes and certain combinations of foods that you like to serve together. You may decide to have set menus that you serve on a rotating basis.

Be careful to have enough variety so that guests staying multiple days are not served the same thing twice.

Presenting the fabulous breakfast you want to serve to your guests requires planning, preparation, and practice. In the next sections I help you pull it all together with tips, suggestions, and ideas to make breakfast one of the many pleasant memories of your guests' visit.

Putting together menus and shopping lists

Planning your menus at least one week ahead of time helps you with your shopping so you're not left scrambling anything but eggs at the last minute. The innkeepers at the Inn at Riverbend in Pearisburg, Virginia, created the chart in Figure 10-1, which allows you to see a week at a glance and makes it easy to create your shopping list. Use this example to create your own table.

The type of shopping you do depends on where you live and the size of your inn. No matter what, however, you need to

- ✔ **Keep a running list of items you need.**

- ✔ **Make sure to keep certain "must-have" items on hand.** (See Table 10-1 for a list.)

- ✔ **Serve your guests local, fresh items as well as items that they can't get at home.** Shop locally. You might visit farmers' markets or a local coffee roaster.

Guests love fresh fruits and vegetables of the season. Serving seasonal selections when they're readily available is often less expensive than buying out-of-season items that need to be shipped in. Some fruits, such as blueberries, freeze well, so you can wash, dry, and freeze them when they're in abundance.

✔ **Buy in bulk when you can.**

✔ **Check into the feasibility of ordering from a food distributor,** either on your own or by combining your order with those of other local inns. The savings can be substantial, and distributors usually deliver.

	Sunday	Monday	Tuesday	Wednesday	Thursday	Friday	Saturday
Fruit	Poached pears w/yogurt and pomegranate	Sliced melon, kiwi, strawberries w/lime sauce	Fresh fruit cup	Vanilla yogurt w/blackberries, blueberries, and strawberries	Asian pear, pineapple, and berries	Honeydew w/prosciutto	Sautéed apples w/honey, sour cream
Bread	Apple streusel cake	Sour cream pumpkin cake	Banana raisin bread	Wonton apple wraps	Sour cream pound cake	Cranberry scones	Blueberry crumble cake
Entrée	Strawberry stuffed French toast	Poached eggs on baby spinach	Belgium waffles	Breakfast sushi	German apple pancake	Ham and cheese strudel	Sour cream banana pancakes
Meat	Grilled pork sausage	Sliced Virginia Ham	Grilled pork sausage	Included above	Chicken apple sausage	Included above	Grilled pork sausage
Garnish or Side	Whipped cream, powdered sugar	Sliced tomatoes	Whipped cream	Candied ginger	Powdered sugar	Mesclun greens, tomatoes	Sliced bananas, pecans, whipped cream
Sauce, Syrup, or Topping	Raspberry coulis	Grated cheese	Three-berry sauce	Herb hollandaise, Sweet soy	Sautéed apples and juices	Basalmic glaze	Maple syrup
Juice	OJ/White grape	OJ/V8	OJ/Apple	OJ/White cranberry	OJ/Cranberry pomegranate	OJ/V8	OJ/Apple

Figure 10-1:
Weekly
Menu
Planning.

Courtesy of Linda P. Hayes, Owner/Innkeeper, Inn at Riverbend

Fruit can rarely be served the day that it's purchased because it needs time to ripen. If you plan to serve cantaloupe, for example, make sure you purchase it a few days ahead of time so that it's mouth-watering and juicy when you serve it.

Generally, a serving size of fruit is ¹/₂ cup, not including garnish — for example, one-sixth of a medium cantaloupe served as melon balls. For hot entrees, allow two eggs if scrambled and at least 2 pieces of bacon, sausage, or Canadian ham if you serve meat. Sweet entrees, such as pancakes, waffles, and French toast, are usually served in smaller portions — for example, two pancakes or two pieces of French toast — and can be served along with something savory, as simple as a scrambled egg with grilled sliced peaches on the side. As you go along, you'll get a feel for how much your guests eat, and you can adjust your serving sizes accordingly.

Keeping basic ingredients on hand

As an innkeeper, you quickly learn to expect the unexpected and to be prepared for it. When it comes to breakfast, this means keeping an ample supply of breakfast staples on hand. (See Table 10-1 for a handy list.) Then when the oven suddenly stops working, your carefully prepared recipe doesn't turn out as expected, or you find yourself with a guest who can't eat anything you've prepared, you'll be ready and able to use your creativity to whip up something on the spot.

Table 10-1	Breakfast Ingredients to Keep On Hand	
Almonds (sliced)	Bacon	Baked goods in freezer
Baking powder	Baking soda	Berries (frozen)
Bisquits (frozen)	Bottled water	Brown sugar
Butter	Cereal	Cheese (cheddar)
Cinnamon	Cloves	Coffee (regular and decaffeinated)
Confectioners' sugar	Cream cheese	Dried tomatoes
Egg Beaters	Eggs	Flour
French toast bread	Fruit	Granola
Half-and-half	Herbs and spices	Honey
Jams	Juices	Lemonade
Low-calorie sweeteners	Margarine	Milk (2% and skim)
Oatmeal	Oil	Orange extract

Table 10-1 *(continued)*

Pancake mix	Raisins	Soda
Sugar (10 lbs.)	Syrup (sugar-free)	Teas (selection)
Vanilla extract	Vegetarian meat/ sausage	Walnuts
Whipped cream	Yogurt (vanilla and flavored)	

Staying quality-conscious

If you've been wondering whether you have to bake everything from scratch, don't worry — most innkeepers don't. What you do need to keep in mind is the importance of offering quality, delicious, fresh food that you can serve to your guests with pride. Certain store-bought items are delicious and are great shortcuts when you scrutinize your choices. As long as the items you offer taste fresh, your guests will be happy. Some of your baked goods can come from a box, mix, food distributor, or local bakery, and your guests will never know the difference.

Nevertheless, guests aren't expecting to be served warmed-up, pre-made food that you buy at a local wholesale store. True, many of these products are fantastic and can be used to supplement your own preparations, but B&B guests expect more than a complete breakfast warmed from a box or plastic container. What you serve for breakfast reflects on the quality of your bed & breakfast, so don't miss the opportunity to impress your guests. By serving a quality breakfast, you also distinguish yourself from local chain hotels, many of which offer institutionalized bed & breakfast packages.

Guests will often ask you for your recipes. Don't be embarrassed to tell them you used a mix, and be sure to tell them any special adaptations that you made to the recipe. One innkeeper jokes about some of her "secret recipes." When guests ask her for one of these recipes, she tells them the recipe is so secret even she doesn't know it!

Accommodating guests' dietary needs and restrictions

Always ask your guests about allergies and dietary restrictions when you take their reservations. If something is important to guests, they should tell you at this time.

Asking about preferences is another matter. You may find that your question about dietary preferences is interpreted by the guest as, *"What do you want me to make special for you?"* Some innkeepers serve a large enough variety of food items to accommodate even picky eaters. Other innkeepers feel strongly that the bed & breakfast experience means catering custom menus for their guests. Don't judge yourself on how you decide to handle this. Simply be prepared with reasonable alternatives so that guests have the flexibility to request necessary modifications and still have an enjoyable, satisfying breakfast.

Many food allergies are life threatening, and you must take them seriously. Guests with serious allergies are accustomed to following a strict diet to avoid foods that produce a severe allergic reaction. They will immediately tell you this when making their reservations if you ask them about allergies.

A quick Internet search makes it easy to find recipes for nearly any dietary request (for example, you might search for "gluten-free breakfast recipes"). Special dietary requests that you may be asked to accommodate include

- ✔ **Vegetarian:** Vegetarians don't eat meat. Some eat fish, and most eat dairy products and eggs. If your staples include cereal, fruit, eggs, and yogurt, you should be able to accommodate these guests easily. This request is so common that many innkeepers don't even consider it an issue. You'll probably find that you can adjust most of your recipes easily by leaving out the meat, and even your non-vegetarian guests won't miss it. Another option is to keep some meatless sausages in the freezer. You can pull them out at the last minute if you'd like to be extra-accommodating.

- ✔ **Vegan:** Vegans are strict vegetarians who eat no animal or dairy products at all, so this request is a bit more challenging. An excellent source for vegan recipes is www.vegweb.com.

- ✔ **Gluten-free:** Guests following a gluten-free diet usually do so for the treatment of a medical condition or a wheat allergy. Sometimes they'll bring their own gluten-free bread, and they'll usually tell you what they can eat so you can plan your menus accordingly.

- ✔ **Popular diets:** Low-carb, high-fiber, low-fat, and low-sodium diets are popular eating styles that many guests adhere to, either by choice or for health reasons (although many drop their resolve when on vacation). By having cereal, yogurt, and the other essential breakfast supplies listed in the earlier "Keeping basic ingredients on hand" section at your disposal, you should be able to accommodate these guests easily.

- ✔ **Lactose-intolerant:** Guests who are lactose intolerant need to avoid dairy products, including milk and cheese, but can usually tolerate soy milk.

- ✔ **Kosher:** Some guests seek out B&Bs that keep, prepare, and serve food by kosher standards. This is a niche market that you may decide to cater to. Sometimes guests who keep kosher at home are more flexible when traveling, but they still do not want meat and dairy served together.

Extra special breakfast touches

Here are some menu-planning ideas that can make your guests' stays special:

✔ Plan seasonal menus. Lighter menu options are appreciated in the summer months, whereas heartier fare is common during the cold-weather seasons.

✔ Record what you serve during your guests' visits, and make different specialties when those guests make a return visit (unless they rave about the dish — then see the next bullet).

✔ Make a note of each guest's favorite menus and delight them by serving them on a return visit.

✔ Rotate between sweet and savory menus during a guest's stay.

✔ Accommodate guests' dietary restrictions and preferences, such as low-carb, vegan, and so forth. (See more on special request menus later in this chapter.)

Some inns, such as Coppertoppe Inn & Retreat Center in Hebron, New Hampshire (www.coppertoppe.com), pride themselves in accommodating not only guests' allergies but also guests' food preferences. Part of what their inn is known for is serving vegan, vegetarian, kosher pareve, and allergy-avoidant meals. When they know that a guest has a severe allergy, such as a peanut allergy, they advise their other guests not to bring these foods in to protect the guest with the allergy. Guests choose the inn just because of this. When guests who have allergies find a place where they can eat safely and enjoy their meals, they are very loyal and supportive and are a frequent source of referrals.

Preparing ahead: Mise en place

Part of your job as an innkeeper is to make everything appear effortless so that guests can relax and enjoy their getaways. Breakfast is a highlight of many guests' B&B stays, but they won't enjoy it as much — even if it's absolutely delicious — if you appear frazzled and they feel you're being put out. So here's the secret: Prepare ahead. Being organized also allows you time to interact with your guests before and after the meal and help them plan out their day. (See Chapter 12 for important communication skills and tips on interacting with guests.)

You can prepare ahead in a variety of ways, including

✔ **Freezing:** Your freezer is a fabulous appliance that you won't be able to live without, so make sure it's big enough.

- Bake ahead and freeze breads, muffins, and cookies, which can be thawed by leaving them out overnight and then heated if necessary before serving.

- Freeze batter for quick preparation of cookies and muffins.

- Make extra servings of sauces and then freeze them in individual portions that can be thawed as needed.

- Separate and freeze individual portions of cheese and sausage.

- Keep your freezer stocked with items to accommodate guests' dietary needs, such as vegetarian meats.

✔ **Anticipating:** Be ready for last-minute menu substitutions by keeping essential staples on hand. See Table 10-1 for ingredients you should always have available.

✔ **Organizing:** Have everything ready and laid out the night before. This strategy not only limits the amount of noise you make preparing breakfast in the morning, but also frees you up to handle any guest needs that may require your attention. Breakfast time is show time, and the show must go on. Before you turn in for the night,

- Set out everything you'll need to prepare breakfast in the morning — paring knives, pans, ingredients, and equipment.

- Set up coffee and beverages for early risers.

- Set the table, including serving pieces.

Experiment with freezing ingredients, dishes, and individual portions of various foods. Don't test these techniques on your guests. Instead, play around with freezing different items to find out what freezes well and which dishes you can prepare ahead. Don't forget to mark, date, and rotate items in your freezer for freshness.

Creating signature breakfast dishes

A breakfast specialty can be a valuable marketing tool. Guests will often remember your specialty, and it can become part of the brand image that comes to mind when guests think of your inn. You can designate something as a signature dish because

✔ It's a particular favorite of yours and/or your guests

✔ It's made from ingredients that your area is known for

✔ The recipe has some significance to the inn itself

If you create a signature dish, make sure you publicize it on your Web site and in your marketing material.

Create a section on your Web site to publish many of your favorite recipes. A popular way for people to find recipes is by searching for them online. When you publish yours on your Web site, guests looking for recipes may find them and get to know your inn. Make your recipes easily downloadable in a format such as a PDF file and, of course, make sure the print version includes your inn name and Web address.

You can also make recipe cards for your most-requested recipes. Recipe cards are a great memento for guests and a guarantee that they'll remember your inn when making the recipe at home (again, be sure to include your inn's name and Web site on your recipe cards). Recipe software programs such as Accuchef (www.accuchef.com) make creating recipe cards a cinch.

Preparing Some Guest Favorites

As an innkeeper, you should maintain a file of favorite "go-to recipes" that you're comfortable making. You can assemble them into formal menus or mix and match them depending on your mood, what's in season, ingredients that you have on hand, and what you think your guests will like. Be on the lookout for recipes that make a great presentation, yet are simple to prepare. If they can be assembled ahead of time, that's a big added bonus. To get you started, I've included favorite sweet, savory, and vegetarian menus and their recipes in this section.

When you need inspiration, other innkeepers are the best place to find it. Ask them about their favorite recipes or cookbooks that they use (see Chapter 1 for help in finding other innkeepers to talk to). You can find numerous inn cookbooks at a bookstore, at the library, and online. You can also check out some of the popular online directories where innkeepers share their recipes with other innkeepers and the public (www.bbonline.com, www.bnb finder.com, www.iloveinns.com, www.lanierbb.com and www.bed andbreakfast.com all have extensive recipe sections).

Sample sweet menu with recipes

This sample sweet menu and the accompanying recipes are courtesy of Journey Inn Bed & Breakfast in Hyde Park, New York (www.journeyinn. com). The menu includes:

✔ **Fruit course:** Baked Pears with vanilla yogurt

✔ **Main course:** Baked Apple French Toast served with locally made maple syrup and sausage

✔ **Baked goods:** Banana Walnut Bread served with locally made jams

✔ **Beverages:** Coffee (caffeinated and decaffeinated), a selection of teas presented in a tea chest, orange juice, cranberry juice, ice water

What I like about this menu is:

✔ **Use of local items:** Journey Inn Bed & Breakfast always serves locally made maple syrup and jams that they find at local farmers' markets and from local produce vendors.

✔ **Vegetarian adaptability:** This menu becomes a vegetarian meal if you leave off the sausage or serve a vegetarian sausage.

✔ **Easy advance preparation:** All three recipes can be prepared ahead of time, which makes for quick assembly in the morning.

☉ Baked Pears

For this recipe, everything including the knife, pan, and nonperishable ingredients can be set out the night before, for quick preparation in the morning. This fragrant recipe fills the house with a wonderful aroma. Your guests will be drawn to the breakfast area by the enticing smell of cinnamon, nutmeg, and cloves as the pears bake in the oven.

Preparation time: 5 minutes

Baking time: About 30 minutes

Yield: 5 servings

5 ripe Bartlett pears	*Ground cinnamon*
$\frac{1}{2}$ cup firmly packed dark brown sugar	*Ground nutmeg*
$\frac{1}{2}$ to $\frac{3}{4}$ cup orange juice	*Ground cloves*
3 tablespoons butter	

1 Preheat oven to 350 degrees Fahrenheit.

2 Slice pears in half; remove the core and the stem, but leave the skin on.

3 Line the bottom of a large glass baking dish with brown sugar. Place the pears, cut side down, on the brown sugar.

4 Pour orange juice over the pears and dot each with butter. Sprinkle generously with cinnamon, nutmeg, and cloves.

5 Bake in preheated oven for 30 minutes or until the pears are tender.

6 Place each pear in a bowl. Pour some of the sauce on each pear.

Go-with: *Serve with vanilla yogurt.*

Per serving: *Calories 255 (From Fat 69); Fat 8g (Saturated 4g); Cholesterol 18mg; Sodium 10mg; Carbohydrate 50g (Dietary Fiber 4g); Protein 1g.*

🍎 Baked Apple French Toast

You can prepare this Baked Apple French Toast the night before so it only needs to be popped into the oven the next morning. You can bake the pears and French toast at the same temperature in the oven, and the aroma will guarantee hungry guests arrive at the table!

Preparation time: *Approximately 20 minutes*

Baking time: *40 to 45 minutes*

Yield: *7–9 servings*

2 to 3 tart apples (Granny Smith)	*5 eggs*
¹/₃ cup brown sugar	*Several dashes of nutmeg*
¹/₂ cup butter	*1¹/₂ cups milk (or half-and-half)*
1 tablespoon corn syrup	*1 tablespoon vanilla*
1 loaf French bread, sliced into 20 to 24 ³/₄-inch slices	

1 Preheat oven to 350 degrees Fahrenheit.

2 Peel, core, quarter, and then slice apples.

3 Combine sugar, butter, and corn syrup in a saucepan and cook over medium heat until syrupy. Stir to incorporate the ingredients.

4 Pour into a 9-x-13-inch baking dish. Place apple slices over syrup mixture; then place bread on top of apple slices. Whisk together remaining ingredients and pour over bread.

5 Bake uncovered in preheated oven for 40 to 45 minutes.

Go-with: *Serve with a side of sausage. I recommend precooked patties — they're real time-savers because they only need heating on top of the stove.*

Per serving: *Calories 463 (From Fat 185); Fat 21g (Saturated 11g); Cholesterol 194mg; Sodium 508mg; Carbohydrate 57g (Dietary Fiber 3g); Protein 13g.*

☕ *Banana Walnut Bread*

This was one of the first recipes Journey Inn Bed & Breakfast made for guests and throughout the years it has remained a guest favorite. The recipe can be prepared in batches, up to 4 weeks ahead of time, and pulled out of the freezer as needed. Allow the well-wrapped bread to defrost overnight on the counter. Simply warm before serving in a warm oven (approximately 275 degrees Fahrenheit) for 10 to 15 minutes.

Preparation time: *35 minutes*

Baking time: *About 1¼ hours*

Yield: *Approximately 24 servings (12 per loaf pan), depending on the thickness of the slices*

1¼ cups sugar	2 teaspoons vanilla extract
½ cup butter, softened	2½ cups all-purpose flour
2 eggs	1 teaspoon baking soda
1½ cups mashed ripe bananas(3 to 4 medium)	1 teaspoon salt
½ cup buttermilk	1 cup chopped walnuts (optional)

1 Move oven rack to low position so that tops of pans will be in center of oven. Preheat oven to 350 degrees Fahrenheit. Grease bottom only of two 9-x-5-x-3-inch loaf pans.

2 Using an electric mixer, mix sugar and butter in a large mixer bowl. With mixer running, stir in eggs until well blended. Add bananas, buttermilk, and vanilla. Using mixer, beat until smooth.

3 Stir in flour, baking soda, and salt, using electric mixer on low speed, just until flour is moistened. Stir in walnuts using mixer on low speed or stirring by hand. Pour batter into pans.

4 Bake in preheated oven about 1¼ hours, or until toothpick inserted in center comes out clean. Rotate pans after 30 minutes and test after 1 hour.

Per serving: *Calories 286 (From Fat 80); Fat 9g (Saturated 5g); Cholesterol 56mg; Sodium 322mg; Carbohydrate 48g (Dietary Fiber 1g); Protein 4g.*

Sample savory menu with recipes

This menu and the accompanying recipes are courtesy of the Inn at Riverbend in Pearisburg, Virginia (www.innatriverbend.com). The menu includes:

- ✔ **Fruit course:** Honeydew Melon with Prosciutto
- ✔ **Main course:** Ham & Cheese Strudel
- ✔ **Baked goods:** Cranberry Scones

✔ **Beverages:** Coffee (caffeinated and decaffeinated), a selection of teas, choice of two juices (orange and either pressed apple, V8, white cranberry, white grape, or pomegranate cranberry), ice water

What I like about this menu is:

✔ **The choices are simple, yet elegant.** The honeydew with prosciutto, mesclun greens with balsamic glaze, and sliced plum tomatoes require very little preparation yet are fresh and delicious items.

✔ **The menu can easily be adapted to a vegetarian menu** by eliminating the prosciutto on the melon and substituting another vegetable for the ham in the strudel.

✔ **The scones can be prepared ahead of time and frozen.** This is a great item to have in the freezer because you can pull out and bake exactly as many as you need at the last minute.

✔ **The prep (chopping) for the strudel can be done the night before** and the strudel can quickly be assembled and baked in the morning.

✔ **Nothing ever goes to waste.** For example, if you have melon left over from the melon and prosciutto recipe, you can cube the melon and use it in a fruit cup or use thin slices as a plate garnish the next morning. Leftover prosciutto can be chopped and added to scrambled eggs, omelets, or quiches.

Honeydew Melon with Prosciutto

The combination of the sweet honeydew melon and the prosciutto offers a cool, fresh taste to start the day.

Preparation time: *10 minutes*

Yield: *12–14 servings, depending on size of melon*

Honeydew melon   *Prosciutto, sliced thin –1 slice per guest serving*

1 Cut and seed melon, making slices ¹/₄- to ³/₈-inch thick.

2 Wrap 1 piece of prosciutto around 2 melon slices.

Tip: *Since melons are rarely ripe and ready to eat when purchased at the grocers, buy the melon several days ahead and allow it to ripen on the counter.*

Per serving: *Calories 72 (From Fat 16); Fat 2g (Saturated 1g); Cholesterol 13mg; Sodium 302mg; Carbohydrate 11g (Dietary Fiber 1g); Protein 5g.*

Ham and Cheese Strudel

This strudel offers a nice variation from the usual savory breakfast with an easy preparation and an elegant presentation.

Preparation time: *30 minutes*

Baking time: *About 25 minutes*

Yield: *8 servings*

2 Pepperidge Farm puff pastry sheets

1 pound ham, finely chopped

1 16-ounce package shredded Mozzarella or Monterey Jack cheese

1/2 cup crumbled feta cheese

4 stalks celery, washed, trimmed of greens, and finely chopped

1 large tomato, diced

1 egg, beaten with a little water

1 Preheat oven to 375 degrees Fahrenheit. Remove pastry sheets from freezer and thaw for 20 minutes.

2 Roll each pastry sheet into a rectangle, smoothing out the folds.

3 Mix together ham, cheese, celery, and tomato, then divide into two portions.

4 Spread one portion to within 1 inch of the long edges of one pastry sheet. Fold the long edges to overlap just 1/4 inch and then press the short ends together and seal with your fingers. Repeat with remaining portion and pastry sheet.

5 Turn pastries over so the seam side is down. Brush with egg beaten with a little water.

6 Bake in preheated oven until golden brown, approximately 25 minutes.

Go-with: *Serve with a small handful of mesclun greens, a thin slice of an orange tomato and a red tomato, and balsamic glaze drizzled over the top of the greens and tomato. The glaze can be found in specialty gourmet stores or by searching for "balsamic glaze" via the Internet to order online. Amounts for the greens, tomato, and glaze depend on the number of guests that you are serving.*

Per serving: *Calories 320 (From Fat 202); Fat 22g (Saturated 12g); Cholesterol 101mg; Sodium 419mg; Carbohydrate 10g (Dietary Fiber 2g); Protein 20g.*

☙ *Cranberry Scones*

Scones originated from a Scottish quick bread that is said to have taken its name from the Stone of Destiny, which supposedly is the place where Scottish kings were once crowned.

Preparation time: *15 minutes*

Baking time: *About 15 minutes*

Yield: *16 scones*

2 cups all-purpose flour	*¹/₂ teaspoon salt*
5 tablespoons sugar plus 1 tablespoon for topping	*6 tablespoons chilled, unsalted butter, cut into pieces*
2 tablespoons baking powder	*²/₃ cup plus 1 tablespoon half-and-half*
¹/₂ cup halved, fresh cranberries, drained on paper towels	

1 Preheat oven to 425 degrees Fahrenheit.

2 In a bowl, whisk together flour, 5 tablespoons sugar, baking powder, and salt. Cut in butter with a pastry blender or two knives until mixture resembles coarse crumbs. Stir in half-and-half until just moistened. Gently fold in cranberries.

3 On a lightly floured surface, knead dough gently, 5 to 10 times. Divide the dough in half and pat into two ¹/₂-inch-thick rounds.

4 Cut each round into 8 wedges. Place wedges on a baking sheet, 2 inches apart. Brush tops with remaining tablespoon half-and-half; then sprinkle with remaining tablespoon sugar.

5 Bake in preheated oven until golden brown, 12 to 15 minutes. Let cool on a wire rack.

Tip: *Fresh cranberries can be halved, drained, and frozen ahead of time.*

Tip: *Because fresh cranberries are seasonal, using dried cranberries is a wonderful substitute year-round.*

Tip: *Make and freeze the wedges ahead of time, and then pull just the amount you need from the freezer in the morning. Bake per the directions above.*

Per serving: *Calories 129 (From Fat 51); Fat 6g (Saturated 4g); Cholesterol 16mg; Sodium 126mg; Carbohydrate 18g (Dietary Fiber 1g); Protein 2g.*

Sample vegetarian menu with recipes

The following menu and accompanying recipes are courtesy of the Birchwood Inn in Lenox, Massachusetts (www.birchwood-inn.com). The menu includes

- **Fruit course:** Pear Cranapple Crumble
- **Main course:** Mediterranean Frittata
- **Baked goods:** Aunt Norma's Sour Cream Coffee Cake
- **Beverages:** Piping hot specially blended coffee, selection of teas, freshly squeezed orange juice

What I like about this menu is:

- **Do ahead prep:**
    - On a rainy day or while waiting for the plumber, you can make up a double, triple, or even quadruple batch of the topping for the Pear Cranapple Crumble and freeze it in a large zip-top bag.
    - Vegetables for the Mediterranean Frittata can be prepared the day ahead.
    - The coffeecake can be made a day ahead and wrapped well. It also freezes nicely.
- **Seasonal versatility:** The Pear Cranapple Crumble is an autumn dish that can easily become a summer dish by substituting peaches, plums, nectarines, and blueberries for the apples and pears.

☺ Pear Cranapple Crumble

This recipe originated in the Northwest Territories in Canada and was passed on to the innkeeper by a teacher both of her sons had. Over the years she has continued to make little changes to improve upon the original recipe, making it one of her guests' favorites.

Preparation time: 15 minutes

Baking time: 1 hour

Yield: 12 servings

1 cup brown sugar

1 cup all-purpose flour

¼ pound (1 stick) unsalted butter

1 cup rolled quick oats

3 large baking apples (Spartans and Rome Beauties are best; Cortlands and Granny Smiths also work well)

2 large Bosc pears, ripe but still firm

1 cup cranberries

Juice of 1 lemon

⅓ cup honey

Fresh nutmeg

1 Combine the brown sugar, flour, and butter in a food processor with the chopping blade and pulse several times; then place this mixture in a bowl. Add the oats and mix well with a spoon. Set aside.

2 Preheat oven to 350 degrees Fahrenheit. Grease a large (10-cup) baking dish.

3 Cut the apples and pears into ¼-inch-thick slices, leaving the peel on. Combine the apples and pears with the cranberries in a large bowl.

4 Add the lemon juice and honey. Toss. Spoon the fruit mixture into the greased baking dish. Spoon the crumbled topping on the fruit. Grate fresh nutmeg on top.

5 Bake in preheated oven for 1 hour.

Tip: In the fall, buy twice as many bags of cranberries as you need — one to use and one to freeze.

Tip: You can transfer the topping mixture to a zip-top bag and store it in the freezer for up to a month.

Vary It! The Birchwood Inn uses 12 crème brûlée dishes for a shorter cooking time (just ½ hour) and a more impressive presentation.

Per serving: Calories 285 (From Fat 77); Fat 9g (Saturated 5g); Cholesterol 21mg; Sodium 9mg; Carbohydrate 53g (Dietary Fiber 4g); Protein 3g.

Mediterranean Frittata

Any innkeeper, new or old, needs lots of kitchen tools and gadgets. They make life a lot easier and often add fun to cooking. They also give you greater flexibility to add new items to your repertoire. Frittata pans (available at Williams-Sonoma) are among innkeepers' favorites. Two sizes are available: a large size to serve 6 and a medium size to serve 4. Each set has two pans: a deeper pan for starting the frittata and a shallower pan for flipping and finishing the dish. Although you can make the frittata with one frying pan, flipping part way through cooking, the frittata pans are a great investment that pay dividends in rave reviews!

Preparation time: 15 to 20 minutes

Yield: 6-7

5 tablespoons butter

1 leek, coarsely shredded

1 zucchini, sliced medium-thick

1/2 can artichokes, quartered

1 roasted red pepper

6 eggs

1/4 cup heavy cream

Kosher salt

Fresh pepper

2/3 cup grated parmesan (the prepackaged supermarket variety works just fine)

1/2 cup finely chopped parsley, divided, or 1/4 cup finely chopped basil and 1/2 cup finely chopped parsley

1/4 cup finely chopped, pitted Calamata olives (optional)

1 Melt 2 tablespoons of the butter in a large skillet, and sauté the leek for about 3 minutes over medium-high heat. Add the zucchini to the leeks and continue cooking for another 2 to 3 minutes. Be careful not to overcook the vegetables. Crunchy is preferable to soft.

2 Spoon the leek and zucchini into a bowl. Add the artichokes. Cut the roasted red peppers in strips and place in a separate small bowl. If you are preparing the vegetables the night before serving, cover the two bowls and refrigerate.

3 Lightly beat the eggs in a medium-large bowl. Add the cream, salt, and freshly grated pepper. Beat until well mixed. Add the cheese. Mix the leeks, zucchini, artichokes, roasted red pepper, and olives together. Measure 2 cups of the vegetables and add to the frittata. Add 1/4 cup of the parsley or basil to the egg mixture. Stir to blend.

4 Heat 2 tablespoons of the butter in the deeper frittata pan over medium to medium-high heat. Add the frittata mixture and spread evenly. Cook the frittata, frequently pushing the edges with a wooden spoon to allow the uncooked mixture to flow to the edges, as you would an omelet.

5 Melt the remaining tablespoon of butter in the shallower pan. When the mixture is fairly well set but wet on the top (approximately 10 minutes), take the second pan and lock it on top of the first. Leave the two pans locked together for approximately 3 minutes. Holding the two pans together carefully, remove the pans from the heat. Flip the frittata so that it is now in the shallower pan (do this over the sink, in case of leakage). Return the pans to the heat and remove the first pan. Continue to cook until the center is fairly dry.

6 Remove from heat and let sit for a few minutes. Slice into 6 pieces. Toss the remaining parsley onto each plate and plate the frittata.

Go-with: *Accompany the frittata with oven-roasted rosemary potatoes, halved cherry tomatoes dipped in parsley, cherry tomato crisp, or grilled vegetables.*

Tip: *You can prepare the vegetables a day ahead and refrigerate them overnight.*

Per serving: *Calories 264 (From Fat 189); Fat 21g (Saturated 12g); Cholesterol 259mg; Sodium 444mg; Carbohydrate 8g (Dietary Fiber 1g); Protein 12g.*

☞ *Aunt Norma's Sour Cream Coffeecake*

Four generations of the innkeeper's family have enjoyed this moist and "cinnamon-y" coffeecake. Both the recipe and Aunt Norma are family treasures, and the recipe is a favorite of guests at the Birchwood Inn.

Preparation time: *15 minutes*

Baking time: *30 to 55 minutes, depending on pan used*

Yield: *18-24 guests (although 12 guests have been known to devour it, leaving nary a crumb)*

1⅞ cups (2 cups minus one tablespoon) all-purpose flour	1½ teaspoons vanilla
1½ teaspoons baking powder	1⅛ cups (1 cup plus 1 tablespoon) sour cream
1⅛ teaspoons baking soda	½ cup chopped walnuts
Pinch of salt	½ cup brown sugar
¾ pound butter, softened	1½ teaspoons cinnamon
1½ cups sugar	⅛ cup powdered sugar
3 eggs	

1 Preheat oven to 350 degrees Fahrenheit. Grease and flour a 9-x-13-inch pan or a silicone Bundt pan. (The silicone Bundt pan yields prettier results than the 9-x-13-inch pan, but either one will suffice. *Don't* use a regular Bundt pan, because the topping will settle to the bottom and stick to the pan.)

2 Combine the flour, baking powder, baking soda, and salt in a medium bowl.

3 In the bowl of an electric mixer, mix the butter and sugar. Add the eggs and vanilla, and mix thoroughly.

4 Add the dry ingredients and the sour cream to the mixture in Step 3 alternately, beginning and ending with the dry ingredients and mixing on medium speed. Pour the batter into the greased and floured pan.

5 Stir together the walnuts, brown sugar, and cinnamon to make streusel topping. Sprinkle the topping on top of the batter; then swirl the topping through the batter with a knife. If you are using a Bundt pan, swirl the topping very shallowly or it can sink to the bottom, making it difficult to remove the cake intact.

6 Bake in preheated oven for approximately 30 to 35 minutes if using a 9-x-13-inch pan (50 to 55 minutes if using a Bundt pan) or until cake tester comes out clean. Cool; invert on serving plate. Sprinkle with powdered sugar.

Per serving: Calories 334 (From Fat 189); Fat 21g (Saturated 12g); Cholesterol 48mg; Sodium 149mg; Carbohydrate 35g (Dietary Fiber 1g); Protein 3g.

Moving beyond Breakfast

In the beginning, you may want to be everything to every guest and to offer every service imaginable. In general, I caution and encourage you to stick with what you are — a bed & breakfast — and do this well.

Wait until you're established before taking on the extra work and responsibility of serving additional meals. If you're planning to serve lunch and dinner on a regular basis from the beginning, I encourage you to reevaluate your business plan and determine whether you're really going to be running a country inn and restaurant, rather than a bed & breakfast. Running a country inn and restaurant should only be considered with the necessary staff, equipment, permits, and knowledge, and then you should be clear to your guests that you are not a bed & breakfast.

My caution here does not, however, mean that you have to limit your culinary hospitality to just breakfast. Offering complimentary snacks and beverages can give your bed & breakfast a competitive edge.

Offering complimentary snacks and beverages

A hallmark of the bed & breakfast experience is hospitality. Extra touches such as complimentary snacks, treats, and beverages are distinguishing features that differentiate a bed & breakfast stay from a hotel stay and, sometimes, one inn from another.

Providing welcome refreshments

Guests don't typically find fruit, cheese, cookies, or other welcome treats upon their arrival at a hotel, unless they're repeat guests at a high-end establishment. Yet these complimentary amenities are common at many bed & breakfasts. You can do something as simple as offering a drink (cold or hot, depending on the season) with or without a cookie or other treat. Providing any type of refreshments is a sure way to start your guests' visit off with a smile.

Offering complimentary snacks and drinks

Guests often cringe at the price of items in a typical hotel mini bar, so complimentary snacks and drinks are highly appreciated amenities — even more so when they're homemade. You may decide to make these items available 24 hours a day, a setup which should be considered when designing your inn.

Don't display an overabundance of anything that's complimentary. Guests are unlikely to feel guilty taking more than they need from a full cabinet, yet they're hesitant to take the last piece of anything. Groups tend to be more indulgent, so when hosting a group, use extra care regarding the amount of complimentary items you put out at any one time.

Creating a social environment

At many inns, the innkeepers create a social environment by offering afternoon refreshments, afternoon tea, or after-dinner socials (check local liquor laws and your insurance company if you plan to serve alcohol). This is often a time for guests to mingle with each other and with you. Many guests consider these times a highlight of their stay — something they can't get at a typical hotel.

You may find these hours of relaxed guest interaction to be your most enjoyable times as an innkeeper. This is a time to find out how your guests' stays are going. You can also take the opportunity to enhance their stays with your first-hand knowledge of the area and your suggestions regarding activities and restaurants.

Serving lunch and dinner

Unexpected circumstances may land you in the kitchen whipping up a quick lunch or dinner, even though you don't intend to serve them. I know of several inns where guests have been snowed in, and it has been difficult and dangerous for the guests to leave for meals. The innkeepers in these situations spontaneously put together a fabulous lunch or dinner for their guests and were surprised at how easy and enjoyable it was.

If preparing an impromptu lunch or dinner for guests is a possibility, be sure to have the necessary ingredients and staples on hand. These can be items in the freezer, nonperishable items such as pasta, or a combination of the two, such as pasta and frozen meatballs and sauce.

I've also heard stories of innkeepers whose guests smelled their dinner and the innkeepers subsequently invited them to join them — again, surprised by how easy it was to serve a few extra people. In some of these cases, this gave the innkeepers the idea to offer dinner packages that could be arranged in advance and added on as part of the guest's stay. (See Chapter 17 for more information on adding services.)

Adding extra meals isn't a decision you should make right away. Start slowly. Not only are extra meals a lot of work, but many other factors also play a role in determining whether it ultimately makes sense at your bed & breakfast. Following are the most important considerations:

✔ **Are you zoned for these services?** Be sure to check your local zoning ordinances and health department restrictions to see whether you're able to offer additional meals and, if so, whether there are restrictions.

✔ **Do you have adequate staff?** If you're already understaffed and can barely get everything done, let alone find any time for yourself, serving additional meals is a bad idea.

✔ **Can you price the meals so that you make a profit?** Factor in all the expenses — ingredients, staff (don't forget the value of your time), permits, and so on — and make sure you can make a profit.

✔ **Do guests want extra meals?** If your area has many wonderful restaurants, your guests may be happy to have breakfast at your inn and enjoy the local flare by dining at different restaurants for lunch and dinner during their stay.

Part IV
Up and Running: Day-to-Day Operations

The 5th Wave   By Rich Tennant

"I showed Patrick where the pots and pans are. Now he wants to know where to go to sharpen and hone his compensation package."

In this part . . .

This part is your guide to the day-to-day operations of your bed & breakfast. It includes what you need to know about establishing your own reservation process, using reservation software, and making reservations smooth for both you and your guests. I give you advice on taking care of the guests, even those few that tend to get out of hand. And because you can't avoid cleaning, I give you some suggestions to make this necessary evil as painless as possible. If you discover that you need a break or must get extra help, I give you some suggestions on where to find it.

Chapter 11

Communicating with Potential Guests and Taking Reservations

Keeping your bed & breakfast full is the key to being a successful inn-keeper. To help ensure that your bed & breakfast stays full, you need to communicate effectively with potential guests, take reservations efficiently, and handle cancellations with ease.

In this chapter I help you determine whether you want to take reservations by speaking with every guest, by handling everything through e-mail, by utilizing online, real-time booking capabilities, or some combination of all of these methods. No matter how guests make their reservations, many will also call you and/or visit your Web site. This phone call or Web visit is the beginning of their personal experience at your inn, so I give you tips on how to make a great first impression and turn inquiries into reservations. And because some reservations will inevitably fall through, I offer concrete suggestions for managing those last-minute cancellations.

Making a Good First Impression

You don't get a second chance to make a first impression, so you want to be sure that your phone is always answered professionally and your Web site looks its best. Your chance to make a good impression starts the minute the guest picks up the phone to call you or sees your bed & breakfast on the Web.

To make the best impression, think of each phone call and each Web visit as another chance to sell yourself and your inn. Your guests don't know you, and your bed & breakfast is just one of the many places they can choose to stay. In addition to having questions about your availability, your rates, and your rooms, potential guests are also checking you out, so make sure your phone is always answered in a professional manner and your Web site is easy to use with inviting text and appealing pictures. Making a good impression is imperative in turning the looker into a booker!

Your guests' experiences are determined in large part by the personal service you offer. Find out whether this is their first bed & breakfast experience and whether they've been to the area before, or ask why they are visiting and what their expectations are. Most reservation software will allow you to customize the guests' reservation request to find out the reason they are visiting your area, and on the phone it's easy to work these questions into the conversation without sounding nosy. Most guests will ask you upfront about your availability or your rates. Try responding with something like, "While I'm checking that for you, may I ask

- ✔ Whether this is your first visit to the area?
- ✔ Whether this will be your first stay at a B&B?
- ✔ What brings you to the area?

Many guests will have the same needs and requests, so keep a list handy of restaurants, spas, activities, and so forth that you can comfortably recommend. This shows how knowledgeable and helpful you are, and makes the call go smoother.

The recommendations you make are a reflection on you, so before making them, either try the services yourself (speak with your accountant about tax-deductible business expenses) or only suggest services that many other guests have given good reviews of. Don't forget to add these references to your Web site as a handy resource for guests, to develop partnerships with other local business, and to build content for optimizing your Web site (Chapter 15 has more information on getting optimal search engine placement).

Use guest questions as feedback. If many guests are asking the same question, this is a signal that you should include this information on your Web site. If you have numerous guests calling for something that isn't applicable to your inn or area, ask them why they thought this was available. Probing to find out where a misunderstanding is originating enables you to make clarifications, especially if the confusion is coming from your Web site. Correcting the misleading information helps to avoid unhappy guests in the future.

Your inn will not be the right choice for all guests. For example, you may not be able to accommodate young children if your inn is full of antiques. When your inn is not a good match for the guest, be upfront and tell the guest so, and then make alternate suggestions. You may say something like, "I'm not sure that we're able to meet your expectations. You may want to try the Main Street Inn or the Inn On the Way. May I give you their numbers?" You'll spare yourself an unhappy guest and avoid a potential nasty online review, while making brownie points with your neighboring innkeepers, who may have a guest to refer your way in the future.

Representing Your B&B Over the Phone

You're anxiously anticipating the first calls from guests, but have you thought about how you're going to handle them? Many B&B guests, even those who book their reservations online, will want to speak directly with you. They may

- ✔ Have questions about the inn or the area
- ✔ Want to know which room is *your* favorite
- ✔ Want advice on the best place for dinner
- ✔ Want to "size up the innkeeper" by hearing your voice before they commit to staying with you

When a potential guest calls, you have to both gather and share quite a bit of information. Having a script or procedure to follow when you or your staff are taking reservations over the phone ensures that you get the necessary info the first time (you don't want to annoy guests by asking a second time for information they've already given you).

Put together an actual script to use for phone calls, and then role-play some practice calls with your friends so you know what to say when the real calls come in. Have your staff practice calls with you so that they can build their confidence interacting with potential guests over the phone, and you can be sure they're conveying the message and tone you want your guests to be greeted with. Check the Cheat Sheet in the front of this book to be sure you don't skip essential reservation information.

Check out Chapter 8 for more info about representing your B&B online.

Answering the phone in a friendly, professional manner

Guests are calling a business, and your phone greeting should reflect this by including the name of your bed & breakfast. You don't want a guest to have to ask: "Is this Mount Victoria?" Say something like, "Good Morning (afternoon or evening); thank you for calling the award-winning Mount Victoria

Bed & Breakfast Inn. This is Lisa. How may I help you?" Use a strong, clear phone voice and imagine putting a smile in your voice. These inflections add to the first impression guests formulate about your inn.

Use enticing adjectives in your greeting, such as award-winning, historic, or majestic (if they're true), to set your inn apart from the crowd. These simple words are extremely powerful, low-key selling tools that reiterate to potential guests that they're calling a special inn.

Ask the potential guest for his name, jot it down, and use it often in the conversation. The bed & breakfast experience is about personalization, and there's no better way to personalize it than by taking the time to remember and use someone's name.

Part of answering professionally is answering early. Answer the phone before the third ring. Fair or not, subconsciously, guests make an assumption about your inn when the phone rings multiple times. Put yourself in the guest's shoes and think about how you feel when you call a business and the phone rings and rings. If you're busy and can't get to the phone, make sure your answering machine or voice mail greets the guest with a professional message before the third ring (see the later section, "Relying on answering machines or voice-mail systems" for details).

When you're busy with another guest, serving breakfast, dealing with an overflowing toilet, or otherwise unable to devote your full attention to guests who call, let them know their calls are important and ask for permission to call them back. Try something like, "I'm helping another guest at the moment; may I call you back in 10 minutes so I can answer all your questions?" This lets guests know that when they stay with you, you're going to take good care of them. Or consider, "I'm taking a batch of cookies out of the oven. May I call you back in 5 minutes?" The guest will probably imagine the wonderful smell of the cookies coming through the phone.

If you use these techniques, be sure your voice is pleasant and that you call guests within the time that you specify. Letting them know that they're important encourages them to wait for you, rather than dial the next inn.

Probing for a potential guest's needs and expectations

Engaging guests in conversations about why they're visiting your area, what their expectations are, and what they're looking for in an inn gives you the chance to help them plan a trip they can be excited about and, in the process, secure a more definite reservation that's less likely to result in a cancellation. You'll probably discover that when guests find out how much there is to see and do in your area, they're likely to book a longer stay with you than they originally intended. A side benefit of interviewing your guests is ensuring that they'll be happy at your inn and you'll be happy to have them.

Being a good listener makes you a good salesperson — one who's able to match the right guests to your inn and your inn to your guests' expectations. If a guest tells you that he and his wife are taking their first getaway together in ten years since they had children, you could ask whether they'd like suggestions for a romantic restaurant in town, or offer to schedule a couples massage for them at a nearby spa. The amount of personalization that you offer is up to you. Listen to the guests' needs, and decide how you can most closely help them achieve the experience they're looking for by choosing your inn. These are the extras that guests remember when they make referrals and write online reviews.

Sharing all the wonderful things your inn offers

Sell the experience before discussing price. When speaking to potential guests, you're selling your inn, your area, and yourself. Be prepared to offer tips and suggestions for restaurants, attractions, and activities.

Tell guests at least three features of a room before telling them the price. If you tell guests that your rooms range from $129 to $295, few of them will opt for the $295 room unless you give them a reason. So try saying something like, "We have a Jacuzzi suite with a fireplace and private bath available; does that sound like what you'd be interested in?" Then you can tell them that room is $295. You can always offer your smaller rooms or rooms with fewer amenities if the guest's response indicates that price is an issue.

Asking for the reservation

A good salesperson knows you're much more likely to get an order when you ask for it. Taking the guest through the booking process is no different than walking a purchaser through any other sale. Without seeming presumptuous, you can offer to make the reservation for the guest by asking, "May I go ahead and confirm that for you?" The section "Taking Reservations," later in this chapter, goes into this part of the process in more detail.

When guests are noncommittal, it's okay to ask why they're not ready to make a reservation. An easy way to accomplish this is to ask, "Is there anything I didn't mention that you're looking for?" Asking this question enough times gives you good feedback about your reservation skills. If guests continually mention the same thing, then you know it's something you should be including earlier in the conversation. However, their hesitancy may not have anything to do with what you have or haven't told them — they may just be gathering information, sounding you out, or shopping around.

Don't pressure a guest into a reservation. Guests who make a reservation because they don't want to tell you no often end up cancelling those reservations. If a guest is hesitant, ask if he'd like to think about it and get back to you. If the guest wants you to hold the reservation, doing so for a brief period (never more than 24 hours) is usually fine, as long as you have a clear understanding with the guest that it is a temporary hold and not a reservation. For more on this topic, see the sidebar "Don't contribute to a cancellation problem."

Handling calls you can't answer

Several tools are available to help you respond to guest inquiries when you're busy with other guests, attending to emergencies, or otherwise engaged, or when you simply need some personal time to yourself. When you can't answer the phone, consider the alternatives outlined in the following sections.

Relying on answering machines or voice-mail systems

Put your answering machine or voice mail to work. Appeal to your guests by considering the following when creating the message your guests will hear:

- ✔ Offer a short, pleasant, informative greeting. Include enticing adjectives (see the previous section "Answering the phone in a friendly, professional manner").

- ✔ Customize your message according to whether the call is received during the day or after hours. During the day, you might say, "We're assisting other guests, but we're anxious to speak with you." After hours, your message might say, "We're sorry we can't speak with you personally right now; please leave us a message, including a phone number where we can reach you during the day. You may also check our Web site at (and give your Web site address slowly)". Some innkeepers provide even greater personalization by changing their message when they're running errands letting guests know when they'll return calls, and others add seasonal customization such as updates on fall foliage and snowfall.

- ✔ Briefly describe highlights of your inn or area (for example, "We're located across the street from the Vanderbilt Mansion and three miles north of the Culinary Institute" or "All of our rooms offer ocean views").

✔ Invite callers to visit your Web site and slowly give your Web site address. While guests like the personalized service B&Bs offer, in today's busy world they want to know quickly whether rooms are available, and most are eager to secure a reservation. Many guests want an immediate answer, and will call the next inn if they don't reach you. Allowing guests to book reservations instantly online will satisfy many of these guests. (See the "Taking reservations online" section later in this chapter.) If you use reservation software for this purpose, include this in your message. You might say, "Please visit our Web site (and slowly give your Web site address) to check availability and make a confirmed reservation."

✔ Last but not least, always encourage callers to leave you a message so you can call them back to handle their inquiries. (Remember they may have already seen your Web site and be calling with questions or want to confirm information). End the message with, "We look forward to speaking with you personally."

Considering an answering service

Forwarding calls to an answering service such as Calling Inn (`www.calling inn.com`) ensures that guests speak with a live person who can answer the most commonly asked questions about your inn. Some answering service companies can even take reservations or reservation requests for you if you want them to. This type of service is especially valuable if you work outside of the inn and are not available during normal business hours to answer and return phone calls. Unlike an answering machine or voice mail, a live person can give guests instant information. However, they can also give incorrect information. The only way to know if an answering service is right for you is to try them out, so ask about a trial period before signing a contract with them.

Taking Reservations

Taking reservations is as important to innkeepers as taking orders is to a waiter. It's an essential component of your business. The reservation process usually represents your first contact with potential guests, so it's an exciting part of your business as well. When it comes to taking reservations, you have a lot of choices as to how you go about it.

There is no right or wrong way to take reservations. You get to choose whether to take all reservations by phone, let guests request reservations by e-mail, allow guests to book rooms online in real-time, or use a combination of these techniques. The best reservation method is the one that makes you feel most comfortable and makes the most sense to you.

A lot of the information that you request from guests is determined by what reservation system you use and how the data is arranged in the software. (See Chapter 6 for information on choosing a reservation system, which may display only availability or be a complete Property Management System.) However, some essential information must be covered no matter how you take the reservation:

- Dates of arrival and departure

- Names of guests staying in the room

- Review of any policies pertaining to check-in and check-out times, smoking, children, pets, and so forth, as applicable

- Contact information for guests before arrival and cellphone numbers in case you need to reach guests on the date of arrival

- An agreed-upon arrival time, and your notification requirements should that time change

- Dietary restrictions (ask about allergies and dietary restrictions rather than preferences, or you'll be a short-order cook)

- Review of your policies regarding deposits/prepayments and cancellations/refunds

- The next step the guest should expect (for example, receipt of a confirmation letter or e-mail, depending on your system)

This is a good time to find out whether your guests will be celebrating a special occasion like an anniversary or birthday, affording you the chance to make their stay extra-special with a card or even a simple "Happy Anniversary." A little personal attention goes a long way.

Taking reservations by phone

Even if you offer the most gorgeous and inviting Web site (see Chapter 8 for complete information on setting up a Web site for your B&B), guests will quickly lose interest in your B&B if they don't receive a warm greeting when calling your inn. Each time you pick up the phone, think of it as going on an interview. Your interaction with guests while you're making their reservation creates a personal connection, and starts your guests' visits off on the right foot long before they arrive at your B&B.

As you collect the information you need from a guest (see the preceding section), write down when the reservation was taken. This detail can come in handy if any questions come up regarding your cancellation policy.

Don't contribute to a cancellation problem

It's easy to be so enthusiastic about your inn that a guest has a hard time telling you "no." In these instances, guests may give you a credit card number to hold a reservation for several months into the future, even though they're not really committed to coming. In your mind, once you take a reservation, the room is sold. Yet the guests may be thinking that they don't have to cancel until 14 days prior to their planned arrival, so going ahead and making a reservation just gives them options.

Listen carefully to a guest's questions and ascertain the level of commitment before taking the reservation. It will be a lot harder to fill that same room with only 14 days notice, and you'll be doing the same work twice. Even though you should ask to help the guest make a reservation, you should never push for it.

Ask what telephone number you may reach the guest at if you need to contact her concerning the reservation. You don't want to spoil a surprise or let out a secret by calling someone other than the person who made the reservation with you. Additionally, you should have your guests' cellphone numbers in case you need to reach them on the day they're traveling to your inn.

You also need to know who will be staying at your inn, but you can't always assume a couple are husband and wife. On the other hand, asking for the name of a guest's partner may rub the guest the wrong way when he or she *is* a husband or wife. Consider simply asking for the names of the guests who will be staying in the room.

Taking reservations online

The B&B industry has been much slower than the airline and hotel industries to adopt confirmed, real-time, online reservations systems, primarily for two reasons:

- ✔ Innkeepers prefer to speak with their guests personally
- ✔ Innkeepers fear *double bookings* — reserving one room for two different groups — which can occur if you don't have an organized system for keeping track of your reservations. Arriving guests don't want to hear that there's no room at the inn.

But regardless of these factors, guest demand is pushing the trend of real-time, online reservations forward. How much information and control you give to online guests regarding your availability and making reservations are choices you need to make.

In today's information-rich world, guests are looking for immediate confirmation. They don't want to take the time to find out about an inn until they're sure the inn has a room available that fits their travel schedule.

Most guests determine when they want to travel first and do research secondarily to determine where to stay. Rarely does this process work in reverse — with a guest first choosing an inn and then deciding when to travel based on the inn's vacancies.

You have three main options when you're using the Internet to aid you in taking reservations. The following sections give you details on each option.

You shouldn't feel pressured to handle reservations in a manner you're not comfortable with. Some innkeepers feel that if their reservation process requires them to speak with every guest personally, they lose reservations because many guests book with the first inn that has availability. Other innkeepers feel that by speaking with each guest prior to the reservation, they're better able to ensure that the guest is right for the inn and the inn is right for the guest. Each system is explained in greater detail in the following sections. If you're really unsure which system makes sense to start with, speak with other innkeepers who have inns similar to yours in terms of size, occupancy, and innkeeper involvement.

Showing availability only

When you show guests availability only, you display a calendar of when you have rooms available and when you're booked. (Some calendars show availability by date only, whereas others display availability by room.) These calendars can be displayed on your Web site and on many other online adverting pages, such as directory listings (see Chapter 8 for information on online directories) and some association Web sites.

The calendar merely shows when rooms are available and when they're booked. Guests can quickly scan the calendar for this information, but they can't request or confirm a reservation until they contact you.

You should consider this option if you're an innkeeper who wants to speak with your guests before confirming their reservations or if you don't want the responsibility of having to update your computer system immediately upon taking a reservation. This also works well if you don't want guests to see that a particular room is booked and bypass your inn without having the opportunity to sell them a different room. You also may use it to let guests know when you have no rooms available so you aren't bothered with calls for rooms that are already booked. If you choose this type of system, make sure it clearly tells guests how to contact you to make a reservation.

Taking reservation requests

In addition to showing guests your availability (see the preceding section), either by date or by room, these systems let guests submit a reservation request by e-mail or through a form online. Requests are not confirmed reservations until you confirm them with the guest.

Innkeepers choose this option for a variety of reasons. The guest's request starts the reservation process, yet it still gives the innkeeper the option to speak with the guest before the reservation is confirmed. You don't need to worry if you're unable to update your availability in real-time because the guest is only making a request, not a confirmed reservation. As a result, you can't double-book a room, even if your system is not updated.

A word of caution about the reservation request system: You need to make it clear to guests that they are only making requests and not confirmed reservations. Software programs that cater to the B&B industry automatically send a guest who makes a reservation request an e-mail that acknowledges the request and tells the guest what to expect next, such as a call from you to confirm the reservation. These e-mails specifically state that this is not a confirmed reservation; however, you should follow up quickly because guests often don't read these details and assume they have a confirmed reservation.

Confirming real-time reservations

This system allows guests to book online as soon as they find an inn they like, even if it's in the middle of the night. Many innkeepers choose this format because they feel they would lose the reservation otherwise. Guests prefer this system because they know that once they've found an inn they like, they can make a reservation and receive a confirmation immediately without directly speaking with you.

Your real-time room inventory and availability is stored on your software vendor's server if you use a Web-based system and on your computer if you use a desktop application (Chapter 6 explains the different systems). This feature allows you and the general public to view your inventory at the same time. It makes sense for innkeepers to have a high-speed Internet connection because although online reservation systems may work using a dial-up connection, the process is very slow.

When you receive a room request by phone, you must keep the caller on the phone while you put the reservation through the system to make certain a confirmation number is generated. No confirmation number means no reservation.

If you don't put the reservation through while your guest is on the phone, you run the risk of an online guest booking the room before you do! Say, for instance, that you're interrupted or distracted and you don't book the room requested by a caller right away. In the meantime, a guest viewing your inventory online makes a reservation for the same room and date you promised to your caller. The online guest has already received the confirmation number, so the room belongs to her, not the person who contacted you by phone earlier in the day. This may seem unfair, but real-time reservations systems operate strictly on a first-booked, first-served basis. The fact that you're the owner of the inn does nothing to alter this.

You can have your real-time availability programmed so as not to allow same-day bookings. An online note will then display, telling the viewer to call the inn directly for same-day room availability. This prevents a double booking from occurring in the event that you have drop-ins (sometimes called *drive-bys* or *walk-ins* — people who drop by without reservations hoping you'll have a vacancy for them on the spot). You won't run the risk of other guests showing up later that night for the same room because they were booking it online while you were checking in the drop-ins.

After you are accepting confirmed, real-time reservations, you may opt to participate in the GDS (Global Distribution System) through most software providers. GDS is the system used by travel agents, and participating gets your property listed on such sites as Travelocity and Expedia. The price, however, is steep — you should expect to pay fees of up to 30 percent for each booking.

Avoiding Cancellations and Managing Vacancies

Busy innkeepers have a tendency to focus on their current guests. But managing last-minute vacancies, whether due to cancellations or lack of demand, is part of your revenue management plan. So no matter how busy you are, keep an eye on your upcoming reservation calendar.

Rooms are your inventory, and unsold inventory has a shelf life or expiration date. If you have five rooms and one of them is vacant, especially on a peak weekend, you're forgoing 20 percent of your potential revenue.

You can take some examples and inspiration from the cruise ship and airline industries in thinking about how to handle your last-minute vacancies. Once a ship sets sail or a plane takes off, all chances of earning revenue on vacant cabins or seats are lost. Just like these industries, you may want to offer last-minute packages and specials. Many of the top online directories (listed in Chapter 8) have last-minute getaway pages where you can promote your last-minute specials. Discounts aren't the only technique to fill vacancies. Keep a careful eye on your future reservation calendar and check out the suggestions in the section, "Filling unsold rooms," later in this chapter. Planning ahead and finding out how to fill your rooms is guaranteed to work better than crossing your fingers and hoping for a walk-in guest.

The best way to keep a full house is to avoid having to sell a room twice. Do everything you can to avoid a cancellation, leaving you with a last-minute vacancy. Keep in mind, though, that while cancellations are disappointing, they're also inevitable, and they're not personal.

Clarifying your cancellation policy

Having a good, clear cancellation policy is the best way to avoid cancellations. (See Chapter 7 for help in setting your policies.) Making sure that guests understand your cancellation policy is your responsibility. Post the policy clearly on your Web site or anywhere else a guest can make a reservation, and include it in your confirmation letters and e-mails.

Be aware that guests, especially first time B&B goers, may be accustomed to hotels where they can cancel up until the day of arrival. You don't double-book your rooms expecting cancellations the way hotels do, so your cancellation policy is different. Some innkeepers like to include wording such as

> *Due to our size and the personal attention we offer our guests, cancellations affect us greatly. Your deposit is your commitment to us that you are reserving this room and our commitment to you that your room will be waiting for you upon your arrival. Please be sure you have read and understand our cancellation policy.*

If you take a guest's credit card to guarantee a deposit, you may need to charge the card if the guest cancels at the last minute or doesn't show. Check with the merchant bank that processes your credit cards to see whether you need to include any special wording or procedures in your policy to ensure you won't come up against any problems in these situations. (See Chapter 7 for information on accepting credit cards.)

While I recommend sticking to your policy in order to protect your revenue stream, if you want to be flexible because of personal circumstances or because you can easily rebook a room, that's your decision to make. In some cases, bending the rules a little can make you a winner in the end.

Filling unsold rooms

When you find yourself with available rooms, especially during your peak season and on weekends, you need to take a closer look at the prices of your rooms, your minimum stay requirements, and your marketing efforts. If your rooms are priced higher than the competition's or if your guests don't perceive them as a good value, you need to reevaluate — and possibly lower — your rates. (See Chapter 7 for info on setting rates.) Sometimes your pricing is fair, but your minimum stay requirement keeps guests from booking with you and causes them to choose the competition instead. Relaxing this requirement may help you book more rooms. However, you need to decide whether the trade-off of more rooms to turn over justifies the increased occupancy.

Most inns aren't doing all they could to market their property to potential guests. The more often guests find your inn, the more likely you are to fill your rooms, so being found is more than half the battle. Once guests find an inn they like, they're unlikely to spend a lot of time looking around to save $5. Spending time marketing your inn (see Chapters 8 and 15) always brings more guests your way.

No matter what you do to avoid cancellations and fill your rooms in advance, last-minute vacancies will occur, so here are several ideas to keep a steady flow of last-minute inquiries to offset your losses:

✔ **Keep a waiting list.** When guests call for rooms and you're already booked, ask if they would like to be put on your waiting list. This leaves the guest with a good impression of your inn — your inn must be popular if it's often booked and keeps a waiting list, plus you're giving them personal consideration.

In addition to putting customers on a waiting list, ask whether they'd like to be put on your mailing list to receive notices of special packages and upcoming events. The fact that you're booked already tells guests that your inn is a great choice, so keep your name in front of them by sending them your newsletter.

✔ **Offer a last-minute or off-peak special.** When you see that you have upcoming availability during slow seasons or as a result of a last-minute cancellation, you can entice guests with last-minute packages (see Chapter 15 for help creating packages).

✔ **Coordinate with other inns in the area.** Get to know the other inn-keepers in your area, and suggest referring guests amongst yourselves. Then when other inns in the area are full, they can refer guests to you to fill your vacancies without those guests having to find you on their own.

Any recommendation that you make is a reflection on you, so only enter into this arrangement if the inn you refer guests to offers an experience that's comparable to staying at your inn. Remember the guest may be a frequent visitor to your area, and if your referral doesn't work out, that guest won't stay at either inn in the future.

✔ **Consider upgrading existing guests upon arrival.** When guests arrive, give them a tour of the inn. If an unbooked room is an upgrade over the room they reserved, be sure to include it in the tour. Oftentimes, guests will ask to upgrade after seeing your better rooms.

If guests don't request an upgrade, you always have the option of earning some brownie points by upgrading them at no extra charge. Only you can be the judge of how often you want to do this. Doing so increases the likelihood of these guests becoming repeat customers and referring your B&B to others, filling future unsold rooms. On the downside, you don't want return guests to come to expect upgrades. Keep the overall picture in mind and don't upgrade the guest until check-in, or you'll lose the opportunity to sell the higher-priced room to this guest at check-in or to a last-minute guest inquiry.

✔ **Create an e-mail notification list.** Invite previous guests to be on a special e-mail list that lets them know when you have a cancellation or last-minute vacancy and are offering a special discount.

Chapter 12

Taking Care of Guests

· ·

In This Chapter

▶ Being an extraordinary host

▶ Handling problem guests

▶ Knowing what a guest wants before they ask

· ·

*N*ow comes the exciting part — what being an innkeeper is all about . . . welcoming guests to your bed & breakfast! How you take care of your guests is integral to the personality of your inn.

In this chapter, you find out how to manage the check-in process to avoid misunderstandings and maximize your guests' safety and comfort from the moment they arrive. I tell you how to make sure they enjoy their time at your bed & breakfast so much that they'll start planning their next visit before they've even checked out! And for those rare occasions when you find yourself hosting problem guests, I give you some warnings about what to expect along with some tips on handling difficult people.

When the Guest Arrives

Your inn is more than just a beautiful setting. While the physical structure is important, what defines your bed & breakfast is the experience that your guests have when staying at your B&B. The arrival of each new guest and the return of repeat guests add to the dynamics of your inn and become a part of its evolving history. Your job is to create a welcoming environment and to facilitate camaraderie among your guests so that everyone's getaway becomes intertwined with the energy and fun of staying at your B&B. Starting off on the right foot with a warm and informative welcome sets the stage.

Use the following information to create a checklist of guest check-in procedures to help you keep the process running smoothly and signal to your guests that you are graciously in charge. Of course, you won't carry the checklist around with you as you're checking guests in, but having a set procedure is helpful not only to you, but also to anyone who may greet guests in your place — whether they be new employees, staff members, or interim innkeepers. When first starting out, it's a good idea to practice check-ins on staff, friends, or family.

Setting the tone with a warm welcome

Your welcome sets the tone for your guests' visits, behaviors, and anticipations. Guests can be turned off at the most spectacular inn if they feel no warmth or hospitality when they arrive. There's no one secret tip to make your guests feel welcome; rather, it's the little things that add up to differentiate a stay at your inn from other inns and hotels. For starters, be sure to perform the following tasks before your guests even arrive:

✔ **Confirm curb appeal.** The outside of your bed & breakfast should be as welcoming as the inside. Guests form an immediate opinion of your inn the minute they arrive, so landscaping, ease of parking, and the exterior of your inn must be maintained. Don't forget to include well-spaced lighting for guests arriving after dark.

✔ **Check your entryway.** Try to see your inn through your guests' eyes as they step inside. Is the front door clean and well painted? Is the entryway clean, uncluttered, and welcoming? Be sure it makes a good, strong first impression.

✔ **Remind yourself of pertinent reservation details.** Review your guests' expected arrival times and familiarize yourself with their names. Also note special dietary requests or special celebrations and verify the details of any packages that they have reserved. Your guests will feel warmly welcomed when greeted by name, and your exceptional hospitality will be evident when their dietary restrictions are accommodated without question and the details of their packages such as massage appointments, flowers, chocolates, and so on are in place.

Guests with a positive first impression of your bed & breakfast are more likely to overlook anything that isn't quite perfect than guests who start out on the wrong foot — the latter are the ones most likely to remember and complain. So to make that all-important first impression a mark in your favor, here are some thoughts from experienced innkeepers on greeting guests:

✔ **Answer the door.** (Many B&B guests ring the doorbell.) Think about how you would feel arriving at a B&B with no one to greet you and not knowing where you should go or how to find the person in charge. Greet your guests with a warm and genuine greeting and big welcoming smile. When possible, open the door before they have a chance to ring the bell.

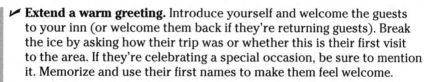

> ✔ **Extend a warm greeting.** Introduce yourself and welcome the guests to your inn (or welcome them back if they're returning guests). Break the ice by asking how their trip was or whether this is their first visit to the area. If they're celebrating a special occasion, be sure to mention it. Memorize and use their first names to make them feel welcome.
>
> Your smile, the tone of your voice, your body language, your appearance, and your immediate availability affect your guests' initial feelings about your inn. Imagine the difference between being greeted by an innkeeper with a mop in hand and cleaning clothes on and being greeted by a neatly dressed innkeeper with a huge smile welcoming you through a wide open door.
>
> ✔ **Ask guests where they are parked and/or give them parking instructions.**
>
> ✔ **Offer to help them carry in their luggage.**

Checking guests in

When guests arrive, they're likely to be weary from traveling and eager to get to their room. Having an organized check-in procedure speeds the process along.

Don't keep guests waiting to check in. If guests are backed up, seat them in the common room, offer refreshments, and check them in by turns.

Be sure to take the following steps as you check in each guest:

1. **Verify/record each guest's full name, home address, phone number, vehicle description, and license plate number on the guests' reservation card/folio (see Step 5 for more information).**

2. **Verify the room selected and the rate of the room plus occupancy tax (mention any discounts, upgrades, or offers).**

3. **Confirm the check-out date and time.**

4. **Swipe a credit card or collect the outstanding balance.**

   As a new innkeeper, you may feel uncomfortable collecting payment during the welcome process, but getting payment upfront avoids the possibility of misconceptions about how long guests plan to stay, misunderstandings about the price of the room, guests slipping away without paying, or guests feeling rushed if they need to check out early while you're preparing breakfast for other guests. Also, it's rather anti-climactic to be enjoying the spirit of friendship after hosting guests, and then giving hugs and saying your good-byes only to butt in with *"Oh, by the way, you need to pay $435.23 before you leave."*

5. **Have guests sign their reservation card/folio.**

    This card/folio is a record of the guests' stay and their notification of your policies. It may be a template from your property management system, a custom form, or a combination of both. It usually includes the guests' name(s), address, phone, e-mail, room, rate, dates of stay, credit card information, vehicle description, driver's license number, policies such as smoking and pets, conditions for damage, cleaning or other charges, breakfast time, and check-out time.

6. **Ask guests if they need help with recommendations or reservations during their stay.**

    What sets your inn apart from other B&Bs and the bed & breakfast experience apart from a hotel stay is you. Proactively offering concierge services is guaranteed to enhance your guests' experience.

7. **Give the guests a receipt, a copy of the card/folio they signed, and all necessary keys and access codes (to the front door, their room, and so on).**

Practice the flow of checking guests in. Decide whether you want to check guests in, collect payment, and then give guests a brief tour of the inn, or whether you want to show guests to their rooms first and let them settle in for a few minutes before officially checking them in. Most innkeepers prefer the former.

Occasionally mistakes are made and you or a staff member will book two guests in the same room. It doesn't matter how it happened (of course you'll want to figure it out later so it doesn't happen again); your immediate concern is to take care of the guest. If you don't have another room to offer, find the guest a room at another inn for the period of the double booking. Make sure it's a room of equal or greater value than the room they had reserved with you, and pay the difference regardless of the cost (or refund any balance if the price is lower). Apologize profusely and try to get the guest back to your inn as soon as possible. Then do something extra for them, such as leaving flowers or wine in the room.

Getting guests settled and taking a tour

Hotels are easy to navigate, but your guests don't know the lay of the land at your inn, so give guests a welcome tour of your inn, including all common areas and outdoor spaces (weather permitting), before showing them to their rooms. Here are some things you don't want to forget on the welcome tour of your inn:

✔ **Show guests the common areas.** Be sure to invite your guests to use these spaces. Let them know that they're often used by other guests so they feel comfortable using them. Point out any related amenities and information, such as:

- Complimentary snacks and beverages like early-morning coffee, afternoon tea, or after-dinner drinks (check the liquor laws in your area if you serve alcohol)

- Board games, cards, DVDs, a lending library, and newspapers

- Frequently requested maps, brochures, and other area information, such as a listing of local churches

- A book with local restaurant menus

✔ **Tour outdoor areas.** Don't forget to show guests patios, outdoor hot tubs, gardens, and so on. Be sure to tell guests where to get towels for the hot tub and where to find umbrellas and cushions if you don't automatically set them up.

✔ **Remind guests of your policies.** A welcome tour provides the perfect opportunity to reinforce and clarify policies regarding breakfast times, smoking, children, and pets. Clearly communicating your policies to guests as part of their orientation helps to underscore your expectations and reduces the likelihood of misunderstandings.

You don't want to beat guests over the head with rules when they're trying to get comfortable, but they do need to know the policies and guidelines. So be sure to establish boundaries ahead of time by providing a copy of your policies when you confirm your guests' reservations, posting your policies clearly on your Web site, and giving guests a copy of their reservation card/folio with your major policies listed on it when they check in. If you want to post one or two policies in the rooms, do so with informational notes tastefully displayed. For example, create them in calligraphy (computers usually have many fancy fonts) and post them in a small, attractive frame. You might also consider creating a Guest Book for each room that includes important information about your inn, your policies, amenities, and area activities. This information is handy for guests to refer to; however, because many don't read it, you shouldn't rely on it to communicate your policies.

✔ **Point out fire escapes and emergency exits.** Tell guests where this information is posted in their rooms (usually on the back of the door) and show them fire escapes and emergency exits during the tour.

✔ **Provide pertinent info about amenities and appliances.** Briefly explain how to use amenities and appliances such as wireless Internet, the TV remote, the heating or air conditioning system, the telephone, the hot tub, and the fireplace. But also leave behind clear, written instructions that guests who are distracted by the details can reference later.

If your inn practices a linen reuse program, now is a good time to explain to guests how to let you know when they want their linens and towels changed. (Refer to Chapter 13 for information on linen reuse programs.)

✔ **Let guests know how to reach you.** Guests need to know how to reach you in the event of an emergency and how to ask you questions about the inn and the area. If you live on-site, remind them of this.

Guests should always know how to reach you, whether you're running errands or out for the evening. When you're away from the inn leave a brief note where guests can see it letting them know how to reach you and/or when you plan to return (the innkeeper's door and the inn's front desk are ideal spots for communicating with current guests, and the inn's front door is a good spot to leave notes for new arrivals or drop-ins).

During the first few hours after guests have arrived, you should expect to be asked questions you've already covered. Be patient and gracious, and use questions as feedback. If you're getting the same questions over and over, it's a cue for you to analyze how you provide the information to guests and ask yourself whether you can make the information clearer.

Part of being a good innkeeper is to periodically ask guests how their room is and whether they're finding everything okay. Asking these key questions within a few hours after guests have settled in helps to put them at ease, demonstrates that you're genuinely concerned about their comfort, and gives you a chance to correct any deficiencies they may bring to your attention.

Accommodating early check-ins

Innkeepers commonly receive requests for early check-ins. "Early" means different things to different people. Sometimes guests arrive early and unannounced — in fact, don't be surprised to have guests show up to check in while you're still serving breakfast to your current guests — and an unrushed, gracious check-in can easily take up to 30 minutes.

As with most things in the B&B world, there are no absolutes. Deciding if and when you want to grant an exception is up to you. If your guests' room is ready, you may decide that their request is easy enough to accommodate. Other times — even when the room is ready — you may decide that an early check-in just isn't possible.

Your check-in policy should be as clear as all your other policies. But no matter how clearly you word it, some people simply won't read it. They're also unlikely to understand how much happens during the 3 to 4 hours you have between check-out and check-in (cleaning rooms and the rest of the inn, changing linens, doing laundry and yard work, baking, running errands, giving tours of the inn, taking reservations, and more). You need to protect this time in order to welcome your guests with your best foot forward.

Common check-out times are 11 a.m. and noon, and common check-in times are from 3 to 6 p.m. or 4 to 7 p.m. Once you've been open for several months, you'll get to know when most guests want to check in and you can adjust your times accordingly. Just make sure you allow yourself enough time between check-out and check-in to clean the rooms to the standard that you set for your inn — without having to rush and feel frazzled.

Having someone else in the house also has a psychological and an emotional impact. If you're between guests, you may need an hour to yourself to eat lunch or make some personal calls. This is okay. Taking time when you can makes you a better innkeeper in the long run.

Sometimes guests will tell you when they make their reservation that they'd like to check in early. Even if you want to accommodate them, you don't know whether the previous guests will be checking out at the last minute and whether you'll have time to turn over the room. In this case, you can suggest that they call you as they get close to the inn on their arrival day, and that you'll let them know then whether or not their room is available.

Other guests may ask to drop their luggage off early. Sounds like a simple enough request on the surface, and for many it is, but beware: In some innkeepers' experience, there's no such thing as *just dropping off luggage*. Dropping off luggage often leads to using the restroom, and many B&Bs don't have a public restroom. This means that guests need to be allowed into their rooms, which means their rooms need to be ready for them — and if that's the case, they might as well check in. With or without a public restroom, dropping off luggage early may or may not be a courtesy you want to extend to your guests.

When you're not ready for guests who arrive early, you have the following options:

- ✔ **Answer the door and step outside to tell your guests that you're sorry their room isn't ready** (whether it is or not). Remember that this impromptu greeting is an important first impression of your inn. Be hospitable, and suggest places for them to have lunch or an attraction they might want to see. Let them know you're looking forward to welcoming them at 3 p.m. (or whatever your designated check-in time is) and that their room will be ready and waiting for them then. How firm you want to be is up to you and how much you need to get done.

- ✔ **When you really need to get something done, you might not even answer the door** — but don't let your guests know you're inside if you use this tactic. Any time you're not able to answer the door or are running errands, leave a note for guests on the front door letting them know you're away from the inn and that you'll return by whatever your check-in time is.

Handling late arrivals

Your reservation procedure should include asking guests for their approximate arrival time, requesting that they contact you if they're running late, and asking whether they have a cellphone by which they can be reached if necessary while they're en route. (See Chapter 11 for complete details on taking reservations.) However, despite the fact that you agree upon a window of time during which your guests should arrive, the unexpected often happens, causing your guests to arrive later than planned.

Some of your guests will give you a courtesy call to let you know that they're running late, but many first-time B&B goers (and others) won't — perhaps they think you have a 24-hour check-in desk. Whatever the reason, you may have plans that prevent you from being at the inn. Just the fact that you need to get up early to prepare breakfast makes waiting for late-arriving guests very inconvenient. While some innkeepers choose to wait and greet every guest personally, no matter what the time, there is a viable alternative. You can institute a self-check-in plan for late arrivals that allows your guests to help themselves.

When guests tells you they plan to arrive after your normal check-in time or call to let you know they're running late, you can tell them how to check themselves in. For guests who arrive late with no advance warning, you can leave a note at the front door explaining your self-check-in procedure. Alternatively, you can leave a note with a phone number to call you. Once you've identified them, you can give them the information for a self-check-in. Systems to enable self-check-in can take on many forms, including

- ✔ A combination key lock on the front door
- ✔ A lock box (ideally one that allows you to set the combination — for example, to the last digits of the guest's phone number).
- ✔ A hidden key
- ✔ An electronic door lock and/or intercom system
- ✔ An unlocked door
- ✔ A key in an envelope

Naturally, the neighborhood in which your inn is located determines how secure you feel with any of the preceding self-check-in procedures.

To make the self-check-in procedure run smoothly, do the following:

- ✔ Leave a welcome note for the guests with information on the location of their room and when breakfast will be served. You should leave lights on throughout the inn and the grounds so they can easily find their room.
- ✔ Leave the lights on in the guests' room and put a sign on their door with the room name, so there are no misunderstandings as to which room is reserved for them. Keep all other room doors closed — and preferably locked. You don't want your guests looking around and choosing another room.

Send out an e-mail the week before your guests' scheduled arrival, letting them know you're looking forward to their visit and confirming their arrival time. Include a reminder to give you a call if their arrival time changes.

Interacting with Your Guests

Hosting personal friends and family members in your home is quite different from hosting guests who pay to stay at your bed & breakfast. Successful innkeepers know that taking care of guests is much more than offering a lovely room in a beautiful home and cooking wonderful food for guests to rave about. B&B guests choose bed & breakfasts over hotels because of the experience. You, the innkeeper and host, are a big part of the guests' experience. Your attention to their needs, whether it's offering additional amenities or respecting their desire for privacy, shapes their experience at your inn. Ultimately, your interaction with your guests determines their desire to return and to refer your B&B to others.

Making guests want to come back again and again

Going the extra mile is the key to delivering the genuine hospitality that makes guests want to come back again and again, as well as refer you to their friends. Showing care and concern for your guests' comfort and happiness is the secret to making your bed & breakfast number one in your guests' eyes. Consider it a compliment if your guests are planning their next trip to your inn before they've even checked out. Here are some tips and ideas to make that happen:

- **Ask open-ended questions.** Most B&B guests are the nicest people in the world, and they don't want to be thought of as complainers. As such, they may be reluctant to tell you if something is wrong with their room or if they need something. You can draw guests out by asking open-ended questions, such as *"How is your stay going?"* or *"How is your room working for you?"* Successful innkeepers know to ask, *"How is your ice holding out?"* rather than *"Do you need more ice?"* The first question is more of a conversation generator than the second, which elicits only a simple yes or no response. Guests quickly pick up on your willingness to be of service to them, and it sets the stage for a pleasant stay.

✔ **Show interest in your guests' enjoyment.** Guests notice when you care enough to inquire whether they're enjoying their getaway, and this type of hospitality is guaranteed to make your inn stand out. For example, the Walnut Lane Inn in Lyman, South Carolina (www.walnutlaneinn.com) has installed an inexpensive motion detector in the corner of the front door that rings in the owners' quarters. Not only does this let the innkeepers know when someone is coming or going, it also allows them to greet their guests after dinner to ask how their dinner was and to confirm breakfast times.

✔ **Make restaurant or activity suggestions and offer to make reservations for your guests.** Providing this service helps you in several ways:

• The guests appreciate the personal attention you're offering by making suggestions and reservations. They also appreciate your letting them know when you think they wouldn't enjoy a particular restaurant or activity, and why.

• If you send numerous referrals to any one establishment, your guests are likely to be treated especially well, which is a nice reflection on you.

• Giving referrals may beget referrals. When you make the reservations yourself, other local businesses know that the referral is coming from you. You never know when they may be in a position to send a referral your way.

✔ **Serve a light breakfast for early check-outs.** Often, guests who need to leave early will tell you not to worry about their breakfast. However, they're usually extraordinarily appreciative of your extra hospitality if you can offer a light breakfast or "breakfast-to-go" before their departure.

✔ **Offer guests amenities and extras they wouldn't typically receive at a hotel.** For example, if you're near a beach, provide complimentary beach chairs and umbrellas. If there are bike trails nearby, consider offering the use of bicycles (check with your insurance carrier to be sure you're covered in the event that a guest is injured). If you're near a train or bus station or airport you may want to offer a pick-up service for your guests, provided they don't need a car during the remainder of their stay. (Check with your insurance carrier to be sure that you are adequately covered when transporting guests.) Other common amenities innkeepers offer their guests are the ability to borrow DVDs and access to a full cookie jar!

It's important to recognize, however, when abundance is too much. Guests love the feeling of getting a good value and being spoiled, but to be a successful innkeeper and business owner, you must always keep a careful eye on expenses. You need to be sure that the cost of the amenities you provide to your guests is justified in the rates you charge. (See Chapter 3 for help in creating a plan for your business, including estimating the cost of amenities.)

> ✔ **Display a level of thoughtfulness that's out of the ordinary.** For example, at Sunrise Landing B&B in Dundee, New York, (www.sunrise landingbb.com), the innkeepers offer to take each guest's picture. They then surprise them by putting it in a gold foil frame as a take-home memory of their stay. On the back of the picture they put the inn's business card with their contact information and Web address. Guests love the thoughtfulness of this gesture, and it keeps the inn foremost in their minds when friends ask them for a referral.

When guests choose your inn, they are choosing you, your hospitality, and your concierge services over hotels and other inns in the area, so pay attention to your guests. Always be on the lookout for little extras you can add that will make your guests not only want to return, but also refer you to their family and friends.

Knowing when to be quiet

Despite your desire to anticipate and fulfill your guests' every need, one of the most important skills you should have is knowing when to be quiet. This is tough for many innkeepers, because most have very outgoing personalities. However, from time to time you'll get guests who, for whatever reason, simply prefer to be left alone.

Be aware that sometimes you'll read the situation correctly and sometimes you'll get it wrong. For example, when a guest gives you a one- or two-word answer, you may be dealing with a person of few words or it may be an important cue that the guest doesn't want to engage in conversation. This is where people-reading skills come in handy. When you have guests that you think would prefer to be left alone, simply let them know you're available if they need you. You might say something like, "There are extra pillows and blankets in the closet, and if you need more, or if there is anything else you need, please let me know."

As an innkeeper you need to know when to be quiet and also to sense when there's too much quiet. It can be equally difficult to get a conversation started at breakfast when there's an awkward silence. The weather, local sights, or the food are usually safe conversation-starters. Avoid discussing politics, religion, and environmental issues.

At some point, most guests will ask you why you decided to become an innkeeper. Never answer with your complete life story and the evolution of your bed & breakfast. Start with a very short answer. If the guest asks you more questions, you can give them more details.

Keeping Guests Safe and Comfortable

Guests need to feel safe and comfortable in order to feel taken care of. As an innkeeper, you need to be concerned about a variety of forms of guest safety, including:

- **Your guest's physical safety:** Not only do you need to be sure locks on your doors and windows are secure to keep perpetrators out, but you also need to be sure that guests can move freely around the inn without worry of injury. (See Chapter 9 for information on safety considerations when furnishing your inn.)

- **Your guests' perception of safety:** Guests need the comfort of feeling safe. A guest from a rural environment may feel uneasy at an urban inn in a large city, but you can attempt to alleviate the guest's fears by reassuring the guest with specific suggestions about how to get around and where to go.

- **Compliance with required safety procedures and codes:** Many safety requirements are mandated by federal, state, and local law. Others are required by various inspection and rating agencies. (See Chapter 5 for information on zoning and other legalities.)

- **Food safety:** The last thing you want is for guests to get sick at your inn because the food they ate was bad. Proper refrigeration, storage, and cooking procedures need to be practiced diligently for guests' safety. The health department will inspect your facilities and practices concerning safe food handling, storing, and preparation, and in many U.S. jurisdictions, you will be required to pass the ServSafe Food test (for more info, check out www.servsafe.com).

Guests should know how to reach you or a staff member at all times, even during the night. Good communication is key to a guest's well-being and feeling of safety, and knowing how to reach you is an essential component of this communication.

Being prepared for emergencies

The first few minutes after an emergency occurs are the most critical. You must react to protect your guests, yourself, and your B&B. Learning as much as you can about what to do in an emergency helps you to be prepared. Beyond calling 911, which you should do immediately in an emergency, here are some things to consider ahead of time:

- **Know basic first aid.** Take a first aid training class to know how to help a guest who is choking. Checking with your insurance company and your attorney for legal advice in rendering medical aid is a good idea.

✔ **Keep basic first aid supplies on hand.** Have bandages, ice packs (or frozen peas), antibiotic ointment, and so on available for guests who suffer minor injuries.

✔ **Have smoke and carbon monoxide detectors installed and checked frequently.**

✔ **Stay up-to-date on all zoning, health, and safety requirements.**

✔ **Have fire extinguishers handy, especially in the kitchen.**

✔ **Know what to do in the event of a kitchen fire:**

- Use caution when cooking with grease and alcohol because they're very flammable.

- Don't attempt to extinguish grease fires with water.

- Small grease fires in a pan can be extinguished by placing a lid on the pan to cut off the oxygen supply to the fire.

- Baking soda may be thrown on small grease fires or electrical fires.

- If a fire breaks out in the oven, close the oven door and turn off the heat.

- Don't wear loose-fitting clothing that can easily catch fire when cooking.

- If your clothes catch fire, stop, drop, and roll to put the fire out.

✔ **Prepare an evacuation plan for each room and post it in each guest room.** Show guests the emergency exits when giving them a welcome tour of the inn. In some U.S. jurisdictions, regardless of the size of the inn, you are required to ask each guest whether he would need assistance vacating the building in the event of an emergency.

All staff should be trained for what to do in an emergency and you should conduct drills at least once a year. Does everyone know where to turn off the power, gas, and water, and are there tools readily available to do so? In the unfortunate event that your inn is in the center of a disaster, your staff should be instructed ahead of time not to speak with the press, and it's a good idea for you to speak with your insurance agent before speaking with the press yourself.

Having a contingency plan when a guest's stay is interrupted

Occasionally things that are out of your control happen to interrupt a guest's stay. Instead of wasting a lot of time worrying about what could go wrong, plan ahead by creating a contingency plan. For example, if construction work outside your inn knocks out electricity to the B&B, how will you handle it?

If you've made it a point to get to know the other inns in your area, you're probably all set (see Chapter 1 for recommendations on talking with other successful innkeepers). Innkeepers often help one another by accommodating each other's guests in emergencies. Be sure you know the caliber of the B&Bs that you make these arrangements with, because how you handle the guests' accommodations when plans need to be changed — even if the circumstances are beyond your control — reflects on you and your inn. Despite being friends with many of the innkeepers with whom you may have your guests stay during an emergency, consider staying somewhere else yourself if you have to leave along with your guests. It's often more comfortable for everyone concerned.

Keep emergency phone numbers on hand, and provide a clear way for your guests to contact emergency responders in your area. (See the Cheat Sheet for a list of important numbers to keep in speed dial.)

A great resource for business preparedness and contingency planning is www.ready.gov. Select the option for business.

Handling Problem Guests — And Ohhh Are They Out There!

Some of the most difficult times innkeepers face are the challenges that problem guests bring, knowingly and unknowingly. As an innkeeper, I'm sure you possess a strong sense of pride about your inn and a strong desire for all your guests to have a fabulous stay at your B&B. Problem guests threaten one or both of these strongly held passions. Fortunately, wonderful guests are far more abundant than problem guests.

The problems guests cause range from mildly annoying to serious breaches of your policies. You can prepare for some problems by using waterproof mattress covers and buying a carpet cleaner, but other issues require a more personal touch to resolve. As the host, the owner, and the innkeeper, you must be firmly in charge and able to maintain control to protect your inn and the enjoyment and comfort of all your guests. The best way to do that is to prevent problems by having firm policies and enforcing them as necessary. (See Chapter 7 for help in setting and sticking to your policies.) The following sections describe common situations and how to handle them when things get out of hand.

Always use your best judgment. Accidents happen. Know when to be gracious and when to hold the line.

Friends who are innkeepers and innkeeper associations and forums provide a good source of support. They're a great place to let off steam and bounce ideas around about how to deal with problem guests. Even seasoned innkeepers need to let off steam occasionally. (See Chapter 1 to find valuable innkeeper resources.)

Ignoring your policies

Guests may ignore your policies for a variety of reasons. Each situation is unique and deserves individual consideration. Your job is to make sure your policies are clear and clearly communicated to guests and then to decide which policies require enforcement. Look at each situation and determine how big of a deal it is. Some policies are nonnegotiable because their breach interferes with other guests' enjoyment or causes damage to your inn. Others require simple reminders.

For example, sometimes guests lose track of time. They enjoy breakfast and go back to their room to relax for a few minutes, and then miss check-out time. Gentle reminders usually help in this situation. In the rare instance that guests refuse to leave, you can offer to store their luggage so they can check out. Some innkeepers impose (or threaten to impose) an extra charge, but this method doesn't put more time on the clock for you to turn over the room for the next guest.

Guests smoking in their room requires a stronger response from you. Most innkeepers at the first whiff of smoke will knock on the guest's door and remind them of the no-smoking policy. Smoke is bothersome to other current guests as well as to future guests who will occupy the room, plus it's a fire hazard. So this policy, and others like it, should be strictly enforced.

Acting inappropriately

You want your guests to enjoy themselves, but where do you draw the line? When their behavior can cause harm to themselves or to other guests, when it interferes with other guests' enjoyment or the safety of the inn, you must decide how to intervene. These situations can be tricky because they may not be associated with polices that you can refer to, so you'll need to look at each situation individually before you decide on a course of action.

For example, intoxicated guests may do damage to your inn and interfere with other guests. One intoxicated guest who had trouble closing the front door to an inn severely jammed a small rug under the door in the process. As a result, no one could get in or out. This was a huge fire and safety issue. The innkeeper had been away for a few hours that evening and when she returned, she was luckily able to gain entry through the innkeeper entrance. She then worked for over an hour cutting away the jammed rug.

When asked how to deal with intoxicated guests, most innkeepers recommend making the determination based on whether the person is being a disturbance to other guests or whether he's causing damage to the inn. If there's damage, the party is over and the intoxicated guest must be sternly told this. How you do this is up to you and depends on the circumstances. You may need to insist that the guest retire for the evening or, if the situation is disorderly and dangerous, you may need to call the authorities for help. On the other hand, if you have a spot where guests can socialize without disturbing other guests and damaging important property, direct rowdy guests to this area.

Running group interference

Making sure your guests understand your policies takes on even greater importance when several rooms are rented to a group at the same time that other guests are also staying at the inn.

Recently, an inn with rave reviews from previous guests received two very negative online reviews because a group that had rented most, but not all, of the inn allowed their kids to run and jump in the hot tub while other guests were trying to relax in it. When one of the children told his mom he was going to get sick, the child's parents didn't appreciate that the innkeeper immediately asked for all the children to be taken out of the hot tub. They wrote a negative review because they felt they had been treated unfairly. One of the other guests also wrote a negative review, having felt outnumbered by the group and uncomfortable at the inn. Because of situations like this, many innkeepers accept groups only when renting the entire inn to the same party. Other innkeepers steer completely clear of groups and do not encourage entire inn rentals.

Causing damages

Innkeepers often wrestle with how to handle damages, especially since oftentimes the damage isn't discovered until after the guests have checked out. To protect yourself and the inn, your damages policy must be clear and guests should acknowledge and sign it at check-in (see the "Checking guests in" section for information about reservation cards/folios). When damages do occur, take pictures before cleaning or repairing the damage. Then if you decide to charge the guest a damage or cleaning fee, you'll have supporting documentation if the guest disputes the charge. Often the existence of a damage policy acts as a deterrent to behavior that could cause damage to the inn, so whether or not you decide to enforce such a policy you should have one in place.

Don't be afraid, however, to enforce your damage policy and charge guests for damage to your inn. (Check with your credit card processor to see what documentation is required and what a guest needs to sign in order for you to charge their credit card for damages or a cleaning fee.) Remember, however, that accidents happen and are a part of doing business, so there's a delicate balance here. For less serious violations, gentle reminders are often sufficient, and when minor damages occur, you should usually consider it a cost of doing business.

If your inn accommodates pets, it's not unusual to charge an additional cleaning fee as well as have a specific policy for damages caused by pets. The cleaning fee would be automatic and separate from any charges for damage that the pet may cause.

Being just plain difficult

Ah, the picky eater. Guests have an uncanny way of suddenly being allergic to menu items, being on strange diets, or taking a dislike to certain foods at the last minute. Even if you ask about allergies and dietary restrictions when you take guest reservations, expect to encounter this. Sometimes innkeepers post their menus the night before to circumvent these issues ahead of time; others think this only opens up the situation to problems.

No matter how you handle your menus ahead of time, there are still guests who, when served the meal, say, *"Oh no, I can't eat that."* If you decide to prepare something custom for them, don't be surprised if they leave the table with the special order you created for them uneaten as well. You should also be aware that this becomes an open invitation for everyone to order something different, turning you into a short-order cook. On the plus side, you'll occasionally find the guest who never eats sweets gobbling up your crème brûlée French toast!

But by far the most difficult people are those with a narcissistic attitude. These are the people who believe that the universe revolves around them and no one else. They display belligerent behavior, make demands just for the heck of it, ask for things for the sheer pleasure of throwing the stuff around, ask for food they don't intend to eat, question your policies, take two spaces to park their car in the parking lot — I think you get the picture. Sometimes you can swing their mood by continuing to be cheerful and friendly, and sometimes you just know that you can only go so far. Most importantly, don't let them intimidate you into skimping on your check-in policies. This is why it's a good idea to always

   ✔ Have guests sign *before* giving them their room key.

   ✔ Confirm upon check-in the number of people in the party and the number of rooms reserved.

- ✔ Remind guests of your smoking policy.

- ✔ Remind guests that if everyone parks politely in the parking lot, there will be room for all guests to park.

- ✔ Settle charges upon check-in.

On the flip side, prepare yourself for overly friendly or lonely guests who follow you everywhere, making it difficult for you to get anything done or just plain driving you crazy. Of course, you don't want to hurt their feelings, however sometimes you need to tell them "I need to excuse myself to get rooms ready for the next guest" or "If I don't excuse myself to run some errands, we won't have anything for breakfast tomorrow". Offer to give them recommendations for area activities, show them the lending library of books, DVDs, or magazines, and politely yet forcefully leave so that you can get your work done or enjoy a little time to yourself.

Checking Guests Out

If you've taken care of securing the method of payment when you check guests in, check-out is less formal, which is a nice way to end the visit. Key things you want to do are:

- ✔ Give guests a copy of their final bill.

- ✔ Have guests return their keys.

- ✔ Help guests with their luggage.

- ✔ Offer help with directions and questions.

- ✔ Look guests in the eye, thank them for choosing your inn, and invite them back. Shake their hand (or give a hug if appropriate).

How you say good-bye to each guest depends on the interaction and relationship you've developed with them during their stay. It's your guests' last impression of your inn before they tell others about your B&B, so make it a comfortable, genuine, and positive farewell.

Chapter 13

Maintaining Your Inn

In This Chapter

▶ Organizing your to-do list into schedules and chore checklists

▶ Planning your attack on daily chores and bigger cleaning jobs

▶ Selecting the right equipment for your needs

▶ Taking good care of outdoor space

*Y*our guests come in all shapes and sizes, yet they have one thing in common — they all expect clean and well-maintained accommodations. So cleaning is one area that you can't compromise on. It's up to you to set standards for the cleanliness of your inn — and stick to 'em.

Luckily the best techniques for achieving a totally clean and well-maintained inn aren't a mystery. Here's the foundation of what's required:

✔ **Organization:** Create a schedule and a checklist to help keep you and your staff on track.

✔ **Hard work:** Even with a few shortcuts and tips, cleaning is hard work. There's no way around it.

✔ **Flexibility:** Interruptions are guaranteed when you operate a B&B, so you must be able to address them, prioritize your tasks, and, in the end, still present a clean inn to your guests.

✔ **High standards:** Clean begins with you. You set the standards for your inn. If you have staff, you must lead by example and show them what clean means at your B&B.

The best way to be sure your rooms and other areas are getting cleaned to your high standards is to periodically clean them yourself.

This chapter helps you to make sure that your inn sparkles in the eyes of your guests (even the neatniks). In this chapter, I help you to create organized schedules so you can stay one step (or more) ahead of your endless cleaning and maintenance tasks — both inside your inn and outside, attending to lawn and garden maintenance. To give you a head start, I share schedules from other successful innkeepers as well as explain equipment must-haves and options.

Establishing Schedules and Chore Checklists

Keep your inn in tip-top shape by establishing a cleaning and maintenance schedule so that tasks and issues don't have the chance to build up. This is easier said than done, and you should never lose sight of the fact that running a bed & breakfast is a huge job and responsibility. On many days the tasks will seem daunting and overwhelming. The best ways to stay on top of maintenance are to be organized (or at least start out that way) and to be flexible, accepting the likelihood of interruptions.

I suggest that you create one schedule for each category of task frequency: cleaning and maintenance that needs to be done daily (such as making and cleaning up from breakfast), several times a week (such as watering the lawn), weekly (such as taking out recyclables), monthly (such as vacuuming the bathroom exhaust grates), and less frequently (such as washing windows). Each schedule should contain a checklist of the tasks for that frequency and may call out the rooms or spaces that get such attention. A checklist with each schedule not only gives you a feeling of being in control of the cleaning and maintenance of your inn, but also makes it less likely that you (or your staff) will forget something. After all, it's better for you to discover that renegade dust bunny than for a guest to find it!

When you're a busy innkeeper, it's tempting to jump right in each day and get as much done as you can, but you'll be more productive if you outline each important time block in the day and prioritize essential tasks. Consider these schedules:

- **Daily schedule:** A consistent, organized daily routine cuts down on the amount of time spent cleaning and means fewer headaches for you and a cleaner inn for your guests. The section, "Dealing with Daily Chores," later in this chapter provides an explanation of daily tasks as well as an example of a daily housekeeping schedule with a checklist for daily tasks and the rooms and areas in which they should be performed.

Your daily schedule won't necessarily look like that one, but it's a useful guide. After you create and start to use a daily schedule, you'll find yourself adapting it to work better for you, such as freshening up guest rooms before finishing the breakfast cleanup (remembering, of course, to clear breakfast items from guests' view first!). You can then proceed with a daily schedule that works best for you, keeping in mind that no two days have to be the same and that frequent interruptions are part of the job.

Developing a daily routine and grouping similar tasks helps to keep the inn's rhythm on a schedule so you know, for example, what time is allotted for gardening or errand running or food shopping and when you must shift gears to doing laundry, sending out reservation confirmations, and prepping tomorrow morning's breakfast. Many days you simply can't stick to the same order of tasks, but you'll become a pro at prioritizing what can and can't wait until the next day.

✔ **Weekly schedule:** A weekly schedule lets you see each day and the whole week together at a glance. It can not only tell you who's handling each task on the checklist but also can ensure that all chores are covered. The section, "Weekly cleaning," later in this chapter includes an example of a weekly schedule.

✔ **Less frequent deep cleaning and maintenance schedule:** Periodically you'll need to do a deep cleaning and perform preventative maintenance and upkeep that involves heavy-duty hard work. A schedule with a checklist of such infrequent deep cleaning and maintenance tasks is the easiest way to keep track of how long it has been since a task was done. This schedule also keeps such tasks on your radar to ensure they're not overlooked. You can find out more about the tasks in this schedule in the "Deep cleaning" section later in this chapter.

Be sure to schedule time for bookkeeping, banking, bill paying, and running errands. These tasks may vary in frequency from running errands every few days to paying bills weekly. Don't be surprised to find out that it's the tasks that only you can do that are the ones that get put off, such as entering items in your accounting software.

Without planned schedules and checklists, you may find yourself wasting valuable time doubling back to do forgotten tasks. Your schedules also are great tools for training housekeeping staff or people who simply lend a hand at the last minute.

You decide the order in which you work through the tasks on your schedules based upon the layout of your inn as well as whether guests leave early or wait until the last minute to check out. Experience will help you to develop a rhythm and a desired order of doing things.

Regardless of the layout of your inn or how you decide to schedule your cleaning chores, here are some tips to keep you and your schedules organized:

- ✔ **Clean the same items in one sweep while you have the right supplies with you,** like cleaning all bathrooms before moving on to a different task. (This is an ideal routing and may not be possible if some guests remain in their rooms.) If you're working with a partner, increase efficiency by assigning different jobs to each person. For example, one person cleans the bathrooms while the other strips the beds. This way no one has to stop and change cleaning supplies and tools for each task.

- ✔ **Perform repairs and routine maintenance as needed, rather than putting them off for a later date.** Keeping up-to-date with repairs and maintenance keeps your inn looking good to guests and your appliances and equipment in good working order.

- ✔ **Collect all your cleaning supplies into a cleaning bucket or bag.** You save valuable time in your cleaning schedule when you have all your cleaning supplies with you and don't have to waste time by stopping to go and get something.

It takes most innkeepers several years to establish solid schedules and a routine that makes them feel in control. Don't be discouraged. Know that you'll feel overwhelmed with all that needs to be done in a day, a week, a month, and a year, and seek out support from other innkeepers. (Chapter 1 has advice on finding other innkeepers with whom you can commiserate and from whom you can learn a thing or two.)

Dealing with Daily Chores

You'll quickly learn that an innkeeper's work is never done. Your to-do list may seem endless, but there are certain tasks and chores that must be done every day in order to maintain your inn and to ensure that things are clean and ready for guests. In the next sections, I help you identify and tackle these daily jobs.

Taking the fear out of cleaning guest rooms

Trust me, I know how alarming it can be to find underwear under a guest's bed or a dead fly in the window sill and wonder how long it has been there. You can't catch everything in every room, but having a schedule and checklist and training your staff in the art of cleaning helps to prevent many of these occurrences.

When it comes to guests' rooms, the following two scenarios affect your daily tasks. My explanations include some of the terminology and scheduling procedures that most innkeepers use in keeping their guest rooms clean.

- ✔ **The guest is staying another night:** For rooms in which the guests are returning, *fluffing* refers to making the bed; replacing necessary linens, glassware, and so on; cleaning the bathroom; vacuuming; emptying the wastebasket; and tidying up anything else so that the room is clean when the guests return. Depending on the number of nights the guests are staying, fluffing may also include changing bed linens. In general, bed linens are changed every two to three days unless they're stained. This is the norm; however, you can set different standards for your inn. Depending on whether your inn offers a linen reuse program, the same choice is yours with towels. Otherwise, towels are usually replaced daily.

  Water and energy conservation is a growing concern these days, and a linen reuse program lets you address both issues. Give guests the option of reusing towels. Many inns have small signs in the bathroom that say something like, "We are proud of being a 'green' inn. Towels left in the tub means you want them replaced, and towels left on the hooks means you want to reuse them."

- ✔ **The guest checks out:** When a guest checks out, you perform a *flip* or *turn-over* in order to make the room ready for the next guest. It's a more intense cleaning with the goal of making the room clean and new. A turn-over includes stripping the bed linens; disinfecting the bathroom; washing tub mats; dusting; vacuuming; checking under beds, in every drawer, and in all closets; and cleaning the hot tub and more to remove all traces of the previous guests.

If your arriving guests aren't checking in on the same day as your departing guests, you may pull the linens and wait until the day the new guests arrive to fully turn over the room. It's a good habit to always turn over your rooms when guests depart. If *walk-ins* (guests who arrive without a reservation) are common in your area, you should always do turn-over immediately so your rooms are always ready.

If you do a complete turn-over and the room sits empty for more than a day or two before guests finally arrive, do a walkthrough and freshen up the room with a light dusting and by running the water in the tub and sinks, flushing the toilets, and so on.

The cleaning schedules and procedures for cleaning your guest rooms will be unique to your inn and they will change over time. However, here are some safe assumptions you can make when cleaning guest rooms:

✔ **Hot tubs and Jacuzzis require special cleaning.** In many areas you may need to have board of health approval in order to operate a hot tub or Jacuzzi, and your local health department may have specific standards that you must follow if you offer these amenities, including passing inspections to be sure hot tubs are cleaned properly. Check with your local department of health for cleaning and regulation requirements.

✔ **The fastest and neatest way to make a bed involves two people sharing the job.** You quickly realize how much time you save not running from one side to the other! A bed made by two people comes out neater and crisper, with fewer wrinkles, so it looks better to guests.

✔ **Guests check under beds and behind things to make sure that they don't leave anything when checking out, so you or your cleaning staff must clean under the bed, behind the armoire, and behind the curtains,** among other unseen or hard to reach areas.

✔ **If you have the help of a housekeeper, have her clean the bathrooms (which you check later) while you review the finer details, or touch-ups.** It's your inn, and its presentation is a reflection on you. Focus on the little details, like the following, that make a big impression on guests (or take away from their impressions of your place):

   • **Alarm clocks:** Make sure the alarm isn't set to go off and the time is correct. Don't forget to adjust the time for daylight savings.

   • **Pictures:** Check that pictures are hung straight on the walls, and dust the frames, including the tops.

   • **Dust:** Dust the tops of doors and door jams where dust likes to collect.

   • **Shades and blinds:** Adjust shades and blind heights so that they're all even.

Figure 13-1 is a daily chore schedule from the Inn at the Riverbend (www.innatriverbend.com), a seven-room bed & breakfast in Pearisburg, Virginia. You can use the checklist on this schedule as a starting point and for ideas of how to create your own daily guest room schedule with checklist. The bold items are usually done when fluffing the rooms. The inn also notes arriving guests on the schedule, which serves as a reminder to double-check and freshen up rooms that had previously been turned over but weren't immediately rented to new guests.

Day of the week	Rooms requiring activity							
Activity	Guest Bath	Room 1	Room 2	Room 3	Room 4	Room 5	Room 6	Room 7
Cleaning code (see bottom of page)								
Check under bed for dust and lost items								
Change bed linens/**remake bed**								
Dust all furniture, window sills, ceiling fan								
Vacuum carpet & bathroom floor								
Return TV controls to cabinet								
Empty trash cans and replace liners								
Replace glassware if dirty								
Clean bathtub, shower walls, & rail								
Clean windows and mirror								
Change shower liner if needed								
Clean toilet, sink, counters, & mirror (flush toilet)								
Replace soaps, shampoos, toilet paper, & tissues if needed								
Replace make-up removers, sanitary boxes, & cups in top drawer								
Change bathroom rug as needed								
Replace used towels								
Replace used bathrobes								
Raise blinds, lock windows, & exit door								
Mop bathroom floor								
Is pen by the guest book? If not, replace								
Adjust thermostats in upstairs rooms when unoccupied to 75 (a/c), 67 (heat), empty 60								
Check light bulbs								
Anything left in room by prior guest? (note date, room and report to innkeeper)								
Anything broken? stains? (report to innkeeper)								
Laundry—start washer, move to dryer, fold and iron sheets								
General area dusting, vacuuming								

F= FLUFF   T=TURN THE ROOM   A=GUEST ARRIVING IN THAT ROOM

Housekeeper _____

Innkeeper _____

Figure 13-1: A daily housekeeping schedule with task checklist.

Courtesy of Linda P. Hayes, Owner/Innkeeper, Inn at Riverbend

Moving guests' belongings when cleaning

New innkeepers often wonder whether and how much to move guests' belongings around when cleaning, and the answer is very little. If you need to move money or valuables in order to clean, you should put them back where they were. Neatly folding guests' clothes and leaving them where you found them is often appreciated, but moving them any further could be considered intrusive.

Sometimes guests request that you don't clean their rooms during their stay. They may feel uncomfortable having you clean their rooms, they may be unfamiliar with staying at B&Bs, or they may just be very private people. How you handle this request is up to you. For many innkeepers, it's an easy decision: The guest asks for privacy, and the request is granted. Other innkeepers may say something like, "Are you sure? We like to freshen the rooms for all our guests," or "It's not a problem. We'll just empty the trash and leave some fresh towels for you, if that's okay."

First and foremost, you should always respect your guests' privacy. If guests insist that you don't enter their rooms, you should respect their wishes unless you suspect a serious reason to check that everything's okay in the rooms.

Handling guests' belongings that are left behind

Generally, the best policy is to wait for guests to call about their forgotten items. You can never be 100 percent sure that the items weren't left by a previous guest and simply missed during the room turn-over.

However, depending upon what's left behind and even the quantity, such as prescription medications or more clothes than just one or two items, you should use discretion and make an attempt to contact the guest as soon as possible. (There's nothing like returning lingerie to an assumed wife only to find out the wife was not a guest!) Many times you can reach guests with cellphones before they've left the area, and they can swing by the inn and pick up their items.

Keeping common areas looking their best

It's important that guests feel comfortable in your bed & breakfast, but not all guests have common sense when it comes to knowing how to be respectful and pick up after themselves in the common areas of your inn. Expect some guests to be very tidy, while others drink coffee or tea, have a cookie or some cheese and crackers, and then leave their half-eaten food on the tables in common areas for other guests to look at.

It's your job as innkeeper to continually make sweeps through your inn, including the outdoor areas, to keep things tidy. Deciding when to clean common areas is a balancing act, because although guests expect a clean inn, many are uncomfortable watching you do the cleaning. So try to clean common areas when many guests are away from the inn, such as between check-out and check-in, during the evening, and then again, if needed, at the end of your innkeeping day.

Many guests want to be neat, but they don't know what to do with their dishes when they're finished with them. Set up a collection point in an obvious place, for example, a fancy tea cart next to a wastebasket in the hospitality room or parlor.

A clean kitchen is a happy kitchen

Being able to close the door to a dirty kitchen and deal with it later is a great feeling, especially when a hundred other important things are clamoring for your attention. For instance, you often have to stop loading the dishwasher in order to wish guests a nice farewell as they check out or to answer the phone to take a reservation (or both!). However, closing the kitchen door is only a temporary solution. A clean kitchen not only helps to keep you more organized, but it's also necessary to meet local and state health department guidelines.

There is no "best time" to clean the kitchen; however, all clean, unused foods from your breakfast preparation must be wrapped and placed in the refrigerator or freezer immediately after breakfast. Many innkeepers find that doing the laundry and the kitchen cleanup in tandem works best because they can move between tasks. They first start the laundry and keep an eye on it while they clean the kitchen.

In addition to the obvious daily cleaning tasks in your kitchen, at least every few months don't forget to clean the refrigerator, freezer, and pantry and to rotate items. Also, be sure to continuously throw out unused items as they reach their expiration dates.

Laundry miracles

As you plan for your bed & breakfast, you may wonder, "How difficult can it be to wash sheets and towels?" It doesn't take long to discover the answer to that question . . . it's not as easy as it looks! No matter how much you can accomplish in any given day, you'll sometimes find yourself questioning whether there's a bottom to your laundry pile! Keeping linens spot-free and fresh for the traveling public is very different from washing your family's clothes. A faint spot or two on a pillowcase or sheet that you wouldn't think twice about for your own use may cause a guest to think that the linens aren't clean. For this reason, many innkeepers choose white linens because they can be bleached with no worry about fading.

Easing the task of ironing linens

You may be asking, "What's a mangle?", but if you use one, your question may well be, "How could I ever live without it?" A *mangle* is a heated roller rotary iron (Miele is a popular brand). Sheets, pillowcases, tablecloths, placemats, napkins, and similarly flat items simply roll through the mangle and come out looking professionally pressed. It's a huge time saver! A mangle uses dry heat, so it works best on items that are still damp.

Although the mangle is a miracle appliance in the eyes of many innkeepers, it's big and expensive. For most small inns starting out, a mangle is a luxury. Some innkeepers opt to make this purchase during startup simply because of the time they'll save and be able to devote to other tasks. Other innkeepers hold off on purchasing a mangle until they're more established, and still others never own a mangle. It's a big decision and a large expense, so if you have an innkeeper friend who has one, see if you can try his first. A table-top steam press (ElnaPress is a popular brand) is a less expensive alternative for pressing pillowcases, napkins, and placemats, but it's not large enough for pressing bed sheets or large tablecloths.

Unless you have a separate water source for your laundry, you shouldn't do laundry in the morning or evening when guests may be showering. Planning your laundry time appropriately ensures that guests have adequate hot water and water pressure.

In deciding whether to purchase commercial or household laundry equipment, consider your answers to the following questions:

- ✔ **How much time will be devoted to the laundry each day?**
- ✔ **During what time frame will the laundry be done?**
- ✔ **Who will do the laundry?**

The answers to these questions are intertwined with each other. What's right for your inn depends upon your budget, how many rooms you have, your occupancy rate, how much linen you have per room, and how much staff you have or don't have. Generally, an inn with less than five rooms can use non-commercial equipment, although some inns of this size have two washers and dryers. Commercial appliances are fabulous but they're expensive. For this reason, many innkeepers start out with residential appliances and upgrade later. Another option to explore is an outside linen service for washing, drying, and ironing your linens. Some innkeepers have found the time savings outweighs the cost. Unfortunately, if your inn is in a remote location, this may not be an option for you to consider.

Using household appliances for commercial use may void their warranties.

In general, it takes longer to dry a load of linens and towels than to wash it, so some inns have two dryers. Consider that option depending on how many linens and loads of laundry you anticipate doing daily, because your goal is to crank through large amounts of laundry as quickly as possible on a daily basis with spot-free results.

Finally, launder with soft water. One of the big secrets to soft, fluffy towels that your guests are guaranteed to love is washing your linens in soft water. Hard water is rough on laundry because it contains mineral deposits that cause laundry detergent to become trapped in the fibers of your linens, leaving them with a rough, scratchy feeling. (Hard water also leads to soap buildup and spots on your dishes when they come out of the dishwasher.) Installing a commercial water softener (you can either buy or lease) has many laundry benefits to both the inn and the guests. A water softener uses up to 3/4 less detergent in each wash load, eliminates the need for fabric softener, and produces considerable energy savings because soft water heats faster than hard water.

Fitting In Bigger Cleaning Jobs

Thankfully, there are many tasks that you don't have to do every day yet they're still essential to the maintenance and appearance of your inn and your guests' experiences at your inn. The next sections help you tackle these tasks.

Weekly cleaning

In addition to daily cleaning chores, some innkeepers do a weekly cleaning that involves tasks that need to be done regularly — just not as often as daily tasks (which I cover in the "Dealing with Daily Chores" section earlier). Some innkeepers devote one day each week to giving main areas a more thorough cleaning; other innkeepers handle these jobs throughout the week by spending extra time in different areas each day. For example, Mondays may include giving the dining room a good scrub-down, Tuesdays may include extra attention in the living room, and Wednesdays (or whenever there's turn-over) may include giving guest rooms a heavy scrubbing and disinfecting.

Like your daily schedule, your weekly cleaning schedule is unique to your inn. It's built around how busy your inn is and if and when you have staff to help you.

Figure 13-2 shows the weekly cleaning schedule at the Inn at Riverbend in Virginia. The task checklist is broken down by the day, time, and person responsible. Having such a checklist tailored to the chores at your B&B makes it clear who's responsible for various tasks. It also lets everyone know which tasks are being taken care of and which ones need attention.

Week of: _____	Weekly Schedule							
Weekly Checklist								
(Initials for person responsible)	Mon	Tue	Wed	Thu	Fri	Sat	Sun
6:30 a.m. - 11:00 a.m. Breakfast							
Pick up newspaper/put outgoing mail in box							
Turn any outside lights off							
Open computer programs							
Remove credit card batch report and match							
Pick up old newspapers, glasses—common areas							
Empty dishwasher if needed							
Turn warming drawer on							
Place breads in warming drawer							
Put out coffee, juice, cream, butter, jam							
Cook bacon or sausage, hold in warming drawer							
Make breakfast entrée							
Make fruit							
Check washer & dryer & start load							
Clear & load dishwasher							
Empty juice pitchers							
Restock teas, sugars; clean beverage area							
Create grocery list/Order Sysco if needed							
Start dishwasher if full—after room PU							
Mid day 11:00 a.m - 3:00 p.m.							
Restock guest refrigerator							
Bake cookies, muffins, breads							
Make iced tea, lemonade							
Empty kitchen & guest room trash cans							
Take recyling to garage daily							
Check washer/dryer, pull & fold laundry							
Iron							
Vacuum floors & steps							
Check for new reservations & respond							
Check out guests in property management software							
Clean decks, furniture, tables, railing							
Sweep spider webs							
Empty dishwasher							
Pick up flowers if necessary by 2:00 p.m.							
Set up buffet for snacks, tea							
Put chocolates in rooms							
Remove registrations from book/add keys							
Afternoon Arrivals 3:00 p.m. - 7:00 p.m.							
Check in guests—guest book, payment							
Post guest names in kitchen							
Set up coffee pots for a.m.							

Figure 13-2:
A weekly cleaning schedule with task checklist.

	Mon	Tue	Wed	Thu	Fri	Sat	Sun
Set table for breakfast							
Turn on outside lights at cottage, inn							
Post the menu on the ceramic plate							
Put out glasses & snacks							
Check for new reservations & respond							
Leave late arrival notes if needed							
Evening Closing 7:00 p.m. - 8:00 p.m.							
Start dishwasher if full							
Shut down active programs on computer							
Adjust interior evening lights							
Turn off buffet counter lights							
Lock front door unless you have late arrival							
Outdoor							
Take garbage out on Wednesday p.m.							
Take trash to the dump							
Check pond & fill as needed							
Dead head flowers							
Cut grass & trim							
Spray for bugs							
Weed beds							
Water and trim indoor plants on Tuesday							
EXTRA TO DO's							
Organize package extras							
Pack picnic lunches							
Schedule massages							
Create late arrival notes							
Prepare special events							

Courtesy of Linda P. Hayes, Owner/Innkeeper, Inn at Riverbend

Deep cleaning

Deep cleaning is your heavy cleaning and maintenance. It includes moving furniture to vacuum behind it, washing curtains, cleaning ceiling fans, and changing air filters, among other tasks. You can tackle heavy cleaning on whatever schedule works best — it's usually done twice a year or more.

You'll always be tempted to put off the big cleaning and maintenance jobs, so I recommend penciling out a schedule and checklist for them. When you write it down, you're more likely to actually do it. And unless your B&B is closed for a month or longer each year, you need to be continuously diligent about non-routine cleaning so that it doesn't pile up and become overwhelming.

As your inn becomes more popular and your occupancy goes up, you need to devote more time each day to cleaning because everything in your inn gets more use — from carpets and the furniture to doors and banisters. Bigger jobs don't have to be done all at once. Some innkeepers do them room by room; others do them job by job or as they see the need. Fitting big jobs in when you can lets you set the schedule that works for your inn. Here's a list of deep cleaning and maintenance tasks, along with general recommendations for frequency (note, some of the frequency recommendations depend on occupancy):

- Wash windows and screens, as needed and depending on the weather (such as more often in the spring when rainstorms bring down pollen)
- Wash deck and outside areas, as needed
- Clean outdoor hot tub according to manufacturer's instructions and health department regulations
- Paint touchups, as needed
- Repaint portions of the inn, annually
- Wash curtains, as needed or annually
- Vacuum thoroughly by moving all furniture, several times a year
- Flip and rotate mattresses to prolong life, every three months
- Wash comforter covers, every two months or as needed
- Wash pillow protectors, blankets, and mattress covers, every two months or as needed
- Wash shower curtains, every two months or as needed
- Clean carpets, annually
- Vacuum lampshades, every month
- Tighten hardware, every three months or as needed
- Clean glass on framed wall art and dust frames, every two weeks
- Clean fans and radiators, at least twice a year
- Clean baseboards, every few weeks or as needed
- Dust books on bookshelves, every few weeks
- Replace drawer liners, annually or as needed
- Clean appliance grease traps and filters (including the coils on or in your refrigerator or freezer if you have a commercial kitchen); follow manufacturers recommendations which are usually every three to six months for traps and filters and every six months for coils

✔ Clean wood-burning fireplaces by scooping out ashes after every use (into a metal can with a lid because embers can stay hot for days) and then vacuuming ashes that are left; have a chimney sweep clean the chimney and check for safety issues annually

✔ Check and clean logs in gas fireplaces, approximately every five years

✔ Check fire extinguishers and sprinkler systems, annually

✔ Test emergency lighting, at least twice a year

✔ Replace batteries in smoke and carbon monoxide detectors, at least twice a year

Buying Cleaning Equipment that Makes Your Job Easier

Cleaning and caring for your inn is hard work, so anything that can make your job easier is your friend. For cleaning and maintenance, you need strong, powerful equipment suitable for the job at hand, but when given a choice, choose the quieter model, because it's often in use when guests are around.

Your wish list of tools and equipment to make your job easier may look something like this:

✔ **Oversized washer:** Generally, front-loading washers are preferred because they use less water. However, commercial front-loaders are more expensive and usually bigger than top-loaders. Talk with a commercial vendor in your area about your options.

✔ **Oversized dryer:** Linens take longer to dry than to wash, especially robes, blankets, and towels.

✔ **Oversized dishwasher with sanitizing cycle:** Most health departments require dishwashers to have a sanitizing cycle.

✔ **Mangle (rotary iron) or steam press:** Refer to the sidebar "Easing the task of ironing linens" for information on these appliances.

✔ **Over-the-range exhaust hood:** In non-commercial kitchens, this hood helps to keep grease from building up on kitchen walls and cabinetry.

✔ **Vacuum cleaners:** Each floor of your B&B should have its own light-weight but powerful conventional vacuum so that you don't have to haul one vacuum up and down stairs.

✔ **Carpet cleaner:** Having your own carpet cleaner is cheaper in the long run than hiring an outside service, and it allows you to shampoo carpets on your schedule.

✔ **Backpack vacuum:** This helper makes jobs where you need to maneuver with extra flexibility easier, such as cleaning stairs, crevices, tops of window frames, overhead lighting, and so on. Because it's strapped to your back, you won't need to worry about being tangled in the hose or bumping furniture like you would with a canister vacuum.

✔ **Small hand-held sweeper:** For a quick cleanup of a small area, a hand-held carpet sweeper will save you the trouble of pulling out the big vacuum.

✔ **Carpet spot cleaner:** A small spot cleaner (such as the Bissell Little Green Carpet Cleaner) gets marks and stains off carpets and furnishing in between full carpet shampooing (which is usually an annual job).

✔ **Heavy-duty (commercial) mop and bucket:** These items reduce splashing and are sturdier, which prevents tipping, and a sturdy mop will clean larger areas and hold up well when used frequently. Use this equipment to clean kitchen and basement floors.

Purchase maintenance contracts on important equipment such as your big-ticket items like washers, dryers, and dishwashers (it's usually not worth the expense on smaller, easily replaced equipment). Follow manufacturers' instructions by performing recommended preventative maintenance, such as changing filters and routine cleaning, which saves you money, particularly on your furnace, air conditioning system, plumbing, and large appliances.

Caring for the Lawn and Garden

The outside of your inn is one area you can't afford to neglect. The important thing is to present your guests with a neatly manicured lawn and garden and tidy, well-maintained outdoor spaces. In the B&B business, it's called *curb appeal*. When guests arrive at your inn, you want their first impression to be "Ah, we chose the right inn. It looks so nice." Your goal is to create an immediate reaffirmation of their choice to stay with you.

When you're talking about work in the outdoor spaces of your bed & breakfast, cleaning and maintenance tasks blend together into overall caretaking. As with the indoor cleaning and maintenance tasks, however, some things should be done daily, like checking for trash that may have blown around, and other things need your attention less often, like trimming back landscaping.

Taming landscaping

One of the quickest ways for your inn to look unkept is to have overgrown bushes, vines, and shrubs. In order to keep this foliage in check and to keep bushes trimmed and away from walkways, you need the right landscaping equipment.

Some of the landscaping equipment that you add to your wish list will depend on the size and layout of your property and, of course, your budget, but you can definitely start with some essentials. Make sure you have a lawn mower and edger (if you have lawns), as well as a shrub trimmer and a blower (if you have lots of walkways to keep clear of leaves). You also need the usual hand tools such as pruning shears, shovels, rakes, and brooms.

Clear your yard of hazards on which guests can trip or otherwise be injured. Watch out for ivy and vines on the ground in particular — they're some of the easiest things to trip over when strolling outside. Keep ivy and other beautiful vines cut back and away from parking areas, steps, and walkways.

Landscaping maintenance is one big task that you may prefer to leave to the professionals, hiring a landscaping company to do the maintenance for you. Many innkeepers find that the time savings and the professional results outweigh the cost of hiring a professional lawn service.

Depending on the setup of your inn's water supply, you may need to balance when your lawn and gardens are watered with when your guests are showering in order to ensure adequate water pressure for their showers. If you're in the country and use well water, it may be possible to have the outdoor water source come from a well or irrigation source separate from the water inside your bed & breakfast.

If your inn has an automatic sprinkler system for the lawn and garden, be mindful of the time of day it comes on — you don't want a guest to be drenched unexpectedly while out for a stroll! Set it to come on in the early morning, just before the sun and your guests rise (and want showers), or in the evening when most guests are not outside.

Tending to outdoor furniture

Rule #1 with outdoor furniture is to keep it clean. Wipe it down frequently, often in the morning and again in the afternoon, depending on your area. It's a good idea to keep separate rags and brooms for cleaning outdoor furniture, decks, and patios than those that you use inside the inn because you'll find that they get dirty quickly.

If you're located in an area where outdoor furniture is used seasonally, consider storing it in a garage, shed, or other dry, protected place during the winter and rainy times of the year. Covering it with tarps and leaving it in the yard or on porches is unsightly and creates a bad impression of your inn. Remember, if something is off limits to guests, such as outdoor furniture during the off season, keep it out of reach and out of sight of guests.

Chapter 14

Getting Help When You Need It

*G*ood employees are invaluable assets. They're the ambassadors of your business when their job is to interact with guests, and the backbone of a smooth-running inn when they're doing maintenance and housekeeping. Their performance helps to shape your guests' experiences at your bed & breakfast. They also free up your time so that you can do other things.

But if you've never been a boss before, the nuances of interviewing and managing employees can be scary. This chapter lends a hand. In it I help you figure out what tasks are best to outsource, and I give you pointers on interviewing, training, and— when necessary — terminating your employees.

Knowing When You Need Help

In the beginning, few inns can afford the luxury of hiring outside help. However, at some point, when extra money becomes available, you're likely to consider hiring additional staff to help improve your living situation — and maybe even take a vacation! There is no exact right time to hire help, but the following sections outline the times when you may need to consider it.

You can't judge an inn by the number of people it employs. Some innkeepers choose to forgo paying themselves a salary in order to hire outside help. Each innkeeper has his own goals and makes personal lifestyle choices with tradeoffs between rewards and consequences.

Keeping up with day-to-day chores

If you're running a small inn, you may need to take care of day-to-day jobs, maintenance, and general upkeep of your B&B for some time, but the time to plan for outside help is now! Anticipating when you can hire help should be part of your business plan (see Chapter 3). Your plan may call for reaching a set occupancy rate before hiring help, but you may not be able to afford to wait if you're having trouble keeping up. For example, figure out a way to get extra help when the inn is not being cleaned up to your standards, you're falling behind on your marketing, and, most importantly, before you become burned out.

Of course, if you're running a larger inn or if you're also working outside the B&B, hiring help may be necessary even before you begin welcoming guests. If so, then budgeting for help in your business plan is a must. Start a running list of tasks for the efficient operation of your inn. As you get ready to hire help, identify the jobs that can most easily be turned over to someone else, or that must be assigned to others. Start with the tasks that you physically won't be able to do if you're working outside of the inn and those that you like the least, and keep for yourself the ones that you can do best.

Using this list, create a job description. Is this a description for a house-keeper, a cook, an assistant innkeeper, or a combination of several of these positions? Next, think about who would be the ideal candidate to fill the position — an aspiring innkeeper? A retiree? Someone looking for part-time work during the day? Your goal is to match your needs with the position first, and then, when you get to the hiring process, with the person.

During the high season

Many inns, especially those in popular tourist destinations, have a great need for extra help during *high season,* when you and all other hospitality businesses in the area are the busiest. During these times you will be competing with other local B&Bs, hotels, and restaurants for extra help. Therefore it's a good idea to plan ahead, remembering that high season can be for an extended period of time or a holiday weekend. The busier you are, the more help you may need. Start early to look for help by asking for referrals from your staff and other innkeepers, deciding where you might run an ad, contacting local colleges, and so on.

If you have trouble hiring seasonal employees, take a tip from Alyce Mundy at Dunscroft By-The-Sea in Harwich Port, Massachusetts. Alyce has had success hiring foreign students on J1 Visas. Under the program, called "Work and Travel USA," the students work for 4 months and travel 1 month. CIEE (Council on International Educational Exchange) is one of the sponsors (www. ciee.org). The program has turned out to be a very economical way for many inns to find hard-working seasonal help who perform innkeeping duties from making beds to mowing lawns to cleaning pools at a reasonable cost.

When you need to take time off

Being able to leave your B&B with the peace of mind that comes from knowing your business is in good hands can only happen if you plan ahead. If you don't have staff in place that can run the inn efficiently, you need to find someone you trust to run the inn in your absence before the need arises. Then you need to get organized by documenting your procedures so that others can fill your shoes while you're away.

Numerous professional interim innkeepers (also known as inn-sitters) make a full- or part-time career out of taking care of other people's inns. Oftentimes, these folks are retired innkeepers themselves. The section "Handing over the whole enchilada: Hiring an interim innkeeper," later in this chapter, explains what to look for when you hire an interim innkeeper.

Identifying Tasks to Outsource

When you get to the point where you need or can afford extra help, ask yourself these questions to determine what help you need:

- **What can someone else do so that I can do what no one else can do?** For many innkeepers this means giving up cleaning rooms, setting tables, doing laundry, or some combination of these tasks so they can focus on marketing, bookkeeping, and how their business is doing overall.

- **What can someone else do better than I can?** These could be tasks such as maintenance, repairs, or cooking. The best way to find good people is by asking other innkeepers and business owners in your area for recommendations. The portable Cheat Sheet at the front of this book provides a place for you to fill in important phone numbers and keep them at the ready.

- **What is it that I hate to do?** If you're lucky, this list will include tasks on the previous two lists. For many innkeepers, these are tasks such as laundry and cleaning. Chances are, however, if it's an undesirable job to you, it will be to others as well, so make sure you periodically do the job yourself to be sure it's being completed to your desired satisfaction.

B&B guests choose a bed & breakfast inn for the personal attention they receive from the innkeeper, so don't become an absentee innkeeper unless you outsource your job to an assistant innkeeper who's available to interact with your guests and provide them with the same service that you would. Regardless, hiring out or outsourcing does not relieve you from supervising to be sure things are done correctly.

Hiring Help at the Inn

Finding and training the right people is work — but the goal is to free up some of *your* work, so it should be worth it. Good inn owners know a secret. Hire people who interact well with guests, employees who have the ability and intuitiveness to provide a warm and caring atmosphere, so that guests are not always clamoring for your attention.

Finding good folks

Good employees can be hard to find. Here are some resources for finding people to fill your job openings:

- ✔ **Ask for referrals from other innkeepers and small business owners.** Use your networking skills and ask around. If you're looking for part-time help, you may be able to share someone already employed by another inn.

- ✔ **Ask people who are employed in the same position you're looking to fill** (or ask other innkeepers to ask their employees for you). Good people often know good people. For example, your wonderful house-keeper may have a sister or cousin who is looking for work.

- ✔ **Contact local colleges and schools.** Colleges, universities, and schools can be excellent sources of eager and competent staff. Check hospitality programs at colleges and universities for potential assistant innkeepers, and check culinary schools for help with food preparation.

- ✔ **Check out relevant Web sites.** Many employers and employees get connected online. The usefulness of a Web site is determined by the type of position you're trying to fill. For instance, sites such as Craigslist (www.craigslist.com) are popular in larger metropolitan areas for advertising job postings for tasks such as housekeeping, cooking, and maintenance. Innkeeper forums are better resources for industry-specific jobs such as recruiting assistant innkeepers and managers. (See Chapter 1 for help in finding an innkeeper forum.)

- ✔ **Inquire at temporary agencies.** These can be great resources, especially if the work is part-time or sporadic. Temp agencies can be a great last-minute option, especially for housekeepers. You can't trust just anyone at your inn, so check references of the agencies ahead of time and find out what type of screening they do for the workers that they send to you.

- ✔ **Peruse online directory job postings.** Many online directories have postings of both positions available and people seeking employment. (See Chapter 8 for a listing of online bed & breakfast directories.)

✔ **Contact your state and/or local B&B associations** and see whether they maintain a list of available help or postings for help wanted. The Professional Association of Innkeepers International maintains a classified section at `www.paii.org`. Click on Classifieds and then Innkeeping Careers to see postings.

Inheriting employees

You're the new guy on the block and the current inn employees are as unsure about you as you are about them. They offer knowledge and expertise about how things at the inn work, and you offer the potential for future employment. If you have a training period with the previous owners (see Chapter 4), use this time to observe current inn employees. Watch how they do their jobs and interact with guests. You want to be on the lookout for things that may have been okay with the old innkeepers but are not okay with you, such as how rooms are made ready for arriving guests and so on.

You may want to notify all employees in writing that from the first day you take ownership, all staff and management will be placed on a 30-day "New Owner Introductory Period." This provides a time for you and the employees to get acquainted with each other, and it allows you the opportunity to observe the work habits and job attitudes of the employees. It also gives you the advantage to decide which employees you will keep (some of whom may become your greatest asset), who you'll need to coach, and who you'll need to terminate. Remember, the inn is yours now, and even good employees will need to be trained in the way you want things done. See more information on training employees later in this chapter.

Interviewing potential employees

Interviewing and hiring the right employees takes a little bit of skill and a lot of luck. Hiring employees who come to you as referrals is ideal (though not always possible), and even these employees should go through the same interview process as those who come to you through other sources. Your objectives in the interview process are to make sure that you're hiring the best person to get the job done, and to ensure that the person you ultimately hire knows what to expect and is prepared to do the job. In order to accomplish both of these goals, here are some things to keep in mind:

✔ Create a clear job description that includes the purpose of the job; skills, experience, and/or education required; job duties and responsibilities; physical demands; hours; and so on.

✔ Have the applicant fill out a job application. Anything that is important for you to know should be written on the application. The application is a legal document; a resume is not. One of the most important things you can discover from the application is previous employment history. Chances are if the person switches jobs every three months, you'll quickly be looking for a new employee.

✔ Review the job description with the applicant and ask specific questions, using examples from the actual job. For instance, if you're interviewing for an assistant innkeeper, ask applicants how they would check in a guest. Their answers are not important in terms of accuracy (it's impossible for them to know how you do it); rather, they give you a sense of the logic and reasoning with which they would approach the task. Ask yourself whether they're using common sense and a customer-service-oriented approach to answer the question. This is what you're looking for.

✔ Take applicants around the inn, showing them in detail the tasks their job would require. Ask them to give you examples of how they have performed similar tasks at other jobs. Ask them what they liked least about previous jobs. Let the applicants do a lot of the talking — you want to gather as much information as you can about them. If an applicant tells you all customers should be treated with respect, ask for examples of ways they've treated customers with respect in the past. This way you know that they're not just telling you what they think you want to hear; rather, they intuitively understand the job.

Keep yourself out of legal hot water by knowing what questions you legally can and cannot ask in an interview. Asking personal questions about someone's age, affiliations, disability, ethnic/national origin, gender, sexual orientation, race, religion, military record, and family or marital status is illegal. Be aware of gray areas. For example, while you can't ask job candidates their nationality, you *can* ask, "Are you authorized to work in the United States?" You can't ask about marital and family status, but if overtime may be part of the job, you can ask, "Would you be able and willing to work overtime?" If you have staff members help you interview potential candidates, make sure they, too, are aware of the personal, social, and medical information that's illegal to ask about in a job interview.

You should get and check references prior to hiring anyone to help you at your inn, although they often don't tell you a great deal. This is because people don't like to speak unkindly about others or are concerned with the legal ramifications of doing so. At the very least, verify the dates of employment that the applicant has given you and ask whether the applicant would be eligible for rehire. Many inns also do a background check before making an official offer of employment. You must obtain the employee's permission before conducting a background check. A background check verifies previous employment and criminal records by jurisdiction.

Independent contractors versus employees

Many innkeepers are confused and intimidated by trying to figure out the difference between employees and independent contractors. It's important for you to correctly classify the people who work for you so that the appropriate income is reported to the IRS. In a nutshell, it boils down to answering the following simple questions:

✔ Who dictates how the work is to be done?

✔ Who sets the hours and the days of the week to work?

✔ Who sets the rate of pay?

✔ Who provides the materials and equipment to perform the tasks?

If the answer to the preceding questions is you, then the person doing work for you is an employee and you are the employer. You must obtain an employer ID number from the IRS and from your state. You deduct the appropriate payroll withholdings from each payroll check that you give your employee based upon the information they provide in the W-4 form. As an employer, you also provide on-the-job (workers compensation) insurance and W-2s at year-end showing the total wages your employees received. It makes no difference how much or how little your employees earn; how few or how many hours they work; whether they're temporary, seasonal, on-call, part-time, or full-time; or even if they last only one day on the job! They are your employees.

If, on the other hand, the answer to the questions in the preceding list is "the people doing the job," those people are most likely independent contractors. You provide a W-9 to them to be completed and returned to you so that you have their name, their company name (if any), and their social security number or other tax ID number. You provide independent contractors a 1099-Misc at year-end showing the total amount you paid to them in the previous year if you paid them more than $600 during the year and they are not registered as a corporation.

If you're unsure, the best resources to consult are IRS Publications 15 and 15-A. To find these publications, visit the IRS Web site (www.irs.gov) and enter 15 or 15-A in the search box.

Deciding what to pay

Deciding what to pay is always tricky. Asking other innkeepers for the ranges they pay for similar positions and looking at ads from larger hotels can help you establish a range to use as a guideline.

The people you're interviewing usually are considering not only a job at a B&B, but also one in the lodging industry in general. So your wages must be competitive, not only in salary but also in terms of benefits. Employees usually don't take a job based on salary alone. You can entice employees with benefits such as living in, free meals, various forms of insurance, incentive or bonus programs, discounts, flexible work hours, and so on. You should consult with your CPA, accountant, or tax advisor to determine whether the value of any of the benefits you offer your employees must be included as income for the employee.

The amount you must pay your employees varies by state. The federal government sets a minimum hourly wage, plus many states have their own minimum-wage laws. *Nonexempt employees,* or employees that are usually nonprofessional employees who are paid hourly, must be paid whichever rate is higher. The Department of Labor's Web site (www.wagehour.dol.gov) contains a wealth of information, including minimum-wage exceptions, information on overtime pay, and state minimum-wage requirements.

Payroll taxes and costs are a part of doing business. Doing payroll is simply another skill you need to acquire. Most bookkeeping software can easily run payroll for you, along with figuring all the taxes. Your CPA or accountant can easily help you set up a system to do payroll on your own or using your bookkeeping software.

Don't pay employees in cash "under the table." First, it's illegal, and second, it skews your financial statement, which will only hurt you in a future sale of the business.

Training your employees

Your employees are an extension of your business, and training them is an investment in your business. Your employees should be trained to handle any and all guest requests and situations, clean every room, prepare every breakfast, answer every call, and/or make every repair, depending on their job description and whatever cross-training you decide to provide. The end result of their efforts should reflect the quality and service you want your B&B to deliver. The point is that each employee's actions are a direct reflection on your B&B and you as the innkeeper. This makes it your responsibility to be sure that they know what to do in all situations, and that they follow through.

Setting standards and sticking to them

Being a manager of others is often a hard job for an innkeeper. Innkeepers, by nature, are overachievers and oftentimes very independent. Sometimes those with this type of personality have trouble delegating and find themselves thinking, *"I can do it better (or faster) myself."* Even people who previously held jobs in the corporate world that included supervising others find the transition to managing inn employees difficult because of their direct and deep personal ownership of the B&B and the guest experience. Don't sabotage the success of your team by being overly controlling. Teach employees how things should be done and then give them the flexibility and freedom to get the job done. When things are not done to your satisfaction, coach, teach, and lead by example rather than dictating corrections.

To get the help you need, your employees need to know what you expect. Because your B&B is a small business, your employees may need to be cross-trained. Organization is key. The procedures for nearly everything you do in the running of your inn should be documented. Keeping this information current makes it easy to set expectations for employees. (You'll also be ready when you need to leave the inn in the care of an interim innkeeper.)

As you go through the chapters of this book, use the lists you create to build a manual for your bed & breakfast. Use the daily housekeeping schedule you create in Chapter 13 to train housekeeping staff. These employees need not only a schedule and a checklist, but they also need to know your policies regarding such matters as the number of towels or bottles of shampoo to place in each room. Make sure anyone who answers the phone or takes reservations is familiar with the etiquette that you establish for your inn (see Chapter 11). Those who interact with your guests should also know your policies (see Chapter 7), which should be explicitly expressed in the manual. Your manual should also include guest check-in procedures and phone numbers to use in an emergency (see Chapter 12). These lists and procedures — and the resulting manual — reflect the standards you set for the running of your B&B.

Even that which seems obvious to you may not be obvious to others when it comes to how you want something done. Employees need and deserve training. Here are some other things to keep in mind:

- ✔ **Review your employees' job descriptions with them and give them a copy so they can refer to it.**

  Including every conceivable task in a job description is difficult, so it's a good idea to include wording such as the following at the end of the description: *This description is intended to illustrate the kinds of tasks and levels of work difficulty required for the position and does not necessarily include all the related, specific duties and responsibilities of the position. It does not limit the assignment of related duties not mentioned.*

- ✔ **You'll have the best results if you're the one to initially train new employees.** This helps them understand the importance of their job and your expectations.

- ✔ **Manage by walking around.** Be present, and let employees know you're checking their work.

- ✔ **Be clear on policies and perks.** Employees won't know if they're overstepping their bounds unless you clearly define what is okay and what isn't. As an example, helping themselves to extra shampoo and soaps is probably not okay and should be clearly communicated.

- ✔ **Use performance reviews as a way of coaching.** Set predetermined times to review employee performance. Schedule annual or semi-annual reviews during your slow periods.

Teaching customer service as a way of thinking

Good customer service is something you need to teach employees to incorporate as a way of thinking. Having a *yes mentality* is a good way to start. This means taking every question or request a guest asks and beginning the answer with what you *can* do as opposed to what you *can't*. For example, when guests ask for an early check-in, you can tell them, "We can store your bags for you and recommend a local restaurant for lunch because your room won't be ready until 3 p.m." rather than "No, you can't check in early."

Helping employees understand the difference between a bed & breakfast stay and a traditional hotel stay is another key to customer-service training. The importance of good customer service cannot be underestimated in providing a quality bed & breakfast experience (see Chapter 12).

Handing over the whole enchilada: Hiring an interim innkeeper

Interim innkeepers, or inn-sitters, are individuals you can hire to run your inn in your absence. They're familiar with how to run a B&B. Many have been innkeepers themselves, whereas others have been trained to be professional interim innkeepers. When you hire an interim innkeeper, the most important thing is to be sure you're leaving the inn in good, capable hands.

Finding an interim innkeeper

Several resources are available to help you find someone capable of filling your shoes. Consider the following:

- ✔ Check with your state B&B association for a list of interim innkeepers.

- ✔ Visit the Web site of the Professional Association of Innkeepers International at www.paii.org for a listing of interim innkeepers. From the home page, click on Vendor Marketplace under the Resources tab, and then click on Interim Innkeeper.

- ✔ Contact the Interim Innkeepers Network (www.interiminnkeepers.net) and search for member interim innkeepers by state or availability.

Figuring out what to pay an interim innkeeper

Interim innkeepers set their rates individually. Talk to prospective interim innkeepers about your inn and the job functions you want them to perform in your absence. Most interim innkeepers have a base rate and negotiate the daily rate from there, depending on a number of variables such as the size of your inn, whether you have a housekeeping staff or expect them to clean the rooms, your occupancy rate, and so on.

Negotiating a rate isn't an exact science. To get in the ballpark, you may want to ask other innkeepers what they typically pay. Then, by working with a professional interim innkeeper who understands what the job entails, you can arrive at a price that you're happy with.

Covering all your bases

Make sure you have a complete checklist of everything relating to your inn, procedures, guests, and vendors. Your interim innkeeper shouldn't have to search for passwords to access your availability information, or waste time hunting for someone to call if the plumbing springs a leak. Interim innkeepers should have everything they need at their fingertips in order to run your inn smoothly in your absence.

Many innkeepers want to meet their interim innkeeper ahead of time. You can ask the person you choose to come and work with you for a few days before taking over the inn.

Taxes and insurance are additional items you need to consider, and possibly deal with.

- ✔ **Taxes:** When you hire an interim innkeeper, you need to find out whether that person is an independent contractor or a corporation, an LLC, or a partnership with a Federal Tax Identification Number (FTIN). If the interim innkeeper is incorporated, you only need to pay the bill, but if he is an independent contractor or an unincorporated partnership, you also need to prepare a 1099 for that person for tax purposes. (See additional information on independent contractors in the sidebar, "Independent contractors versus employees.")

- ✔ **Insurance:** Many interim innkeepers carry their own insurance. If this is the case with your interim innkeeper, you should be named as an additional insured. Choosing an interim innkeeper who has his own insurance is recommended; however, if the interim innkeeper you choose doesn't have insurance, you may be liable for workers comp and possibly unemployment. Check with your insurance carrier to see whether you need to do anything to be sure you and your business are adequately covered in your absence.

As with any business dealings, always spell out all the details of your arrangement with your interim innkeeper in a written contract.

Terminating Employees

Bad hires can ruin your business. The actions of every employee are a reflection on you. Guests don't care whether a problem lies with you or an employee; they only care about the experience they have at your inn. When an employee is creating a negative impact on your guests, you have no choice but to address it, and, if attempts to rectify the problem fail, to let the employee go.

Your best bet in dealing with difficult employees is to take steps to nip the problem in the bud. At the first indication of a problem, you should verbalize your concern with accurate information and examples. Discuss the problem with the employee, and clearly state the actions required to improve and keep the position. Document the conversation in the employee's file.

In the following days or weeks, continue to document, document, document, and be clear about your expectations. If termination is the outcome, you want to have a strong case for the reasoning behind your decision in case the employee decides to contest it.

Review the employee's progress, and terminate the employee if progress is not made.

Innkeepers are notorious for keeping less than satisfactory employees far past their "expiration dates." As a people-oriented person, you hate to give up on someone, but the overall harm to your business needs to take precedence.

If you take steps to get an employee on track and she doesn't improve, either that person isn't capable of improving or, more likely, doesn't want to. Often an employee in this situation develops a bad attitude, which may be contagious to other employees and bring down the morale of your team.

If you let the problem go on, guests aren't the only ones who will suffer: Other employees will think it's unfair for one person to get away with not having to do her job. If this isn't enough motivation to encourage you to deal quickly and seriously with employee performance issues, think about the instantaneous and permanent mark a bad online guest review leaves against your inn. You're paying someone to do a job and the guest is paying for an experience — neither should be negotiable.

Part V
Taking It beyond Breakfast and the Basics

The 5th Wave   By Rich Tennant

"Our customer survey indicates 30% of our customers think our service is inconsistent, 40% would like a change in the breakfast menu, and 50% think it would be real cute if we all wore matching colored hats."

In this part . . .

Your inn is always developing and maturing. Just because your business is up and running doesn't mean that you don't need help and support, or that you don't have questions. If you want to continue to grow your business (and I hope you do!), this part helps you do so by discussing taking your marketing to the next level, expanding your current inn, or even buying another. I also encourage you to take care of yourself both personally and professionally to keep you going as an innkeeper — and a good one at that — with suggestions to avoid burnout. Then, in anticipation of when it's time to move on, I help you to determine the best time to sell your inn and what you need to know when you're ready for that step.

Chapter 15

Assessing Your Success and Building on It

When someone asks you how your inn is doing, do you have an answer for them? Do you know? Equally as important as staying on top of bookkeeping and cleaning bathrooms, you need to take time periodically to analyze your successes and, yes, your disappointments. Just when you think you're ready to wind down after a busy season, you need to gear up and decide how you can take your business to the next level.

This chapter helps you to take a good hard look at where your business is and where you want it to go. I encourage you to compare your results to your projections and then figure out how you can use this information to make your business more successful. As an innkeeper, you're fortunate to have many advertising choices, but these choices are confusing, so I show you how to determine which advertising is working. I also introduce you to advertising and marketing strategies beyond the basics.

Analyzing Your B&B's Performance

If you didn't create a business plan before starting your bed & breakfast, it's not too late. A business plan is a road map for your business, and if you've been running your bed & breakfast without a clear direction, now is the time to chart the course (see Chapter 3 information on creating a business plan).

If you've already created a business plan, then you know it's a work in progress that's bound to change as your business grows and develops. Get it out, dust it off, and take a look at how you're doing.

Comparing results to expectations

You're probably wondering whether you're on target to meet the goals that you set. Are you meeting or exceeding your occupancy projections? How about your revenue and expense projections? Using your accounting software, you can run simple reports to see where your business stands, and you can compare these reports against the projections and expectations that you set. If you keep your records by hand you can and should create these same reports manually or in a spreadsheet.

To get this information, create a P&L (profit and loss statement). Set the date range for the period that you want to analyze. Then compare your total revenues, total expenses, and net income (or loss) with what you had anticipated in your business plan. If you're ahead of expectations, congratulations! If you're behind, don't worry — this chapter gives you many ideas to boost your results in the coming year.

You can run similar reports to analyze your occupancy rates in comparison to your projections by using your property management software (see Chapter 6 for information on property management systems), or conduct your own analysis using your records and ledgers. Looking at your occupancy by month enables you to quickly spot times of lower occupancy so that in the coming year, you can ratchet up your marketing in anticipation of these periods.

Tracking trends and the unexpected

Unexpected results can be good or bad news, and both provide important information on how to grow your business. During periods (or in areas) where your overall results are better or worse than you expected, your natural question should be "Why?" Perhaps you over- or underestimated these figures when setting your projections. That's fine, because now you have some hard numbers to use for the future. More than likely, you'll find both good and bad news in comparing actual figures with the projections you initially set. Look at the better-than-expected results and see if you can identify any patterns, such as:

 ✔ **Do you have a particular room that has a higher occupancy than your other rooms?** If so, ask yourself why. Do you have better pictures of this room on your Web site? Is the price lower in comparison to your other rooms or similar rooms at other B&Bs? Is this your favorite room or the room that you perceive to be the best? With this information, ask your-self whether you can make changes to your other rooms, or the percep-tion of your other rooms, that would increase their occupancy rate.

✔ **Can you attribute the periods during which you exceeded your occu-pancy projections to anything in particular?** For example, did a local corporation book numerous rooms with you? If this is the case, don't rest on your laurels — be proactive. Contact the corporation to find out whether they need rooms annually or on a regular basis and, if so, offer to make those reservations now.

✔ **Do you see a pattern in the reasons guests visited you?** If you find you have a large number of honeymooners visiting, are you keeping track of their anniversaries? Do you have a system to send anniversary greetings letting them know you hope to see them back at the inn to celebrate the occasion? Include an enticing special offer or an incentive like a special gift to welcome them back.

Crunching numbers is great; however, knowing *why* guests have chosen your inn or area can help you to attract similar new guests. You won't know this information if you don't ask, and you can't track it and analyze it if you don't record it. Many property management software systems can do this for you, or you can create your own records using an Excel spreadsheet.

If your results are below the projections that you set, look back over the year and see if weather or economic factors existed that could have had an effect on your income and occupancy. Maybe you cut back on advertising during that particular period, or maybe you did nothing different and similar proper-ties also experienced the same general decline in occupancy. No matter what conclusions you draw, you can use this information to be proactive for the same season next year or in case you experience similar conditions again. (See the section "Creating packages: Bundling services that sell" later in this chapter for info on using packages to boost low occupancy.)

Adjusting expenses to increase profits

The benefit of being familiar with your bills, expenses, and projections is that you know where your money is going. That makes it easier to figure out which expenses you can control. Some ideas for cutting back on your expenses include

✔ **Serving a plated breakfast rather than a buffet.** A plated breakfast results in less waste and more portion control, so you can decrease food costs by making this switch.

✔ **Limiting dryer time.** It's easy to throw a load of linens into the dryer and set the timer for an hour when, in fact, the linens will be dry in half that time. Remove them promptly to cut down on ironing, which also saves time and electricity.

✔ **Performing routine maintenance and making repairs promptly.** A well-maintained inn does more than make a good impression on guests. It also keeps appliances in good working order and extends their useful life. Fixing leaks and adding insulation as needed saves on utility costs.

✔ **Storing individual serving sizes.** Keeping individual serving sizes of food items that you periodically get requests for — say, individual cans of V8 — allows you to accommodate the occasional guest who wants it without having to throw out a large, unused container if no other guest requests it for a week. This lets you cut down on waste without cutting down on service.

✔ **Cutting down on serving sizes.** Look at what guests leave on their plates. Reduce the serving size of items that you find many guests aren't eating, whether it's that extra sausage or those breakfast potatoes.

If guests are leaving items on their plates, it doesn't necessarily mean your serving size is too large. It could also mean they don't like the item or the item's quality. To serve the best breakfast possible, replace items on your menus that are frequently left on guests' plates. Lack of quality at your B&B costs you even more than you can save by cutting expenses.

Yield management

Most large chain hotels — and the travel industry in general — use a rate factoring technique called *yield management*. Yield management (also known as *revenue management*) simply means that you raise and lower the prices of your rooms based on supply and demand. For example, if you're located in a college town, yield management suggests that you should raise your rates when special events occur, such as moving in or out days, parents' visiting weekend, graduation, football weekends, and so forth, when you know demand for your rooms will be high. Yield management also suggests that if you have four rooms and three have been rented for a particular weekend, you should raise the price on the fourth room. The idea here is that when you know that demand for your rooms will be greater than availability, you should charge more for them.

Yield management is also used during periods of low occupancy, such that you lower your prices during periods of less demand or on unsold rooms as the check-in date gets closer. The logic is that getting a lower rate for the room is better than getting nothing at all if the room sits empty.

However, yield management isn't for everyone, nor is it the only way to look at pricing. For example, in the case of the college events noted above, you might use a different logic and rationalize that the guests who come on those special weekends will return every year that their children are in school (not to mention that their kids may return as alumni) and, in the interest of rewarding their patronage, you may decide you don't want to charge your repeat guests more.

You may even decide that having many different rates is just too complicated, and therefore leave your rates unchanged despite increased demand.

Setting next year's projections

Setting your projections for year two and beyond is done in much the same way as your initial projections (for a review, see Chapter 3). Unless you have a crystal ball, guesswork will still be a big part of your projections, but after the first year, you have the benefit of knowing

- ✔ **Occupancy:** You now have real historical data to factor in.

- ✔ **Advertising performance:** Advertising takes awhile to take effect. In the beginning, every idea presented to you may sound like a great opportunity but after being open for a year or two, you find it easier to see

    - The types of advertising that work for you (print or online ads, association referrals, or a combination of various categories)

    - Which companies or campaigns within these categories are producing results (later in this chapter I help you determine which advertising is effective).

    What works changes over time, so continuously review your advertising results.

- ✔ **Revenues and expenses:** *Budgets* are educated guesses or projections of your revenues and expenses. Enter your estimates in the budgeting component of your accounting software and run comparisons to previous time periods.

- ✔ **Referral and repeat guest rate:** Are you getting referrals and repeat guests? If so, you're on the road to success! You can expect this effect to mushroom and produce good results going forward.

Guest rooms are a perishable commodity! Each night they're not rented is an opportunity lost.

Evaluating Guest Satisfaction

Guest satisfaction is an important measure of your success. After all, any business without satisfied customers won't be in business for long, and this is especially true in the bed & breakfast industry. Measuring successes and deficiencies are a part of doing business. Larger businesses require huge budgets to measure customer satisfaction but, luckily for you, finding out what your guests think is relatively easy. Not only can their feedback help to make you a better host or hostess for future guests, but if used properly, it can also be a powerful marketing tool. (See Chapter 8 for some great information on how to solicit guest feedback and use it as a marketing tool.)

Use guest satisfaction feedback to help you understand the following:

✔ **Are your guests who you think they are?** Reading any and all guest comments that are posted online and listening carefully to those communicated directly to you tells you whether your guests are who you think they are and whether you're providing the services and amenities they want. Watch for key phrases like

- *I would have liked to have seen. . . .*

- *I thought the innkeeper would. . . .*

- *The description on the Web site was not accurate.*

This information provides you with invaluable free training on how to be a better innkeeper, while improving your guests' experiences and, in the process, increasing your repeat and referral business.

✔ **What are you doing wrong?** No one likes criticism, but all negative comments should be viewed as valuable feedback. If you receive a similar complaint from more than one guest, you're doing something wrong. Most likely, what the guests are expecting is not in sync with what you're offering. This means you are failing to adequately communicate what a stay at your inn is like. Reevaluate all your communications with your guests, including your reservation system, your Web site, e-mail communications, confirmations, policies, and brochures, and change anything that is misleading or spell it out more clearly so that guests know what to expect.

Oftentimes, innkeepers feel that negative guest reviews are either untrue or very unfair. You work hard trying to please your guests, and negative comments hurt, especially when they're posted online for the world to see. Do yourself and your reputation a favor and let your anger subside before you post a management response. Don't take criticism personally, and think before you write. I know — easier said than done — but otherwise you may regret it. Once you post something online, it's a permanent record that can be seen by any and all potential guests and referrals.

Taking Your Online Marketing to the Next Level

The many facets of marketing your bed & breakfast can be overwhelming when you're first starting out (see Chapter 8). It's a lot to absorb, but remember that it's a work in progress. The most successful innkeepers are those who have the following characteristics in common:

- ✔ They never stop learning.
- ✔ They continually delve deeper into more targeted and sophisticated advertising techniques.
- ✔ They're always open to new ideas.
- ✔ They drop anything that isn't working.

If your bed & breakfast is like most, the majority of your new business will come from the Internet. Enhancing your online marketing is the fastest and most cost effective way for most inns to improve occupancy rates. You owe it to yourself and the success of your B&B to know as much as you can about online marketing.

Being part of an inspected and approved program is a successful marketing strategy that brings additional business to many inns. Once established, you can apply for membership in organizations such as Select Registry or Canada Select that require inspections and/or acceptance. Many state associations also require that inns admitted for membership be rigorously inspected and approved.

Adding pay-per-click advertising

Pay-per-click is a form of online advertising whereby you only pay when a guest clicks on your advertisement. Pay-per-click ads are usually displayed on the top pages of Web sites and along the side pages of popular search engines like Google, where they're generally identified as "Sponsored Results." Pay-per-click ads involve an investment of your time to set up and maintain. Then to get them to work efficiently, you must devote some time each month to reviewing the results and making appropriate adjustments.

The concept is based on *search terms*, which are the words or phrases people are most likely to enter into search engines to find you. When you do pay-per-click advertising, you decide on the search terms or phrases that will best find you. Then through a process known as *bidding*, because you have to be willing to pay more than other inns in order to be displayed, you set the maximum price that you're willing to pay if a guest clicks on your advertisement. Be aware, though, that if your price isn't high enough, or if other inns are willing to pay more for the same term, or if your ad fails to attract enough clicks, the search engine company will drop you for that search term or phrase.

To get started, you simply create an account, choose your search terms, set the price you're willing to pay for each click, and write a description for your ad. For best results, pick targeted terms and write a custom description so that only truly interested guests will click on your ad, and you won't be paying for clicks from uninterested people.

Making pay-per-click work for you

The advantage of pay-per-click advertising is that it's a way to get your inn to display in the top results of the search engines. If guests click on your ad, they're taken directly to your Web site rather than to a directory, where they'd also see information about other inns in your area. The idea behind making pay-per-click work for you is to pinpoint the search term that gives you the greatest number of clicks for the smallest price. The more popular the search term, the more each click costs.

Take, for example, the key phrase "Cape May New Jersey." This is a very popular search term; therefore, the cost per click is quite high. Furthermore, the term is too general — it's unlikely that a large number of people who search just for "Cape May New Jersey" are actually looking for a bed & breakfast. Bidding on more targeted search terms not only costs less, but also produces better results. Because Cape May is such a competitive town for bed & breakfasts, even the term "Cape May Bed & Breakfast" is very expensive, although it is highly targeted. The term "Cape May New Jersey B&B" is less expensive, yet still produces results.

Finding companies that offer pay-per-click

Numerous companies provide pay-per-click advertising. They have different interfaces, but once you understand the concept, they're all fairly straightforward and easy to use. Popular pay-per-click adverting companies include

- ✔ **Google AdWords:** www.adwords.google.com
- ✔ **Yahoo! Search Marketing:** http://searchmarketing.yahoo.com
- ✔ **Microsoft adCenter:** https://.adcenter.microsoft.com

Create one list of terms and phrases in a format such as Excel and use it for each company that you create an account with. When you compile your list, think of anything and everything a guest might type in to find your inn. When you set up your account, you're given access to tools that suggest search terms and phrases for you. Pay attention to these — they're based on what guests are actually searching for. As an aside, the terms you bid on should be included in your Web site content as well.

Tracking pay-per-click

Within your pay-per-click account, you can keep track of how often potential guests are clicking on your advertisements and which terms are providing the best return. You can set a daily or monthly budget and even designate what time of the day you want your ads to appear. This enables you to create and stick to a budget, and spread out the running of your ads over a period of time.

Software programs are available that track not only the performance of your pay-per-click ad campaigns, but also the activity on your Web site and all your advertising efforts. They offer various levels of detail. You can ask whoever helps you set up your Web site to help you install tracking software (also known as a traffic report or Web analytics), too.

Another alternative is to have someone else manage the tracking and analysis for you. Companies like Acorn Internet Services (www.acorn-is.com), InnsideOut Solutions (www.savvyinnkeeper.com), and White Stone Marketing (www.whitestonemarketing.com) specialize in helping innkeepers manage and evaluate this type of advertising.

Getting optimal search engine placement

Search Engine Optimization (SEO) consists of the efforts you undertake to get your Web site to place higher among the *organic* (free) listings on a search engine. Figuring out the algorithms currently being used by the search engines to rank sites requires a great deal of time and attention (not to mention the algorithms change frequently), so it's usually better to hire someone to do it for you. If you do want to attempt this yourself, the best advice I can give you is to pay attention to what search engines like in terms of keywords, content, and links (all of which I discuss in the upcoming sections), and then institute only those strategies that make sense.

Don't try and trick the search engines. If search engines think you're doing something to purposely manipulate your Web site into achieving a higher placement, they'll usually penalize your site by listing it lower or, in extreme cases, black-listing your site so that it disappears from the free listings altogether. When you make changes to your Web site with the purpose of improving your search engine placement, make those changes gradually.

Beware of companies that promise or guarantee placement on the search engines and those that want to submit your site to multiple search engines at once. Good search engine placement is a science that takes hard work. The process should be tailored to your inn and your area and, as such, isn't something that can be done in one shot. (See Chapter 8 for Web site designers who specialize in the bed & breakfast industry and in SEO.)

Key search words are key

One thing that has remained a constant in the evolution of SEO is the use of keywords.

- ✔ Periodically review and update the verbiage on your Web site to make sure you're using the most up-to-date keywords as you get to know your guests and what they're searching for. Be sure this information is prominently displayed on your Web site. Not only is this important info that your site visitors need to know, but it also adds popular keywords to your text. This makes new guests more likely to find your B&B when searching on the Internet.

✔ Keep the content of your Web site fresh. Search engines pay attention to how often a site changes, so continually update your Web site text with seasonal activities and fresh content. This not only keeps your site current and appealing to guests, but also helps your search engine placement.

To get on the right track, think of the text on your Web site as talking to your potential guests by providing them with important information, and talking to the search engines by incorporating your keywords into your text. You'll reward both guests and the search engines by having a robust Web site with a lot of content.

Building links is like building a neighborhood

Search engines display Web sites based on the algorithms that humans create. One currently important factor used to determine a site's placement is the number of *links,* or paths to and from other Web sites. Links can be either bad or good. Check out the following explanations and examples:

✔ **Incoming links:** The more good-quality Web sites that link to your Web site, the better your Web site is deemed to be. This makes it important for you to get as many top-notch sites as possible to link to you, especially ones that are within the same industry. For example, a link from your state bed & breakfast association is much more valuable than a link from a company that makes cat food. The logic is that if a lot of major hospitality or travel sites are linking to you, your site must be valuable because people, not computers, add those links.

✔ **Keyword-rich links:** Links to your Web site are even more valuable if the words that make up the link are keyword-rich. For example, a link to your Web site that reads "Cape May, New Jersey Bed & Breakfast" is viewed much more favorably by the search engines than a link that reads simply "click here." Keyword-rich text appears more natural to the search engines and lends credibility to your site.

✔ **Outbound links:** Linking to other Web sites is fine, but having too many outbound links dilutes the ranking of pages on your site. Limit the placement of outbound links on your Web site to those that provide valuable resources to your guests, such as links to activities and restaurants.

Use caution when gathering links. Too many that don't make sense can actually hurt you. Because some site owners have abused this technique in the past, the search engine algorithms are now designed to flag sites with a lot of inbound or outbound links. Stick with partnerships and link exchanges that relate to your business or provide information and resources to guests, and don't add too many at once.

TIP

Ogling Google Analytics

Even if your hosting company provides you with traffic statistics, it's hard to beat the features of Google Analytics (www.google.com/analytics). It's free, comprehensive, and robust.

Google Analytics tracks and records the activity on your Web site through a simple piece of code that your Webmaster adds to each page on your site. To view this information, you log in to your Google account. Each report contains a lot of information, so interpreting it all can be overwhelming. However, the information is so

valuable that it's worth working with one of the hosting companies that's familiar with the bed & breakfast industry to decipher it. (See Chapter 8 for a list of Web site hosting companies that specialize in the bed & breakfast industry.)

Google has numerous other free tools that you or your Webmaster should become familiar with as well. For example, after you create a Google account, be sure your information is correct on Google maps so that your inn comes up in the local search results on Google.

Tracking your Web site traffic

Research shows that your average guest will visit your Web site several times before deciding to make a reservation. In other words, the guest rarely comes to your Web site from one source and makes a reservation or reservation request on the first visit. So how can you track where guests are finding you?

Web hosting companies provide *traffic reports,* which are summaries of the activity on your Web site that give you invaluable information about your guests before you even meet them. Reading these reports clues you in to how guests are finding your B&B. With this info, you can focus your energy and resources in similar places to attract more of the same guests. This data can help you figure out which online advertising is working and worth your investment and which should be dropped. Traffic reports also can tell you about your guests' behaviors when they're on your Web site and whether they're interested in what they see.

Traffic reports come in two speeds:

- ✔ **Basic traffic reports** tell you which advertising is sending guests (traffic) to your Web site, but they don't tell you which guests make reservations. In this case, it's important to look at quality as well as quantity. Don't just look at the number of referrals a site sends you. Determining how interested those guests are is more important, and you can tell this by checking out how many pages on your Web site guests look at and how long they stay on your site.

✔ **Souped-up traffic reports** distinguish the bookers from the lookers and report all the sources that the guest looked at for each actual guest reservation. Services such as Intell-a-Keeper (www.acorn-is.com) and SuperStatZ (www.ew3d.com) provide more advanced tracking software.

Do not place tracking software (often free) that is not password-protected on your Web site. If you do, your competition will be able to see your information, which gives them a competitive advantage.

Traffic reports include several common statistics you can use to help you decipher your report details and understand how your online advertising is performing. One such statistic, referred to as *site usage* or *visitors,* provides an overview of guests' interaction on your Web site including

✔ **Visits (not hits):** This is the number of guests who visit your Web site during the date range that you run the report for. The goal is for this number to rise when compared to the same dates in previous periods (the total for this year, month, or season compared to the same time period in previous years). Always make sure you're comparing the same period from year to year rather than comparing one month to the next.

Numbers are great, but seeing this information in a graph presentation is even more helpful. Many programs, such as Google Analytics, let you set a date range and compare two time periods at once in the form of a graph. (See the nearby sidebar for more info about Google Analytics.)

✔ **Hits:** This is the number of files that load on a Web page.

Keep in mind that each Web page contains many files. Therefore, one page load usually equals many hits and is not a good gauge of the traffic on your Web site. Some sites quote hits, but this data is meaningless in determining how well your Web site is performing. Don't confuse hits with visitors and pages/visit.

✔ **Pages/visit:** This is the number of pages on your Web site that the average guest looks at. The higher this number, the better, because the more pages a guest looks at, the more interested they are in your site and probably your inn. A high number indicates that you're attracting interested guests and that your Web site is keeping their attention.

✔ **Bounce rate:** This is the percentage of guests who leave your Web site almost as soon as they arrive. A high bounce rate means guests arrived at your Web site and immediately decided they weren't interested. If the number is low, you're doing a good job of attracting the right guests to your site — your advertising is on target, and guests like your site enough to explore it. If your bounce rate is high, the good news is that you've found a place to make improvements, either by having more targeted advertising so you're attracting the right guests, or redesigning your site to be more inviting and/or easier to navigate, thereby increasing the number of guests who seriously consider your inn.

✔ **Average time on site:** This statistic tells you how much time the average guest spends on your site. The longer guests stay, the more interested they are.

Traffic is a term that refers to a breakdown of where your guests are coming from and the search terms they're using to find you. Related data includes

✔ **Referrers:** This statistic tells you which sites are sending guests to your Web site. It allows you to see how many guests come from search engines, online directories, chambers, visitors bureaus, associations, and other sources. You can also tell how many guests get to your site just by typing in your domain name.

This statistic is important because rarely can guests correctly tell you where they found you. While guests mean well, they often simply don't remember. They may confuse your Web site with a directory listing for your inn simply because it has pictures, prices, and lots of information.

Some online reservation programs require you to configure referral source choices for the guest to choose from when they're making a reservation. A guest can't identify a source if it's not on the list, so avoid common mistakes like not listing all your advertising sources as choices or not keeping your list up-to-date when you join a new directory or add a new advertising source. Also, avoid listing abbreviations for associations or advertising sources (a guest doesn't know what ABBA is, for example). Even when set up correctly, few guests can remember the name of the site that they found you on and select it from the list.

✔ **Keywords:** This data tells you the keywords or phrases that guests searched to find your site. You want to incorporate these keywords and phrases into the text on your Web site. You can also use these words if you do pay-per-click adverting (see the discussion earlier in this chapter). You should not, however, base your marketing entirely on the most common phrases used to find your site.

Two more statistics are important to your understanding of the traffic on your Web site. They are

✔ **Top entry (landing) page:** This is the page that most visitors to your site see first. It's often your home page, but you'll probably be interested to see how many guests enter on other pages too, such as your recipe or attraction pages. Once you know where visitors are entering, take a look at the bounce rate for each of those pages. Are guests staying on your site or leaving immediately? Be sure your site is easy to navigate so guests don't leave simply because they can't find what they're looking for.

✔ **Top exit pages:** These are the pages your guests commonly visit just before leaving your site. Knowing this can help you identify pages that you should devote some time to making more informative, attractive, or useful.

Networking on the Internet

It's a whole new world out there, and as an innkeeper, you need to keep your priorities in mind. A well-optimized Web site should be your primary goal for marketing on the Internet. Next, you need to monitor your online image on review sites and directories to control the marketing message around your inn. Then, if you have the time to devote to doing it right, you may want to consider interactive forums (such as blogs and Facebook) to generate sales leads. At the very least, you should be aware of the forum phenomenon, knowing that participation can be a great marketing tool, but only if done correctly. Don't feel pressured to be involved, and don't jump in unless you've taken the time to learn the etiquette and are committed to devoting the time necessary to make it worthwhile in promoting your inn.

Tim Brady, owner of Forty Putney Road Bed & Breakfast in Brattleboro, Vermont (www.fortyputneyroad.com) retired as a Chief Technology Officer to become an innkeeper. He offers some of the best advice I've seen to fellow innkeepers:

- ✔ Watch from the sidelines by reading other's posts until you get the hang of how social networking works.

- ✔ Don't participate unless you're sharing knowledge. Do not overtly sell your inn. Be sure your posts include a link to your Web site, which not only helps build links to your site, but also establishes you as an expert.

- ✔ Social networks (MySpace, Facebook, and so on) can be your friend or enemy. Selectively join social networks relative to your audience and area. Again, don't sell; make only knowledgeable comments. Let the interested audience come to you.

- ✔ Post frequent relevant content if you decide to start your own blog. Write conversationally and approve comments of users (not approving comments for reasons other than spam control or inappropriate content is a big no-no). Avoid posts that you feel will spark controversy on your own Web site.

- ✔ Use traveler review sites to your advantage. Check them frequently, post a response geared towards the general reader, and do not become engaged in an argument with the reviewer.

Staying in touch with online newsletters

Periodic online newsletters are an inexpensive way to keep in touch with guests and keep your inn on their minds for return visits and making referrals. A good newsletter is

✔ **Attractive:** Your newsletter represents your inn and should contain images and colors that guests identify with your inn.

A variety of newsletter programs include simple templates that are easy to use and require no programming knowledge. Many Web designers can also create a template for you that matches the look and feel of your Web site. Work with a newsletter program or your Web designer to send out your newsletter so that it's not blocked by SPAM filters.

✔ **Interesting:** True, you're promoting your inn, but your newsletter shouldn't sound like a sales piece. Include information about happenings at the inn and in the area.

✔ **Short:** Include links back to your Web site, your e-mail, and your availability calendar. Take advantage of the "read more" feature, which takes guests to your Web site where you have the full news story. To do this, include an introductory paragraph for each section of your newsletter in the newsletter itself with a "read more" link which takes readers to your Web site for the full article. This not only brings guests to your Web site it also has the added benefit of providing more keyword rich, fresh content on your Web site for Google to index!

✔ **Enticing:** Offer something to entice guests to your inn, even if it's a ready-made package.

Don't send unsolicited newsletters. Obtain your guests' permission before adding them to your mailing list, and always give them the option to opt out. Don't buy e-mail lists — they're a waste of money and can brand you as a spammer.

Taking Advantage of More Offline Marketing Options

Nothing is more exciting than reading about your inn in a newspaper or magazine or hearing it featured on TV or the radio. There's no specific secret to being chosen, but here are some things you can do to increase your chances:

✔ **Create a press kit.** Having a press kit ready when a call comes in ensures you're ready for any press opportunity. Include a fact sheet about your inn including your inn's history, your signature dishes, and some guest comments, as well as your brochure and, of course, your business card.

You don't need to spend a lot of money on a press kit. Get a two-pocket folder that matches the color of your inn, and then have postcards made with a picture of your inn and your inn's name on the front. (You'll get plenty of use out of the postcards and you can order them online — check out www.vistaprint.com.) Use rubber cement to paste the post card in the center of the folder, and arrange your materials inside.

✔ **Add a press room on your Web site.** Having pages devoted to the media makes it easy for travel writers to get information about your inn and download high-resolution photos. Check out `www.sladesinn.com/ reviews-press-room.html` for a good example.

✔ **Handle press inquiries with professionalism.** Take any press call seriously, but be skeptical. Oftentimes travel writers will contact you with the promise that they'll write about your inn in exchange for free accommodations. Ask these reporters for examples of similar articles that they've written and push for details about where the story featuring your inn will be published. While it's understandable that reporters working on a piece will want to stay with you, writers from the top newspapers, magazines, and guidebooks will usually do so anonymously before featuring your inn in a story.

✔ **Contact the media.** Get to know the editors and writers from your local papers and surrounding towns. Invite them to special events and open houses at your inn. Consider offering them a stay during your slow season (check their policies first, though, with regard to accepting free lodging). Periodically create and send the media a press release or your newsletter with a note about happenings at your inn.

✔ **Work with an association.** Reporters are more receptive to hearing about an area than they are to a sales pitch for a particular inn, so work together with your local association to create open houses, tours, and other packages. Then alert the local media and media in surrounding areas.

Ask anyone who writes about your inn for copies of the article and any video; then post them on your Web site press page.

Opening New Doors to Sustain Success

Being creative and staying up to date with fresh ideas will bring a constant flow of guests to your door. Simply embrace and communicate what is unique and special about your inn and then get ready to welcome a host of new and interesting guests.

Catering to a niche market

Catering to a group of individuals with particular likes or needs is called *niche marketing,* and it can bring new guests to your inn that you wouldn't have had otherwise. You may be seeing an opportunity to cater to a niche market if you can answer "yes" to any of the following:

✔ Have you ever turned away guests because of something you didn't offer, not knowing of any other accommodations to refer them to that had what they were asking for? *Could* you offer what they were looking for?

✔ Is there a B&B or hotel that always has numerous guests because of something specific that they offer or groups that they cater to? Is this something you could also do?

✔ Can you identify a trend, such as "going green," that's determining how some guests are making lodging choices?

This type of marketing could include marketing to motorcyclists, to painters by hosting painting workshops, to those traveling with pets, or to any number of hundreds of targeted groups of travelers. Finding your niche (or niches) helps you to distinguish your inn from others in the area and expand your marketing message. Catering to a niche market also provides you with additional places to advertise, thus bringing more guests to your inn. Cultivating your niche is part of building your brand (see Chapter 8 for information on building your brand and establishing your inn's message).

What's pleasing to one group may discourage another. For example, if your inn is pet-friendly, guests traveling without pets or those who aren't fond of animals may choose to stay elsewhere. The important thing is clear communication so that all guests know what to expect. For instance, you may only allow pets in certain rooms but not in the common areas. This is important information for pet owners and other guests to know, so post this type of information clearly wherever your policies are listed (see Chapter 7), remembering you won't be able to please everyone all of the time.

Unleash your creativity and passions as you have fun thinking of ways to attract guests in under-served areas of the market. Do you have a special interest or talent? If you do, you're probably not the only one. Deciding to target other like-minded individuals is another way to fill rooms at your inn, and you'll find it enjoyable as well. Do you love helping brides plan weddings? Are you an artist? Is cooking a passion? There are endless possibilities for niche markets from which you can attract guests and it's easy to get started:

1. **Identify a market segment or unfilled need.**

   Be creative, yet practical. The rewards of niche marketing come when you think outside of the box and brainstorm about ideas for groups of people you want to attract to your inn.

2. **Research the feasibility of catering to the niche market you've identified.**

   Don't waste your time on impractical ideas. There could be any number of reasons that no one else is catering to your niche, including

- **Not enough potential guests are interested.** For example, an inn located in an area known for outdoor active getaways will probably have little success in attracting additional guests for scrapbooking weekends.

- **Your geographic area doesn't offer enough activities catering to the group's interests.** For example, while identifying your inn as gay-friendly might open up new advertising opportunities for you, it won't be an easy niche to cater to if there are no gay-friendly bars or restaurants in your town.

- **Zoning restrictions or regulations are prohibitive.** For example, even if you're fielding calls from brides wanting you to hold small weddings on your beautiful grounds, zoning restrictions may prohibit you from doing so without a conditional use permit, which may be a difficult or impossible undertaking.

3. **Once you find a niche that's workable and likely to attract guests to your inn, clearly define that niche.**

   Decide exactly who you are targeting, why you are targeting them, what you will offer them, and how you will get the word out. For example, if your niche is guests who travel with their pets, the steps you need to take include the following:

   - **Make sure you have appropriate accommodations for the owners and pets you hope to welcome to your inn.** Dogs and cats require different amenities.

   - **Evaluate and adjust your reservation and damage policies.** Make sure they include restrictions and additional charges as needed, such as a pet cleaning fee.

   - **Update your Web site and marketing materials.** Clearly communicating pet policies is important so that guests who are traveling both with and without pets know what to expect.

   - **Update keywords and text on your Web site so that the search engines know you accommodate travelers with pets.**

   - **Create special packages around your niche.** See more on creating packages in the next section.

   - **Find new advertising venues by looking for places to market to travelers who want to bring their pets.** Do Internet searches for terms such as "pets welcome," "travel with pets," "pet travel," and so on to find directories and blogs you can use to get the word out that you accommodate this group of travelers.

   - **Issue a press release.** Companies such as PRWeb (www.prweb.com) and TransWorldNews (www.transworldnews.com) offer economical services to issue online press releases. A side benefit of a press release is that you can include your keywords with links to your Web site.

• **Note any articles that have been written on traveling with pets and contact the writers to let them know about your inn.** (See the earlier section, "Amping up your media exposure," for tips on working with travel writers.)

Packages: Bundling services that sell

Packages are a great way to bundle services together. Ready-made packages present an appealing marketing message, and they're an easy add-on or upgrade for a guest who's already making a reservation to stay at your B&B. Although many guests don't think to ask what else is available for their stay, most are pleased to hear what other special treats you have for them. Guests see packages as something extra that adds to their experience at your B&B, and your revenue increases from the additional service — a win-win for both you and your guests.

You can add packages to reservations taken either over the phone or online. Asking about special occasions when taking phone reservations creates a continuous opportunity to offer add-ons and upgrades to guests. You can also advertise packages on your Web site. Many reservation software systems make it easy for you to offer them to your guests as they're completing their reservations. For example, after the guest has selected a room and is in the final steps of submitting a reservation, the opportunity to add a spa service such as a massage can be offered.

The benefits of creating packages are numerous. Packages offer

✔ **Reinforcement of your brand and your inn's image.** Creating romance packages, for example, reinforces the idea that your inn is a good choice for those seeking a romantic getaway — even if they don't book the actual package.

✔ **Additional revenue.** Packages allow for up-selling. They're also a great way to bundle several items, services, and features together for one price.

✔ **A means to offer discounts without cutting room prices.** By packaging several full-price items together with your room, you can then offer a discount to the guest on the full package and end up with more revenue than if you had discounted just the room rate for the guest.

✔ **Extra promotional opportunities.** Guests using online directories often start on the specials and packages pages, so your inn will be seen first if you're listed on these pages. The directories feature specials and packages in their newsletters and press releases to the media as well, again resulting in extra exposure for your inn. The media may also take info about your packages from your Web site or online directories and provide additional coverage for you.

It's okay to be inspired by other innkeepers, but don't copy their packages exactly. Your packages should be unique to your inn. Refer to Table 15-1 for successful package ideas that combine creativity and niche marketing.

Table 15-1	Popular Bed & Breakfast Packages	
Active Adventure Getaways	Babymoons	Bike Tours
Business Travel Specials	Courses & Classes	Create-Your-Own Package
Culinary Getaway	Dinner Packages	Extended-Stay Discounts
Fall Foliage Specials	Family Reunions	Family Travel Deals
Father's Day Specials	Fun in the Sun	Gas Savings Specials
Girlfriend Getaways	Going Green Getaways	Golf Packages
Group Getaways	Haunted Getaways	Holiday Celebrations
Holiday Tours	Honeymoon Packages	Horseback-Riding Packages
Massage Packages	Midweek Specials	Military Specials
Mother's Day Packages	Murder Mystery	New Year's Packages
Quilting Getaways	Romantic Getaways	Scrapbooking Retreats
Senior Citizen Discounts	Ski Packages	Spa Packages
Spontaneous Specials	Valentine's Specials	Vow Renewal Ceremonies
Winter Specials	Weddings	

Chapter 16

Keeping Your Most Important Asset (You) Fine-Tuned

In This Chapter

▶ Working your business so it doesn't work you

▶ Finding ways to take a break

▶ Continuing the never-ending learning process

Do you work to live or do you live to work? For many innkeepers, this distinction is a blurred one, and that's okay — as long as you're running the business and it's not running you.

In this chapter, I share my favorite sanity-saving tips as well as advice from seasoned innkeepers who've learned (sometimes the hard way) how to set boundaries and keep themselves motivated and happy in the B&B business. I also discuss ways to grow professionally, from joining associations to attending conferences. These resources can give you the support you need and renew your enthusiasm when the business overwhelms you.

Running Your Business So It Doesn't Run You

In the beginning, carving out time for yourself is difficult. Your lists of things to do and bills to pay seem endless, leaving you feeling that there's no time or money left for anything else. Hopefully, your excitement at becoming an innkeeper will carry you through these times, but as the euphoria wears off and fatigue sets in, I caution you to be aware and ready for it. Feeling tired and overworked is hard to hide. Guests sense it in the way you respond to them, and it can show in your dealings with your staff. While these reactions are normal, the trick is to ward off these feelings. When you feel in control, you're working the business instead of letting the business work you.

Longtime innkeepers are a good source of advice because they've been in your shoes. Here are some of their best suggestions:

✔ **Make a list of what you like about being an innkeeper.** Your list will be unique to you, so add to it and change it as your ideas change. You'll have your own reasons, but your list may look something like this:

- I like being my own boss.

- I like not having to get dressed up or having to commute to work.

- I like meeting interesting people.

- I like that I'm never bored and that no two days are the same.

- I like receiving instant feedback and gratification from satisfied guests.

- I like being able to be creative.

✔ **Make a list of what you dislike about innkeeping.** Don't kid yourself; innkeeping is a job and there are aspects that aren't fun. I'm sure your list will vary in length depending on the day — and the guests you've just hosted — so stick to the big things and then look for ways to turn them into a positive. For example, you may not like the feeling that your work is never done, or dealing with demanding guests. Pull back and think about how many wonderful and interesting people you've met because of these long hours and the fabulous compliments you've received.

✔ **Let go of your pursuit of perfection.** There will always be a room that needs painting and a housekeeper who forgets to put a towel in the guest room. Remind yourself that guests don't see most of the things that you think are less than perfect about your property.

✔ **Don't take criticism personally.** The good thing about this business is dealing with people, and the hard thing about this business is dealing with people. Some people are impossible to please (thankfully, these people are a minority). Although it's easier said than done, longtime innkeepers recommend that you not take things personally. They also identify and cater to the types of guests who'll be happy at their inns. (See Chapter 2 for information on matching guests to your B&B's style.)

✔ **Understand that you can't please everyone all the time.** It's impossible to be everything to everyone. Know this and accept it.

✔ **Have a sense of humor.** It's easy to be so busy that you don't take the time to find the humor in a situation and to laugh a little.

✔ **Be sure your circle of friends includes innkeepers, other small business owners, and people who are neither innkeepers nor business owners.** Isolating yourself from other innkeepers and business owners means losing out on a support network of resources and common understanding. Spending time with non-innkeeping friends is a refreshing way to think about something other than your business.

✔ **See your inn through the eyes of others.** Invite a friend over who hasn't seen the inn in a while. Listen to and appreciate the rave comments you're sure to receive. Let them rejuvenate you.

✔ **Look at the big picture.** Understand that guests are going to do what guests are going to do. For example, guests often rearrange furniture in a room. Ask yourself whether it really matters. Is it damaging the property or interfering with another guest's enjoyment? If not, resign yourself to putting it back when they leave.

✔ **Recognize when you need to get away.** See the section "Making time for yourself" later in this chapter.

✔ **Take compliments to heart.** Don't brush off compliments. Hear their sincerity and appreciate your accomplishments, talents, and skills.

Getting extra help

No matter what size your bed and breakfast is, running a B&B is a lot of work. Whether you do it on your own or with a partner and/or staff, the role of innkeeper encompasses many jobs in one. Recognizing this and knowing when you need extra help can not only help you to run a more successful business but it also helps you to *stay* in business by preventing burnout. See Chapter 14 for information on hiring others and outsourcing tasks.

Extra help doesn't have to mean bringing living, breathing beings on board. Another option is to buy equipment that makes your life easier; see Chapter 13 for more information.

Sticking to your policies

For every rule, there is an exception — or is there? Ask yourself: *"Are there too many exceptions? Do I say yes when I really mean no?"* If you find yourself answering yes to these questions, you're not alone. The trick of seasoned innkeepers is knowing when to be flexible and when to stand firm.

Sometimes making decisions regarding your policies is easy, but oftentimes it's not. Most decisions are not clear-cut, and the decision you make may be in contrast to what another innkeeper would do in your place. For example, as a matter of policy, many innkeepers don't rent the entire inn to groups because they've found them to be too demanding. Other inns make it their policy to specifically cater to group rentals of the entire inn. If your policy is not to rent to groups, you made that policy for a reason, so my advice is to stick to it. If you make an exception against your better judgment and it's a disaster, you'll find yourself frustrated with the situation and yourself.

Certain policies are nonnegotiable, and you should always stand firm if the guest is causing damage to the inn or otherwise affecting another guest.

Some of the decisions that cause new innkeepers the most angst are those related to guests who cancel reservations. Do you consider cancellations part of the cost of doing business, do you strictly charge guests a cancellation or no-show fee, or do you do something in between? How you handle cancellations is ultimately up to you. Many innkeepers feel guilty when they enforce their cancellation policies. Remember, however, you're making a business decision.

Sometimes there is no right answer to the question of whether to enforce a particular policy, and you need to handle each situation differently. But it's important for you to become comfortable with your policies so you can enforce them with confidence. You'll save yourself a lot of aggravation and get back time and energy that you can spend more productively.

Getting support from others

The ultimate responsibility of running the bed & breakfast will fall to you, but you don't have to feel alone. Recognizing and using all available resources, including a support system, is important. Family, friends, and the support of other innkeepers are valuable assets. They can often provide help or suggestions, or just provide a listening ear when you need it.

Obviously, you don't want to overburden others. If you feel this is happening, you need to look more closely at the problem and explore solutions. For example, sounding off occasionally about staffing issues is a normal way to relieve frustration, but if it's a constant theme, you need to look at your staff, examine how clearly and firmly you're managing them, and decide what changes you need to make. (See Chapter 14 for help with your help.)

There will be times when family and friends will not understand why you're missing a family or social event. Few people can relate to a 24/7/365 job, except fellow innkeepers, so make it a point to get to know other innkeepers (see Chapter 1 for help in finding an innkeeper support network).

Making time for yourself

Making time for yourself can be as simple as taking a walk or a nap in the afternoon or going out for the evening with friends, having a "date night" with your partner or spouse, or it can mean getting away from the inn for a few days. The problem most innkeepers encounter is giving themselves permission to do this. No matter how busy you are, taking time off is possible and you deserve it.

Should you close your inn or hire a stand-in?

When you're planning a vacation or need to be away from your inn in an emergency, you may find yourself vacillating between hiring an interim innkeeper and closing the inn. How do the costs stack up against each other? Here's a simple exercise to help you find out:

1. Using your estimated occupancy rate and your base room rate, calculate the approximate revenue that you would expect your inn to generate during the period that you'll be away. (See Chapter 3 for help in estimating occupancy and calculating your base room rate.)

2. Double it, because most interim innkeepers also take reservations for future dates that

you'll lose if you're not there to answer the phone. (If many of your reservations are from online bookings, adjust the calculations accordingly to reflect the percentage of rooms booked by phone and e-mail.)

3. Add these two figures together to determine the revenue you'll lose if you simply close the inn while you're away.

4. Subtract the cost of the interim innkeeper to find the cost of keeping the inn open using that person's services. (Don't forget to add in the value of getting a vacation!)

One of the benefits of innkeeping is that you're the boss. If you don't carve out time for yourself and your outside interests, eventually you'll begin to resent innkeeping. You must make a conscious effort and a commitment to yourself to take the time you need.

When you do take some time away from the inn, leave with a free mind by having policies in place. (See Chapter 12 for information on leaving guests alone at the inn.)

Taking an afternoon off for a walk in the park is great, but you also need a vacation, just like everyone else. One option is to close the inn while you're away; however, you lose revenue not only from being closed, but also from guests who are unable to call and make future reservations.

How do you plan to take a vacation and keep the inn running? This is where the use of well-trained staff, a partner who can run the inn in your absence, and/or an interim innkeeper comes in. If you have well trained and competent staff, getting away should not be difficult. If not, don't overlook the effect that a professionally trained interim innkeeper can have on your business. That person can cook breakfast, clean rooms, take reservations for future dates, and handle guest emergencies, whereas dear cousin Charlie may not be up for the challenge. (See Chapter 14 for more info about hiring an interim innkeeper.)

Benefitting from Professional Development

Pick up any small business handbook and you'll read about the benefits of professional development. Running a bed & breakfast is a business and inn-keeping is a profession, so these benefits apply to you. Thankfully, numerous professional resources are available to help you sharpen your skills and find support. Some of the most important benefits of investing your time and money in professional development include:

- ✔ Improving your knowledge and skills
- ✔ Finding answers to your questions and concerns
- ✔ Discovering renewed energy and rejuvenation
- ✔ Networking within your industry
- ✔ Meeting and gaining support from others who face the same challenges you do

Knowledge is power and a key element in the growth and development of your chosen profession. Your fellow innkeepers possess an abundance of knowledge — as do you, even if you don't think so yet. Harness this power by joining a professional association of other innkeepers and by attending an innkeeper conference. Luckily for you, both are easy to do.

Joining a professional association

Innkeepers around the world have joined together to form professional associations that provide support through camaraderie, exchange of ideas, and access to information. When you put yourself in contact with others who share your passion for innkeeping, you'll often find the result is rejuvenating and helps you renew your commitment to your business.

There are local and regional associations as well as associations for many states in the United States and provinces in Canada. Many countries have also formed innkeeper networks. The largest organization is an international association, the Professional Association of Innkeepers International (PAII).

In some areas you have an abundance of choices, and in this case I urge you to select carefully. If you join too many groups or associations at once you won't be able to efficiently take advantage of what each has to offer. If your state has a bed & breakfast association, this is the logical place to start, followed by the Professional Association of Innkepeers International. No matter where you are in the process of running your bed & breakfast, these associations, and their conferences, will provide you with a wealth of information and inspiration.

Search for local, region, and state associations online by entering the key search words "your city", "your town", "your region", or "your state" followed by "bed breakfast association". You may be in luck and find the association this way. If no associations are listed you'll probably find a list of inns in the area. Contact some of these innkeepers and ask about associations that they belong to and recommend. As an aside, this is an excellent time to invite the innkeeper to your inn for coffee or tea — you may have found a new friend for support and friendship, who in turn might invite you to meet other local innkeepers that he or she is friends with.

Associations come in all sizes from small local groups to large national networks.

✔ **Local associations:** You may be able to join an association of innkeepers who operate within a given city or tourist destination. Members of local associations often create joint marketing campaigns, rely on each other for networking and support, as well as group together to support or oppose legislation that affects their inns.

✔ **Regional associations:** Associations at this level help innkeepers with regional marketing and local lobbying efforts. They're often large enough to hold local conferences where you can meet with other innkeepers, exchange ideas, and meet industry vendors.

✔ **State and province associations:** These associations usually hold an annual conference. They can provide marketing for their member inns and, as a group, serve as a strong lobbying association for issues that affect the bed & breakfast industry.

✔ **The Professional Association of Innkeepers International (PAII):** In 1988, innkeepers Pat Hardy and JoAnn Bell created PAII. Today, PAII (pronounced "pie") is an international organization that has grown to over 3,000 members. PAII holds an annual convention, supports a members-only forum, and offers a wide variety of other resources on its Web site (www.paii.org) and to its members.

In addition to innkeeper associations, you may want to consider getting involved in your local community and your chamber of commerce and/or convention and visitors bureau to help you keep up with local events and happenings that can affect your business. Often this networking brings you referrals and local business, too. Many innkeepers find the personal and professional satisfaction of getting out and being with others invigorating.

Attending an innkeeping conference

There is no other industry that I can think of like the B&B industry — where owners pour their hearts, energy, and resources into it with so much intensity that most live on the job. Eventually you may reach a point where you ask yourself, *Can I keep doing this?* If you're at this point, you're not alone.

To resolve your feelings, I urge you to attend an innkeeping conference. The energy, ideas, and optimism are contagious. Speaking with other innkeepers at a time like this can provide the renewed energy that turns you back around and sends all thoughts of putting the inn on the market out of your mind.

Joyce, at the Chambered Nautilus Bed & Breakfast Inn in Seattle, Washington, recently shared with me that in her eighth year, she was ready to put her inn up for sale when a wise innkeeper asked her, *"Why would you do that? You've just gotten over most of the hard part."* Joyce is now in her twelfth year of innkeeping and has shared many of the ideas included in this chapter as a motivational speaker at industry conferences.

A variety of innkeeping conferences are held on the local, state, and national level every year. You don't have to travel far to find one near you. When you attend an innkeeping conference, you can expect to:

- ✔ Learn from experienced innkeepers
- ✔ Network and meet other innkeepers
- ✔ Attend workshops on a variety of topics from baking to bookkeeping
- ✔ Find fresh new ideas and ways of doing things
- ✔ See products and demonstrations by a variety of industry vendors all in one place who can answer your questions in person
- ✔ Have a lot of fun and make lifelong friends

Once you've found the associations that you're interested in, ask about upcoming conferences and mark the dates and details on your calendar. Some regional associations hold conferences, and nearly all state associations either hold their own conference or group together with nearby states for a larger conference. Most associations that hold conferences and the Professional Association of Innkeepers International (PAII) hold annual conferences which usually last two to several days and offer workshops which are geared to aspiring, new, and veteran innkeepers. To choose a conference look carefully at the schedule and evaluate your interest in the sessions that are offered. Then, ask other innkeepers which conferences they recommend.

When you teach, you learn, and you'll be able to share your experiences with others. Sharing your knowledge, enthusiasm, and love for innkeeping with others helps you to grow. No matter where you are in the process of running your bed & breakfast, I encourage you to begin sharing with others. You've already learned something that others would want to know just by reading this book (hopefully many things)! If you're just starting out, attend an aspiring or new innkeeper workshop and share your experiences. If you're a new or veteran innkeeper, volunteer to be on a panel and share your current and relevant experiences with aspiring innkeepers who are following in your footsteps; you'll be recommitting yourself to the profession.

Chapter 17

Looking into Your Future

- -

In This Chapter

▶ Adding more services to make more money

▶ Expanding your current inn or buying another one

▶ Choosing your exit strategy

- -

*Y*ou're over the hump, and you've got this innkeeping gig down to a science. Well, almost. So now what? Are you still energized? Do you want to grow and expand in big ways? Or are you losing steam and thinking it may be time to bow out of the innkeeping business? Both scenarios require advance planning, and no rule says that you can't and shouldn't plan for both at once.

In this chapter, I show you ways to prepare for and achieve both outcomes: moving up and moving out. I discuss ways to grow your business, from expanding your services to adding to the physical size of your inn or — for even more fun — taking on an additional inn. At the same time, I help you to plan your exit strategy so you're ready for the day when you start to think about leaving the business behind.

Deciding when to Grow Your Business

Your business is running smoothly, you're enjoying many repeat guests, you have lots of satisfied guests who send you fabulous referrals . . . so what else is there? Maybe status quo is the best place to be. You sure can't fault yourself for being a success, and don't underestimate the hard work it will still take to maintain your success in the bed & breakfast business. However, if you're wondering what else is there, then you may be ready to take on more, and this section helps you explore ideas and options.

If you're at the point where you think it's time to make changes in your business, the first question you need to ask yourself is *why?* Pull back and examine your motivation. Do you think you should make a particular change because everyone else is doing it, or do you have a great new idea for a service or amenity that you're passionate about adding? You may answer yes to both.

When it comes to growing your bed & breakfast business, being both a leader and a follower can be beneficial, but most importantly, you need to be an independent thinker. Following are tips on how to play each role:

- ✔ **To be a leader:** Offer something no one else is offering. Listen carefully, and make note of amenities or services that guests are asking for that neither you nor your competitors in the area provide. For example, do you receive calls from families looking for a venue to get together for a family reunion? If so, creating a family reunion package might be a great way to attract new guests.

- ✔ **To be a follower:** Check out what other inns in your area are offering and, if it makes sense, do the same. For example, if many inns in your area offer mugs and local jams or coffees for sale and these products are popular with their guests, why not offer similar items from your inn?

- ✔ **To be an independent thinker:** Seek out and offer solutions to needs that no one is asking for. . . yet. Begin by looking at your local community, and consider potential guests that you're currently not targeting. What services are missing? For instance, do local corporations have a comfortable place to hold meetings and retreats? What about clubs and organizations? If not, consider renting your common area or dining room for meetings and events, as long as doing so wouldn't interfere with your current lodging guests. If your inn isn't licensed and permitted to make meals other than breakfast, would it be possible to arrange for meal delivery to your inn for these groups?

Exploring Ways to Increase Profit

Your *profit* is sales (revenues) minus expenses, or what is left at the end of the day. Simply put, increasing your profit means bringing in more money, spending less money, or both. Refer to Chapter 15 for help in decreasing and controlling expenses; then check out the following sections for ways to bring in additional revenue.

Raising your prices

Your bed & breakfast's success depends on having room rates that are high enough to be profitable to you, yet reasonable enough to attract guests and keep your rooms occupied. A high occupancy rate means that demand for rooms at the current price is high. If you raise your rates too high, your guests may bypass your inn and choose the competition or stay fewer nights, causing your occupancy rate to decrease. The trick is to figure out how much you can comfortably raise your rates to bring in more revenue without causing a net loss in profit through decreased occupancy.

Figuring out the price point for safely raising your rates and increasing your revenue is a juggling act. For example, if last year a given room was booked 100 times at an average price of $125 per night, your annual revenue for that room was $12,500. Say the next year you raised the room rate to $150 per night and booked it 95 nights. Your revenue would be $14,250, meaning that a 20 percent increase in your room rate resulted in only a 5 percent drop in occupancy. Not only did you have to clean the room five fewer times, but you also had an overall increase in revenue of $1,750. In this scenario, raising your rates would be a good decision. If, however, you raised the room rate to $150 and you were only able to fill the room 75 nights, your revenue would decline to $11,250, an overall loss of $1,250. (Refer to Chapter 7 for additional help in setting your rates.)

Offering additional amenities

Raising your prices is only one means to increase your revenue. Another way is to add value to a guest's stay. If the added value of additional amenities or services costs you less than the amount by which you raise your rates, you've found another way to increase your revenue stream.

For example, consider creating a romance package (I suggest other package ideas in Chapter 15). The package could include a couples massage and a private in-room breakfast for an additional charge of $250. If you pay the massage therapists $75 apiece, your cost for the package is $150. Your revenue increases by $250 and your profit by $100. (This assumes that the in-room breakfast doesn't have any additional costs associated with it. Many innkeepers prefer serving in-room breakfasts because once the guests are served, they are taken care of for the time being – although you will have to wait until you turn or fluff the room to get the dishes and run the dishwasher.)

Adding services and amenities can be a fun way to increase your business's profitability. Let your creativity flow. Think about new guests that you could target and what would attract them to your inn. Would they be interested in yoga classes? Weekend-long prenatal classes? Spa getaways?

Be careful not to become so excited with an idea that you forget some important considerations:

- **Costs versus revenue:** Does the product or service cost you more to provide than you can reasonably charge for it?

- **Demand:** Is the product or service one that your guests will be interested in?

- **Opportunity cost:** What are you giving up in order to offer the product or service? Could you be making better use of your time and the space at your inn if you weren't providing it? For example, you may think it's a great idea to dedicate a room for massages or as a workout room. Keep track of how many guests take advantage of these services versus the revenue that you are giving up on a room rental or another service that guests would use more. Or you may be an avid biker and think that bike tours are a great idea. However, between the increased insurance cost and the amount of time away conducting the tours, will your new offering make a profit?

Think about new target groups of guests you could attract to fill rooms when bookings are ordinarily low, such as weeknights and during your slow season. A few years after Thurston House, (www.thurstonhouse.com), a B&B in Maitland, Florida, opened for business, the innkeeper noticed that guests traveling on business were asking for services such as the use of a fax machine. The inn added a few common amenities for business travelers and began prominently advertising to this group. Today, many rooms are filled midweek by business travelers, who are also frequent repeat guests and a great source of referrals. Common amenities for business travelers include

- ✔ Work desks with phone/modem hook-ups
- ✔ Complimentary wireless Internet access
- ✔ An on-site fax machine
- ✔ In-room telephones (particularly if you're in a remote area with poor cellphone service)
- ✔ An early-breakfast option
- ✔ Corporate rates
- ✔ A flexible cancellation policy
- ✔ Private bath
- ✔ Acceptance of major credit cards

Think outside the box. Guests are not always who you think they are. Most innkeepers associate business travelers with large corporations. However, many of the business travelers at the Thurston House are pharmaceutical reps, non-profit employees, designers, and furniture reps.

Hosting weddings and special events

Many inns successfully host weddings and other special events, from small elopements to large extravaganzas, while others avoid them like the plague. If you're considering hosting weddings, or other large events, seek out advice from fellow innkeepers who have successfully done so (see Chapter 1 for help in connecting with other innkeepers).

Be sure to check local zoning laws, which may or may not permit you to host weddings and other special events at your inn. You may be able to get the variances necessary to hold these events. Sometimes called conditional-use-permits, they'll spell out the conditions under which you can host special events and may limit the number of events that you can hold each year, the size of the events, and so on. Decisions on variances and special-use permits are usually governed on the local level and the ease in attaining the necessary variances differs greatly by area. Here are some other things you need to consider:

✔ **Parking:** Determine the amount of on-site parking available in terms of width, length, and number of spaces, as well as street or other parking.

✔ **Entrances and exits:** Guests must be able to efficiently get in and out of the property.

✔ **Maximum occupancy:** This is the maximum number of people you can accommodate per room, per floor, per common area, or on the grounds.

✔ **Fire regulations:** These specify required safety and fire protection equipment, emergency exits, signs, and lighting.

✔ **ADA compliance requirements:** ADA stands for Americans with Disabilities Act and sets requirements for accommodating those with special needs. To access the ADA information line for answers to your questions about what may be required, visit `www.ada.gov/infoline.htm`.

✔ **Commercial kitchen requirements:** In many areas, a commercial kitchen is required for catering special events.

✔ **Availability of public restrooms:** You need a sufficient number of restrooms to accommodate event guests.

✔ **How your neighbors feel about it:** Hearings are usually held before conditional or new variances are awarded, and your neighbors can be your best allies — or your worst enemies. (See Chapter 5 for more information on zoning and variances.)

To let guests know about the various types of events you're willing and able to host, post links to pages that detail the relevant information clearly on the home page of your Web site. Not only do these pages provide important information for guests, but they're also keyword-rich, which helps your Web site place higher in Internet searches. Check out the Admiral Peary House's Web site at `www.admiralpearyhouse.com` for an example of a beautiful page devoted to wedding services.

It's important to evaluate whether hosting weddings or other special events is worth your time and energy. For example, if a new wedding business generates only $2,000 in profits per year but takes a huge amount of time and results in wear and tear on the inn, is it worth it? Make sure you track revenues and costs!

Adding a gift shop

Adding a gift shop is a natural step for many innkeepers. Local items, such as jams and coffees, and items displaying the inn's name and logo, such as robes and mugs, are popular. Some factors to consider when thinking about opening a gift shop include

- ✔ **Space versus revenue:** Your highest profit margins are typically on your rooms. Would the space that you plan to devote to your gift shop be better used as an additional guest room? (Don't forget to verify zoning restrictions for the additional guest room or gift shop.)

- ✔ **High overhead:** Opening a gift shop requires an investment in inventory, which means tying up funds.

- ✔ **Inventory storage:** Space is required in order to store additional products.

- ✔ **Zoning issues:** Check with your local zoning officials before investing in a gift shop. Your inn may not be zoned to offer one without a variance. However, this may not prevent you from selling items that you use at the inn such as mugs, jams, robes, and so on by simply letting guests know that they are available for sale, in a display case for example.

- ✔ **Seller's permit:** You need a seller's permit if sales tax is collected on retail items in your location. This permit authorizes you to collect tax on purchases and turn these taxes over to the state.

- ✔ **Natural fit:** You might love antique dolls, but the fact that they're your passion doesn't mean that selling them would be profitable. Know your guests, and only carry items that they're likely to purchase. A good rule of thumb is to sell items you use at your inn.

Many inns have had success selling mugs with their logo from Deneen Pottery (www.cloth-clay.com), a long-time supplier to the bed & breakfast industry. Guests who use the mugs during their stay often purchase them as mementos of their visit, as gifts to bring home, or simply because they enjoy the feel of the mugs. Each mug taken home brings with it an advertisement for the inn at which it was purchased.

Renovating Your Inn

Renovating your inn has exciting possibilities. Maybe you want to open up the back of the inn to expand your breakfast seating area or add more guest rooms. Or you may decide that the cost of adding in-suite bathrooms is a good investment because they'll allow you to increase your room rates now, and add value when you sell the inn later. As you approach these projects, it's natural to have questions like *Where do I start?* and *Can I do renovations and host guests at the same time?* The following sections address those concerns.

Going back to square one

Before starting renovations, you should keep good statistical data to analyze whether the costs are justified. Assuming they are, in many respects expanding and renovating your inn requires taking the same measures you took when you first opened your inn.

To get started, you need to check with your local zoning department to be sure your plans will be approved. Even though your inn is your business — and probably also your home — local zoning ordinances dictate what's allowable in the way of expansion and renovation plans. Although smaller in scope, the renovation process is essentially a new construction project, and it requires you to take the same steps to verify zoning, select a contractor, and so on (see Chapter 5 for detailed information). Even seemingly minor renovations require you to obtain building permits and have the work performed by licensed architects, plumbers, and electricians. (Work performed without the necessary permits or by unlicensed contractors and sub-contractors may void your insurance protection, not to mention cause problems later when you sell the business.)

Check to see that your proposed renovation won't suddenly require you to qualify under all sorts of other compliances that you were previously exempt from. For example, you might be required to install sprinkler systems; outdoor, covered fire escapes; or a full commercial kitchen. A small renovation can easily turn into a major — and very expensive — construction project, if even small changes to the property force you to meet other codes.

Handling guests during construction

Once you've decided to go ahead with your project, you need to decide how you'll handle guest reservations for those guests who will be staying with you during the renovations. Some jobs may be performed on a definite date, but other times you may be on a contractor's wait list or awaiting the arrival of appliances, fixtures, and such. Indefinite factors like these make blocking out exact dates for renovations impossible.

So how do you handle hosting guests? The answer really depends on the type of renovations you're having done and how easily you can work around guests without inconveniencing them. For big jobs, you'll probably need to close during renovation. However, for less-major improvements, oftentimes inns continue to host guests because guests are usually out during the day, when the work is being performed.

Next you need to decide whether to notify guests ahead of time. Innkeepers have differing opinions about how to handle this question, and no single answer fits every situation. Most inns decide to call guests because their first concern is their guests' comfort. You can explain exactly what's going on and what inconveniences the work will entail. This often heads off problems before they can occur. Most guests will react by thanking you for letting them know, while keeping their reservation. However, if guests want to cancel their reservations, let them do so and chalk it up to the cost of doing business. Better to give guests a choice than to risk negative online reviews of your inn and damaging repercussions.

If during the guests' stays the inconveniences are more than you anticipated, make amends by giving guests a discount or other special consideration to thank them for putting up with disturbances. After your renovations are complete, both you and your future guests will be able to enjoy the benefits with no lingering bad memories.

Buying Another Inn

Purchasing a second inn is another way to expand your business. Advantages include having some economies of scale (ordering supplies in bulk, for example) and being able to refer guest overflow from one of your inns to the other. However, you're still looking at twice as much work, and this may require you to hire staff that you may not have needed before.

The most successful way to effectively handle ownership of multiple inns is to buy a property that's geographically close to your existing inn. This strategy allows you to maintain the hands-on control and the provision of personal attention that running a true bed & breakfast commands. One exception worth noting is owning seasonal inns with opposite open and closed periods, and moving between the inns by season.

Juggling inns successfully

Whether you own one inn or several, careful planning and organization are the keys to success. Innkeeper Carolyn Lee provides a good example. In 1987, Carolyn bought Alexander's Inn (www.alexanders-inn.com) in Santa Fe, New Mexico. Nine years later she bought an inn a few blocks away — Hacienda Nicholas (www.haciendanicholas.com) — and six months later the inn across the street, The Madeleine Bed & Breakfast (www.madeleine inn.com). Carolyn wasn't necessarily plan-ning on expanding; rather, the opportunities of the two new inns presented themselves. She was able to make it work and maintain a personal touch at all the inns because of their close proximity to each other. Although each inn had a main innkeeper, Carolyn stayed involved with the guests and breakfasts. After seven years of running three inns, she converted Alexander's Inn into vacation rentals. To be able to visit with all guests, breakfast for the two remaining inns is served at Hacienda Nicholas.

Some of the first steps to take when considering the purchase of an additional inn are:

- ✔ Deciding how you will divide your time
- ✔ Figuring out what additional staff you will need to hire
- ✔ Determining if the second inn will operate independently or if it will be an extension of your original inn.

When It's Time for a Change

All good things eventually come to an end, and you're smart to start planning your exit strategy long before you even think about selling or closing your inn. No matter where you are in the inn ownership process, now is the time to think about your future plans. How long do you plan to be an innkeeper? What will you do after you sell or close your inn? None of these questions are intended to discourage you or to persuade you to sell or close your inn before you're ready, but they're important enough to mention here so that you can start thinking about life after innkeeping.

The best time to think about your exit strategy, whether you plan to sell your inn or retire, is when you're putting together your business plan (subject to change with the times); see Chapter 3.

Selling the inn

The long-term goal of many innkeepers is to create a profitable bed & breakfast that one day they will sell. It seems counterintuitive to think about selling your business while you're putting so much time and effort into starting it, but incorporating good selling points into your plans is smart thinking. It's not something you need to entertain on a daily basis, however. In fact, it's better if you don't, because on tough days (and there will be plenty of those) selling might seem like the only rational thing to do.

Life has a way of surprising us. If you're the managing owner of your inn, life changes are more complicated because your home and business are affected at the same time. Maybe you suddenly can't run your B&B anymore because you or your partner become ill or suffer a debilitating injury, or maybe you simply want to move closer to family. If you need to be away temporarily, consider hiring an interim innkeeper to keep the inn open and running (see Chapter 14). If, however, you decide that selling the inn is your only option, you'll be glad you took the steps outlined in this section and have been gradually preparing for the sale of the inn.

Knowing when to sell

The time to sell your bed & breakfast is not determined solely by market conditions; rather, the ideal time to sell your inn is before you're ready to sell. This time is different for everyone and is meant to warn you against waiting too long to consider selling your inn. If you're like many innkeepers and are emotionally attached to your inn, it's easy to put off thinking about your exit strategy. Periodically examine your long term goals. When you get to the point that you think you can do another 2 to 3 years, it's time to think about selling. Don't wait until you've slowed down, when you've let your marketing initiatives slip, and when your energy and enthusiasm for running the B&B are waning. You'll receive the best price for your inn when it's going strong, when you're putting your best energy into it, and before you become burned out or are in a position where you *must* sell.

Getting your inn ready to sell

Most inn owners sell their inns at some point. Turning loose something that you've put so much of yourself into building is an emotional decision; however, your work doesn't end once the decision to sell is made. Preparing your inn to sell is a crucial process.

Seasoned innkeepers suggest you prepare for the eventual sale of your inn by taking the following steps well in advance of when you intend to put your inn on the market:

1. **Prepare an inclusion list (what goes with the sale) and an exclusion list (what is not part of the sale).**

   If possible, start to replace items you don't want to sell with like items, so the exclusion list is short.

2. **Hire a realtor or broker experienced in selling B&Bs.**

   See Chapter 4 for a list of bed & breakfast sale specialists, or hire the most energetic local realtor you can find and engage the services of an inn consultant (see Chapter 3 for B&B consultants).

3. **Keep your enthusiasm and energy going.**

   You need to keep your inn running full steam with maximum revenues to realize the full value of your business. This includes keeping your advertising and Web site up-to-date.

4. **Maintain the property and make improvements.**

   Clean out garden sheds, garages, basements, and closets. Not only will an uncluttered inn show better, but you'll also be getting ready for your big move.

It's not uncommon for inns to take two or three years to sell, but a quick sale is also possible, and it's best to be ready for either contingency.

Buyers want information. Wow them with your property, your organization, and some comprehensive information about your property and the area. Hire an inn consultant to prepare a professional evaluation or a for-sale packet (see Chapter 3 to find an inn consultant). A thorough evaluation consists of 35 to 50 or more pages. If you want to assemble the information yourself, see Figure 17-1 for an idea of the type of information you should be getting organized to give to prospective buyers.

BRADFORD PLACE INN AND GARDENS - SONORA, CALIFORNIA

FOR SALE INFORMATION PACKAGE TABLE OF CONTENTS

PART ONE.   DESCRIPTION OF THE AREA
         The Central Sierra Foothills of California
         Sonora, California
PART TWO.   BACKGROUND OF REAL PROPERTY
         History Of The Property
         Introduction Of The Property As A Bed And Breakfast
         A Historically Significant Property
PART THREE.   DESCRIPTION OF INN
         The Neighborhood
         The Property
         The Rooms
         The Back Wing
         Other Buildings/Improvements
         A Personal Word From The Owner
PART FOUR.   DESCRIPTION OF BUSINESS
PART FIVE.   DESCRIPTION OF BUILDING
         Building/Property/Equipment Changes
PART SIX.   DESCRIPTION OF SALE
         List Price and Terms
         Orientation, Training, Consultation and Seller Interim Innkeeping
         Proprietary Information
         Summary Of Sale
         Business Transition Check List
         Furniture, Fixtures and Equipment – Included In Sale
         Furniture, Fixtures and Equipment – Not Included In Sale
PART SEVEN.   MARKETING STRATEGIC PLAN – OPENING DAY TO PRESENT
         Initial Marketing Objectives
         Getting The Inn Marketable Before Opening
         Tier Pricing
         Strategic Planning/Increasing Rack Rates
         Advertising and Publicity
         Looking Ahead
PART EIGHT.   HISTORY OF REVENUES AND OPERATING EXPENSES
         Notable Highlights
         Discussion/Room Prices
         Discussion/Operating Expenses and Chart Of Accounts

ADDENDUM.   SELECTED IMAGES
         PLOT PLAN
         FLOOR PLAN: 1ST Story and 2ND Story
         ROOM RATE HISTORY   (03/00 - 2008)
         ROOM REVENUE HISTORY   (01/05 - 09/08)
         OPERATING EXPENSE SUMMARY   (2005, 2006, 2007, 2008)

Figure 17-1:
For-sale
packet table
of contents

Courtesy of Dorothy Musser, Owner/Innkeeper, Bradford Place Inn and Gardens

Deciding what retirement means to you

You should begin planning for your retirement from innkeeping even before you purchase your inn. This may sound like strange advice but in doing so you'll be prepared both financially and emotionally for your retirement from innkeeping.

From a financial point of view you should talk to a tax attorney, CPA, or inn consultant when you set up your business to plan for your retirement along the way because selling may entail significant tax consequences. Additionally, keeping good financial records from the start will make the process of selling your inn and moving on much easier.

Running a bed & breakfast carries many feelings and emotions with it. The sentiments associated with devoting considerable energy, passion, and time to your B&B means that moving on can be difficult. If your exit strategy includes selling the business, picture where you would like to be in the next phase of your life, making the transition easier when the time is right.

Fortunately innkeepers' personalities rarely allow them to do absolutely nothing. Whether you're just starting out or counting the days until your inn is sold, think ahead to what you'll do in retirement. Many innkeepers want to:

- Travel and spend more time visiting family
- Become interim innkeepers
- Stay involved in their communities
- Relax (on rare occasions)

Part VI

The Part of Tens

The 5th Wave

By Rich Tennant

"It's quite a business plan, Ms. Strunt. It's the first
one I've read whose mission statement says,
'...keeps me out of trouble.'"

In this part . . .

*H*ere's where you find ten innkeeper secrets for cleaning that are sure to save you time and money. I also give you ten tips to make every guest feel special and hopefully keep them coming back for more visits. The hardest guest to get is the first-time guest, and after that, you can use the tips I give you in this section to turn them into repeat guests and induct them into your marketing team.

Chapter 18

Ten Cleaning Tips to Save Time, Money, and Your Inn

"Life is too short to spend cleaning anymore than absolutely necessary."

– Betty Gladden,
Professional Association of Innkeepers International workshop

One common aspect of every successful bed & breakfast is cleanliness. All innkeepers share the challenges of saving time and money and effectively maintaining their inns. In this chapter, I give you ten tips and tricks to help you win these battles.

When making up rooms, carry the tools you need in a cart, a bucket, a basket, or a gardening bag with lots of pockets. Basic items to carry along for efficient room cleanup and turnover include stain remover, glass cleaner, all-purpose cleaner, a dust mop, dust rags (or microfiber cloths), and scissors to cut stray strings or threads on towels and bedding.

Putting White Vinegar to Work

White vinegar is a miracle cleaner on glass shower doors, mirrors, vanities, and chrome fixtures at the Red Dog Inn in Beaufort, North Carolina. Using vinegar cuts way down on fumes and saves money over other cleaning products.

Don't use white vinegar on tile grout because it will eventually make pits in the grout. Instead, spray an all-purpose cleanser with bleach on the grout and let it sit a few minutes to kill germs and mildew.

Harnessing the Power of Hydrogen Peroxide

Hydrogen peroxide is great for removing stains without removing color on towels, sheets, and even furniture at the Blair Mountain Bed & Breakfast in Dillsburg, Pennsylvania. It works wonderfully on blood, ink, and red wine stains.

Let the hydrogen peroxide soak into the stain briefly, but launder as soon as possible.

Getting Rid of Pesky Hair

Nothing is more frustrating than cleaning a bathroom only to turn around and find hair that just got pushed around. No matter how much you wipe and clean, hair is hard to get rid of. It sticks to everything, including wet rags, and then reappears just when you think you're done cleaning. End the frustration by vacuuming the bathroom before cleaning it. This will save you a lot of time and aggravation; it does at Prairie Creek Inn in Alberta, Canada.

Wash and dry your rags after every use to get rid of hair and to keep them smelling clean.

Keeping Your Towels in Tip-Top Shape

Guests love fluffy, good-smelling, soft, absorbent towels, so here are some tips from The Turkish Towel Company to keep them that way:

- **Never use fabric softener on your towels.** It coats the threads and makes them nonabsorbent, meaning you'll have to replace them sooner. Instead, add 1 cup of white vinegar to the rinse cycle once a month to restore your towels to full absorbency.

- **If you catch a thread on a towel and pull a loop, simply cut off the pulled loop with a pair of scissors.** High-quality towels are woven in such a way that a pulled loop won't cause the towel to unravel.

Softening Sheets

How many times have your sheets come out of the dryer twisted into a fat, wrinkly rope? Never again. By using white vinegar and baking soda as a fabric softener, you can foil the culprit behind the mess — static cling. Just follow these tips:

- ✔ **Add ¹/₂ cup white vinegar to the wash cycle.** The vinegar prevents lint from clinging to your linens, and it eliminates chemicals from newly manufactured linens.

- ✔ **Add ¹/₄ cup baking soda to the wash cycle.** The baking soda lifts dirt for extra clean sheets.

- ✔ **Add ¹/₄ cup white vinegar to the last rinse.** This dissolves alkali in soaps and detergents and prevents yellowing. It also acts as a fabric softener, reducing static cling. As an extra benefit, it attacks mold and mildew.

Don't use vinegar on silks, acetates, or rayon.

While I'm on the subject of bedding, here's a little more advice learned the hard way: Use waterproof mattress covers. Protecting your mattresses minimizes damage from bedwetting, spills, menstrual accidents, and bedbugs. (Even if you don't host children at your inn, until you're an innkeeper you might be surprised by how many adults still wet the bed.)

Preventing Clogged Drains

Don't let your money go needlessly down the drain. Treat your drains monthly to guard against a build-up of hair and other debris, and cut down on the number of calls you have to make to the plumber.

Mix 1 cup of baking soda with 1 cup of vinegar, and pour the mixture down the drain. Let it sit for 5 minutes; then rinse with hot water.

To prevent soap build-up as well as hard water and odors in your dishwasher, run a cycle with 1 cup of vinegar every month.

Discovering the Miracles of Microfiber

Innkeepers have discovered a secret — they swear by microfiber cleaning cloths to clean everything! Save money and your health by forgoing expensive chemical cleaning products. Microfiber cloths miraculously pick up dust and dirt — rather than just pushing it around — and they're even effective on grease and grime. They're as gentle as they are strong, and they never leave streaks, marks, or scratches.

Treating Stains Immediately

Always treat stains as soon as they're discovered. For example, when you flip back the covers to strip the beds, treat any stains immediately with a stick or spray. For stains that require more intense treatment before laundering, InnStyle (www.innstyle.com), suppliers of linens for bed & breakfast inns, recommends writing the type of stain on a piece of masking tape and using it to mark the location of a stain. This will ensure the stain is not forgotten and make it easier to find and treat it in the laundry area.

Working Wonders on Windows

Use full-strength white vinegar to clean oil, salt, grease, and grime off windows. Wash windows in different directions when cleaning the inside and the outside. When you wash the outside of the window using horizontal strokes and the inside using vertical strokes it makes it easier for you to see areas that you have missed. For regular window cleaning, use 1 cup of white vinegar per pail of water and a good squeegee.

Caring for Carpets

Guests will spill things and, yes, also get sick. Cleaning carpets immediately minimizes the impact of the problem by getting rid of unpleasant odors and making the area useable again.

To treat carpet stains, make a paste using 2 tablespoons of white vinegar and $1/4$ cup of salt or baking soda. Rub the paste into the stain. Allow it to dry, and then vacuum.

For oily stains, use white vinegar full-strength, rinse with clean water, and blot dry. Repeat if necessary.

Use baking soda as a natural deodorizer. Sprinkle it on carpets, let it sit, and then vacuum.

Buy a carpet cleaner. It may become your new best friend.

Chapter 19

Ten Ways to Guarantee a Return Guest

*W*hen your guests' stay exceeds their expectations, you're guaranteed a return visit the next time they're in your area. The secret to keeping guests happy and getting them to return is to do the unexpected, and this chapter tells you how.

Making Guests Feel Special

Your guests begin their stay thinking that you are special; after all, they could have chosen to stay at any number of places, but they chose your inn. Prove them right, and make them feel special in return. There are numerous ways to do this, many of which are unique to your inn and your guests. Start with the mantra, "It's all about the guest," add some personal attention, and take it from there. Here are a few ideas to get you started:

✔ Give all guests a welcome tour of the inn.

✔ Offer assistance with dinner reservations or other arrangements.

✔ Greet guests with a short handwritten note and small treat such as a plate of cookies or dish with some candies in their room.

✔ Thank them for choosing your inn by offering a frequent visitors discount, if you have one. Or simply send them on their way with a few of the brownies or muffins that they raved about during their stay, or give them a recipe card with a recipe that they inquired about.

Upgrading Upon Arrival

Everyone loves an unexpected upgrade. If you have available rooms, treat first-time guests to an upgraded room as an introductory special and return guests as a thank you for staying with you again. The cost to you of offering an upgrade at check-in is minimal (you have a larger room to clean at check-out), but the rewards are happy guests who feel special. Because the guests are staying in a nicer room, chances are good that they'll enjoy their stay even more. You're also giving them the opportunity to try out a better room, which they may book on a return trip. A win-win for you and the guest.

Wait until check-in to upgrade guests. If you upgrade them before check-in, you lose the opportunity to sell the better room.

Catering to Your Guests' Interests

Personal touches differentiate your property from other places your guests have stayed, and those that they could choose in the future. When taking your guests' reservation, ask whether this is their first visit to your area and what brings them to the region. If they tell you they're coming for antiquing, for instance, put some brochures in their room of popular antique stores that you recommend.

Recognizing Repeat Guests

If you discover that certain guests will be making frequent visits to your area, think about extra ways to accommodate them so that staying at your inn is always their first choice.

- ✔ When parents of freshmen stay with you while they're settling their son or daughter into college, invite their child to breakfast. These parents will be visiting again, as will other relatives over the next four years. You want them not only to choose your inn, but to tell other parents about your inn as well.

- ✔ Area seniors living in small senior-citizen housing may have family who are frequent visitors. Extend an invitation to these guests, offering your common or outdoor areas as comfortable places to visit with their relatives.

- ✔ Offer business travelers personal services, such as making reservations for them, printing their boarding passes, or offering the use of a common area for a small meeting.

Make notes on guests who stay with you so that you can welcome them back warmly on repeat visits. Most reservation software systems give you space to do this, or you can record the info manually. Then, when guests visit again, you can ask how their son (by name) is doing at the nearby school and know he's a sophomore and a rugby player, for example. If a repeat guest requests the same room, identify it as "their room" — frequent return guests love that.

Asking Guests How Their Stay Is Going

Periodically ask your guests how their stay is going and whether they need anything. If you inquire about their plans, do so unobtrusively. If they're chatty and open to suggestions, you might offer them insider tips about restaurants in the area, ways to avoid lines at attractions, and so on.

Taking Allergies and Special Diets Seriously

Treat allergies and special diets as a big deal — not as a big deal to accommodate, but in order to reassure the guest that you've prepared something special. Giving vegetarians more vegetables is not the answer; rather, prepare something extra, such as a tofu scramble, or adjust your menu to make it vegetarian. (See Chapter 10 for sample menus that are easily adjustable to accommodate vegetarian guests.) Your regular eaters will never know the difference, but your guest on a special diet will feel very special.

The Internet makes it easy to accommodate all types of special diets. Have a few easy vegetarian, low-carb, low-fat, and gluten-free recipes handy.

Sending a Welcome E-Mail

Guests love personal attention, and you can start to give it to them before they even arrive at your inn. Have a form e-mail prepared that you can quickly customize and personalize for each guest's reservation. Include in the e-mail the dates of your guests' stay, your check-in and check-out times, directions to your inn, and any advance reservations that you have made for them. You can make the e-mail as simple or as elaborate as you want; it's the welcome that counts, so make it sound personal and not like a routine confirmation. Send the e-mail one week before a guest's visit.

Helping Guests Celebrate

You'll have many guests visiting to celebrate a special occasion (make sure to ask whether this is the case when you take the reservation). Have birthday, anniversary, and blank cards graphically designed with pictures of your inn on hand. Then when a guest is staying with you over a special occasion, hand-write a card and have each staff member personally sign it (with their first names only). You can also have sparkling cider on ice and champagne glasses on a nice tray waiting in the guests' room — no liquor license is required!

Get a big smile from the unexpected. As an innkeeper, use your creativity and do something out of the ordinary. Use your judgment as to how personalized it should be. Remember that some people are very private. For example, if a gentleman calls to make a reservation to celebrate an upcoming anniversary, have a small bouquet of flowers in the room with a gift of a CD of smooth instrumental music. Or ask him whether he'd like the same flowers in the room that his wife carried in her wedding bouquet (he probably won't remember what they were, so have him send you a picture). This type of endearing experience will make the couple want to spend future anniversaries with you, not to mention that it's a wonderful advertisement for your inn every time the story is retold.

Making Sure Your Inn Is at Its Best

This idea may seem obvious, but it's too important to leave out. If you offer a welcoming atmosphere, a firm bed, a clean property, spotless bathrooms, and a good breakfast, and if you're honest in your advertisements and your prices are fair, your guests will leave happy and they'll return.

Sleep around … at your inn. Pack a suitcase and stay in your rooms as a "guest." This is a good way to determine whether something is missing, whether storage space and hangers are sufficient, and whether the beds are comfortable. Over time, do this for every guest room.

Leaving a Good Last Impression

Personally shake hands (or, in the right situations, give a hug) and look your guests in the eye while thanking them for selecting your property. Send a follow-up note after their visit expressing your wish that they return (use the e-mail address that you sent the confirmation to, not a mailing address).

For guests who must leave early in the morning before normal breakfast service, offer a simple to-go breakfast if you can't accommodate their breakfast time.

Index